THE BOW BUILDER'S BOOK

The Bow Builder's Book, Revised 2nd Edition

Editor	Angelika Hörnig
Authors	Flemming Alrune
	Wulf Hein
	Jürgen Junkmanns
	Boris Pantel
	Holger Riesch
	Achim Stegmeyer
	Ulli Stehli
	Konrad Vögele
	Jorge Zschieschang
Main Back Cover Photo	Volker Alles
Original Layout	Angelika Hörnig
Collaboration	Hubert Sudhues, Holger Riesch, Volker Alles

Translated from the German by Dr. Edward Force
First published in Germany, ©2001 by Verlag Angelika Hörnig, www.archery.de
Original ISBN 978-3-9805877-7-8

First English edition published in ©2007 by Schiffer Publishing, Ltd.
First edition ISBN 978-0-7643-2789-6

Copyright © 2012 by Schiffer Publishing, Ltd.
Library of Congress Control Number: 2012943327

Type set in Zurich BT

ISBN: 978-0-7643-4153-3
Printed in China

Published by Schiffer Publishing, Ltd.
4880 Lower Valley Road
Atglen, PA 19310
Phone: (610) 593-1777; Fax: (610) 593-2002
E-mail: Info@schifferbooks.com

For the largest selection of fine reference books on this and related subjects, please visit our web site at **www.schifferbooks.com** We are always looking for people to write books on new and related subjects. If you have an idea for a book please contact us at the above address.

This book may be purchased from the publisher.
Please try your bookstore first.
You may write for a free catalog.

In Europe, Schiffer books are distributed by
Bushwood Books
6 Marksbury Ave.
Kew Gardens
Surrey TW9 4JF England
Phone: 44 (0) 20 8392-8585;
Fax: 44 (0) 20 8392-9876
E-mail: info@bushwoodbooks.co.uk
Website: www.bushwoodbooks.co.uk
Free postage in the U.K., Europe; air mail at cost.

TRADITION MEANS NOT PICKING UP THE ASHES,
BUT PASSING ON THE FLAME

RICARDA HUCH

THE BOW BUILDER'S BOOK

Bow Building from the Stone Age to Today

Revised
2nd Edition

4880 Lower Valley Road • Atglen, PA 19310

The Fascination of Simplicity

A bent stick and a string—how often has this scene repeated itself over the past thousands of years? Based on the dating of rock and cave materials, it is quite possible that the first arrow was shot from a bow 20,000 years ago.

What links us through the millennia and all of history is the fascination, the magic, that comes from a bow and arrow. Bending the bow powerfully to send an arrow on its way, the good feeling when it has hit its target.

Having all of these experiences with a self-built bow increases the impact, making it more personal. And replicating a bow from an earlier epoch can help us to gain better understanding of those who came before us.

"...One knows only the things that one tames," said the fox. "The people no longer have time to get to know anything. They buy everything ready-made in the stores. But since there are no stores that sell friends, the people no longer have friends. If you want a friend, tame me!"
From *The Little Prince,* by A. de Saint-Exupéry

In this sense, this book would like to offer instruction and inspiration to tame one's "personal friend made of wood." It presents a set of instructions that readers can follow, but, naturally, they do not have to, for only through experimenting and testing were "new things" discovered 20,000 years ago.

Wishing you much pleasure,
Angelika Hörnig, Editor

Hubert Sudhues (1957–2005)

A LITTLE HISTORY OF THE BOW

Excerpt from a cave painting in the Cueva de los Caballos, Spain.

The invention of the bow is lost in the mythical mist of history: Its place and time of invention cannot be determined exactly through archaeology. The reason for this is the fact that both bows and arrows were made of organic materials, which have not survived the ravages of time.

Only with the use of arrowheads of bone or stone did our ancestors leave behind clearly datable evidence for the use of bows and arrows. Such contact points let us know that the bow has been used by humans for some 20,000 years.

Sticks and stones were man's first tools and weapons. The invention and further development of weapons was necessary, as humans were not only a potential food source to beasts of prey, but were also hopelessly inferior as hunters, in terms of cleverness as well as strength, speed and "natural armaments" (teeth and claws).

The hand axe, probably the oldest weapon of humans, was followed by the spear, but, because it still required close contact with hunted animals, the risk of injury to the hunter was reduced only slightly. The spear, as the first distance weapon, and the spear-thrower (atlatl) allowed increasingly greater distances and effectiveness in hunting, and naturally also in warfare.

The bow, though, allowed a large number of projectiles to be carried in a small space and fired at great distances, more accurately than did an atlatl. With it, the Stone Age hunter could adapt to the changing game population (with the extinction of the mammoth and woolly rhinoceros) and hunt fast-moving animals like reindeer with a good chance of success.

To date, the oldest worldwide evidence for the existence of the bow is the stone-tipped arrows found at the Stellmoor site near Hamburg. These arrows, with shaft, secure attachment system, and flint arrowheads, represent an already developed technology and date to about 9000-8000 B.C. The oldest bow, found in the 1940s in the Holmgaard Moor on Seeland, Denmark, dates to about 8000 B.C. Here too, the design of the bow shows a high level of "know-how."

Proof that the bow, the hunting weapon, was also used very early as a weapon of war is shown by a Mesolithic rock painting (ca. 8000 B.C., left). Two groups of bowmen oppose each other in battle, and a half-reflex (circle segment) bow can be recognized.

In 1991 an archaeological "find of the century" was discovered in the Hauslabjoch in the Ötztal Alps: the glacier mummy of a man ("Ötzi") about 5300 years old, with complete equipment. An important part of his equipment was a longbow, along with a quiver filled with fourteen arrows.

For thousands of years, the bow and arrow remained the main long-range weapon of humans; to be sure, it was valued very differently in various cultures. To the ancient Greeks it was the coward's weapon, for the man who feared close combat.

Scene from Les Dogues, Castellon, France

Among the Teutons as well, the bow was only a hunting weapon; in war, according to Tacitus, it was regarded as childish and malicious. In many Asian cultures, on the other hand, the bow was seen as a royal weapon.

The Assyrians introduced mounted bowmen and, thus, combined the long-range bow weapon with the mobility of the horse. Among the old Persians, every boy had to learn three things: to ride a horse, shoot a bow, and speak the truth.

The European Age of Chivalry was put in question and finally ended by the great battles of the Hundred-Years' War between England and France (Crecy in 1346, Poitiers in 1356, Agincourt in 1415) at the end of the Middle Ages. Even against armored knights, the massed use of the English longbow was decisive. At Crecy the crossbow proved inferior to the English longbow, because of its slower rate of fire (once per minute, as opposed to up to twelve arrows per minute).

From the Cueva Salta-dora, Spain

Similarly, the Mongolian bowmen ("Tartars," from the Greek *"tartaros,"* the underworld), with the mobile tactics of Genghis Khan allowed by the bow, left the heavily armored and thus immobile knights of Europe with nothing to oppose them.

In warfare, the bow was displaced only by the development of guns at the end of the Middle Ages, for crossbowmen and musketeers were easier to train and thus less costly, since the longbowman needed years of training.

In the American Indian Wars of the 19th century, though, the bow was still a dreaded weapon. Only with the introduction of repeating guns could the Native Americans, superior until then in both rate of fire and precision, be defeated. For the same reason, Benjamin Franklin (1706-1790) had suggested during the American Revolution that the ponderous musket be replaced by the long-proved English longbow.

In the 20th and 21st centuries the bow was and still is used by the indigenous peoples of South America, Africa, the Arabian peninsula, India, and the South Pacific (for example, in Papua New Guinea) for both hunting and warfare.

At the beginning of the 20th century, a renaissance of sporting and hunting bow use was brought about by, among others, Saxton Pope. In North America today, there are some 2.5 million archers, many of whom hunt game with bow and arrow, the majority of them using compound bows.

In some European countries (such as France, Italy, and Hungary), bow hunting is also allowed, though not in Germany, Austria, and Switzerland.

Despite all the technical inspiration, in the United States and Europe, since the 1980s the numbers of bowmen using simple longbows and recurved bows without sights or pulleys have increased more and more. The number of traditional sport clubs is growing, so that it becomes easier to practice this form of bowmanship among those who share one's interest.

And the bowyer's art was rediscovered as well. In Europe, in America, and also many other countries, there are again professional bowyers who pass on their knowledge and ability by teaching courses.

And there are those who have discovered archery as an exciting and relaxing hobby. Here, at least, the circles are closing...

Sources: Beckhoff 1963, Daniel 1996, Dutour 1986, Egg 1992, Ehrenreich 1997, Feldhaus 1914, Feustel 1985, Hardy 1992, Heath 1971, Hurley 1975, Kluge 1989, Lennox 1979, Marden 1080, Nickel 1970, Pope 1923, 1930, 1985, Schmidt 1989, Stodiek 1993 and 1996, Sun Tsu 1993, Sunzi 1996, Winkle 1974

CONTENTS

FLEMMING ALRUNE

For some 18 years, Flemming Alrune has been reconstructing archaeological artifacts from Denmark, northern Germany, and southern Sweden. Over the years he has built many bows and arrows from the most varied epochs for museums in many countries. He documents his work in articles for international magazines and in television and film productions. Today he gives courses and demonstrations in bow building and writes freelance for the Danish Historical-Archaeological Center and various museums.

His first brochure, "Bows and Arrows 6000 Years Ago" from 1991, was quickly sold out in Denmark and was often reprinted. In the present book, his second publication, "A Bow From the Middle Ages—Build Yourself a Copy" can be found. The author looks forward to letters and contacts (address in appendix).

BOWS AND ARROWS 6000 YEARS AGO

Translated from Danish by Wulf Hein (in cooperation with Kerstin Wieland and Ole Nielsen)

A question that I am asked over and over when I give a talk or show my bows and arrows is: "Where can I learn to make bows and arrows? Are there books about it that I can get from the library?" There are books on the subject, but they are either written in English or are so technical that they scare a beginner away—usually they are both.

This is the reason for creating a book with simple and easy directions, telling how to make a bow, and make and shoot arrows. Building a bow yourself is not a laborious job, as neither a big workshop nor expensive tools are needed. Time—and care—are needed. Patience is a good thing, and why hurry to get something done when you can enjoy the process and can also be sure of getting the right results. Boys and girls from 13-14 years up, who can work halfway decently with their hands can also build a bow. (*Editor's note:* Thus a bow-building project is also suitable for a youth group or school class.)

WHICH BOW SHALL WE BUILD?

The bow that is described and explained below is a reconstructed copy of a bow discovered near Tybrind Vig on West Funen.

There is a unique magic and excitement in replicating a bow that was in use 6000 years ago. Suddenly it is not just a bow and arrow any more, but also a matter of how people lived then. What did the country look like that long ago? So here is a little bit of "bow history."

THE DISCOVERY

In the seventies, amateur divers discovered a very exciting area in the Kleinen Belt off West Funen, about halfway between Faborg and Middelfart. The place was called Tybrind Vig, and the sea floor there was practically covered with relics and traces of the **Hunting Stone Age.**

In 1978 a fruitful cooperation between divers, archaeologists, and the Moesgard Prehistoric Museum began. A carefully planned "underwater excavation," which lasted more than ten years, was begun. The excavation area was some 250 meters from the present coastline, at depths between two and three meters.

From an undisturbed layer of mud one to two meters under water, many valuable and well-preserved relics were brought to the surface. Unbelievably, they included whole longbows and parts of others, plus several arrow shafts.

The bows, all made of elm, were all about 160 centimeters long. They represented two types, which differed only slightly in shape. All were made of thin, knot-free elm shoots.

The number of annual rings indicates that the wood grew slowly. It is called "shade-grown" and produces the best bows. The arrow shafts were made of hazel. The more technical details are in the section on bow building.

Drawing of the Tybrind Vig bow, age ca, 6000 years, length 167 cm, the model for the described replica.

HUNTING STONE AGE

Editor's note: In Denmark one distinguishes between the "Hunting Stone Age," the time from the origin of mankind to the introduction of farming and livestock raising some 5000 years ago, and the "Farming Stone Age," which approximates our Neolithic Age. The era described here is called the "Mesolithic," the time between the end of the ice age (10,000 years ago) and about 5000 years ago.

The Tybrind Vig discovery was dated at 5300 to 4000 years B.C.: 1300 years of a period called "Ertebølle Time," the last part of the Hunting Stone Age. That means that people have lived here for 6000 years.

How did their land look so long ago?

It was unbelievably beautiful.

A small protected bay linked with the Kleinen Belt by a narrow passage. The hilly land was covered with virgin forest, the forest around the small settlement was dark and impenetrable.

Oaks, elms, and lindens were the big, dominant trees. In glades and along the wood edges grew birches, hazels, alders, pines, and many others.

The people of the settlement lived by fishing and hunting, but above all, that meant "going fishing"—so often that one really ought to call this era the "fishing stone age."

The forest also provided food and clothing. Wild boars, deer, martens, foxes, wild-cats, otters, and lynxes lived there.

Elk and bison were rare. They were already on the way to extinction in this area. An overly thick forest was not their natural habitat. There were roughly the same kinds of fish and birds that we know there today. Small whales and seals formed a large part of the diet.

How I would have loved to see that land!

The Tybrind Vig Bow

Seen from the side

Seen from behind

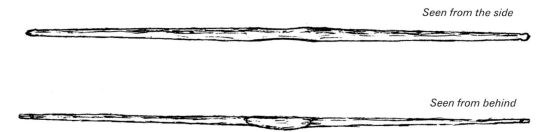

THE BOW

The bow that I have taken as a model was found in one piece and was well preserved.

Total length	167 cm
Maximum width	38 mm
Maximum thickness of grip	36 mm
Maximum thickness of limbs	24 mm

The small tree used for the replica was 14 to 18 years old and had a diameter of 7-8 cm.

The bow is of a "flat bow" type, which means that it is quite wide in comparison to its thickness. From the notches, the limbs increase slowly in width and thickness, reaching their largest size just before they narrow and join the grip.

The bowstring has left no trace behind. It might have been made of sinew, rawhide, or plant fibers.

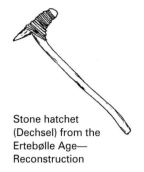

Stone hatchet (Dechsel) from the Ertebølle Age— Reconstruction

THE ARROWS

The arrows found at Tybrind Vig had hazel shafts and quartz heads—so-called "crosscutters."

This unusually effective and strong head is typical of the "Ertebølle Age."

During the next few millennia, until well into the Farming Stone Age, people used arrows with such heads. This says something of their usefulness.

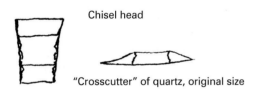

Chisel head

"Crosscutter" of quartz, original size

The arrow shafts are 80 to 100 cm long. At their thickest points they are 9 to 9.5 mm thick, slimming to 7.5 to 8 mm at the ends.

The slots were placed so that they formed a 30-degree angle to the annual rings or marking lines. This decreased the risk of the wood being split by the bowstring.

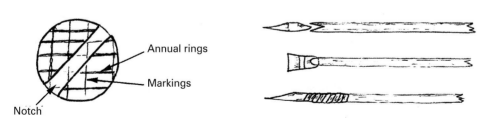

Annual rings

Markings

Notch

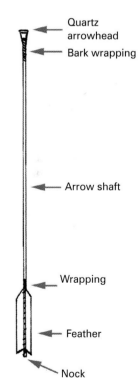

Quartz arrowhead

Bark wrapping

Arrow shaft

Wrapping

Feather

Nock

At other sites, arrows have been found with remains of wrappings on the shafts, indicating that the arrows were feathered.

Forward sections of shafts with arrowheads still attached have also been found. They were bound with inner bark fibers after being pressed into the shaft.

THE TOOLS FOR REPLICATION

After talking about the discovery, we are now ready to move forward 6000 years—into our own time.

We need few tools, and their prices are reasonable. You will find most of them where you live:

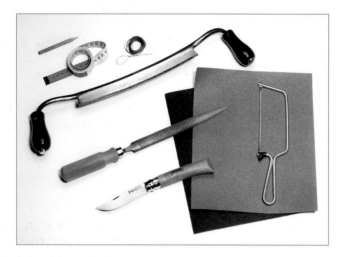

Photo: Volker Alles

You need:
- A saw (to cut down trees)
- A small hand axe
- A knife
- A rasp
- A few varying files
- A draw knife and/or plane
- Coarse and fine sandpaper

The axe, knife, etc., should be very sharp.

You do not need a large workshop. You can actually make bows and arrows in the kitchen (if you get permission). If you work with sandpaper, though, I advise you to go outside, on account of the dust.

Precision

From the start, I would like to stress that it is necessary to be careful and precise. Take frequent breaks and check what you are doing—and decide what to do next.

Be critical, and take your time. Enjoy the process of making a bow—it takes time, but patience is a quality that you can learn.

Don't forget!

Never work on a bow when you are in a bad mood or stressed—you should feel good and be relaxed to get good results.

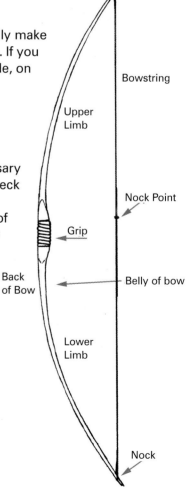

Bowstring

Upper Limb

Nock Point

Grip

Back of Bow

Belly of bow

Lower Limb

Nock

THE WOOD

All the Danish Hunting Stone Age bows that have been found were made of elm, so naturally, we shall use the same kind.

Elm is an excellent bow wood and easy to work; it also grows all over the country, in gardens, parks, and forests, where it is regarded as a weed. There it is found as trees growing wild, and this is where we'll find our wood. But we cannot use just any old tree.

The wood must be "shade-grown," meaning that the tree must have poor conditions for growing, so that it grows slowly and is thus tough and elastic.

We will also find our elms in the shadows of other, taller trees, on poor ground, and on the northern edges of forests.

Such trees develop straight and slender, without many side branches and resulting knots. Because of its slow growth, the annual rings are very close to each other.

All in all, these are qualities that we need.

Field Elm

Editor's note: Since the **elm** is very rare in Germany because of elm disease, and unwillingly cut down by foresters, you may have to settle for other wood. Possibilities are: **yew,** though it is poisonous, hard to work, and unforgiving. Then **mountain ash, ash, false acacia, laburnum** (also poisonous), and **dogwood.**

Good Bow Wood

We need a straight piece of wood, 200 centimeters long, with a diameter of 5 to 8 cm. It should be a small trunk, not a branch. It is a good idea to ask a forester whether he has elms. Explain to him what it is to be used for; then things will go much more easily.

As said, it should have grown in the shade and be free from branches. Don't just take the first one that you find, but walk around and examine many. Take your time making a choice and be critical. It is a good idea to take two or three pieces, so that you have something in reserve and perhaps can make another bow of it.

The time to cut is in January or February, when there is the least sap in the tree. Use a saw to cut it, and be sure to make a smooth cut.

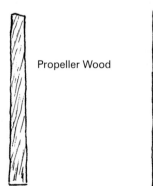

Propeller Wood

Straight Wood

Be sure that you don't get "propeller wood," meaning a trunk that winds around its own axis. That occurs when the top of the tree inclines toward the sun and thus turns.

Curing

The wood must be cured at least four months. Even if it is cut in winter, it will contain too much sap. It must dry out, but under certain conditions.

The trunk should lie outdoors in a dry place, but in the shade and with air moving freely around it. A carport or a hay shack is perfect. It is important that the drying proceeds slowly and follows the temperature and humidity outdoors.

Later, as spring comes, the air dries more—and so does the elm trunk.

Editor's note: The final drying takes place only during the making of the bow, for only then does air touch the actual bow wood from all sides. So take your time making the bow.

Before the wood is stored, both ends should be sealed with a coat of lacquer. Otherwise it will dry too quickly there and the trunk will split.

The bark should also be removed in advance. Don't use a knife, but tear it off with your hands and make sure not to damage the wood under the bark.

While the wood is drying, you have time to read about the Hunting Stone Age and Robin Hood.

Patience! The wood determines the right point in time.

A Little Information about Wood

Elm wood (and any other kind of wood) consists of bark on the outside, a layer of inner bark, then the wood itself, which consists of two types:

Inside is the **heartwood** with the pith in the center. The color is dark brown. The heartwood is dead fabric that no longer transports food and fluid in the trunk.

Heartwood is stiff and can stand compression of the fibers, but not pulling. It has a very unequal distribution in the trunk, and can be missing altogether in thinner trees. In thicker trunks it can be spongy or decayed.

Between the heartwood and inner bark is the yellow sapwood. Inside, it no longer takes part in transmitting fluids, but outside it does. Later, when a tree grows older, the sapwood is turned into heartwood.

The sapwood is younger and more elastic than the heartwood. It bears bending and pressure when pulled, but not when pressed.

Cross-section of a Trunk

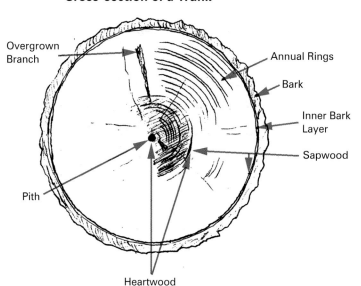

Overgrown Branch

Annual Rings

Bark

Inner Bark Layer

Sapwood

Pith

Heartwood

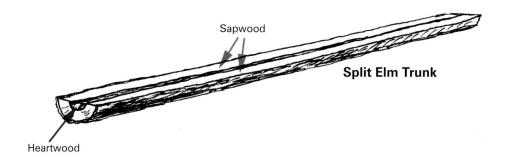

Sapwood

Split Elm Trunk

Heartwood

It is the varying characteristics of the heart- and sapwoods that we'll utilize in our bow. The back of the bow should be in the sapwood, its belly in the innermost part of the sap- or the heartwood.

Locating the Bow in the Elm Trunk

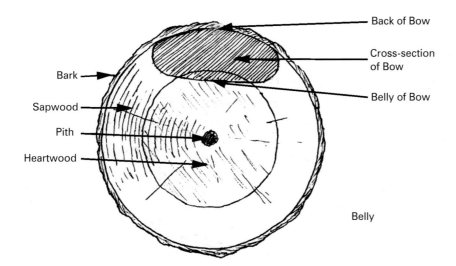

As noted, the varying characteristics of the two types of wood are what we'll use to design the bow.

Sapwood can bear bending, heartwood can bear pressure.

The two types together will unbend and straighten quickly after application of power. This gives the bow the "propelling power," which is its ability to straighten instantly after it has been bent.

The faster it straightens, the faster the arrow will fly.

A good bow should have a good propelling power.

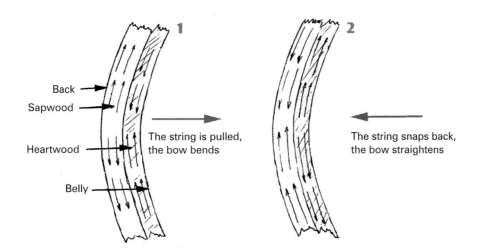

In drawings 1 and 2 you see how the fibers in the bow work.

In crude terms, these are the physical powers that give a bow its propelling power. It is always advantageous to know why and how a thing functions, because then one can understand better why some types of wood are better suited than others.

DIMENSIONS OF THE BOW

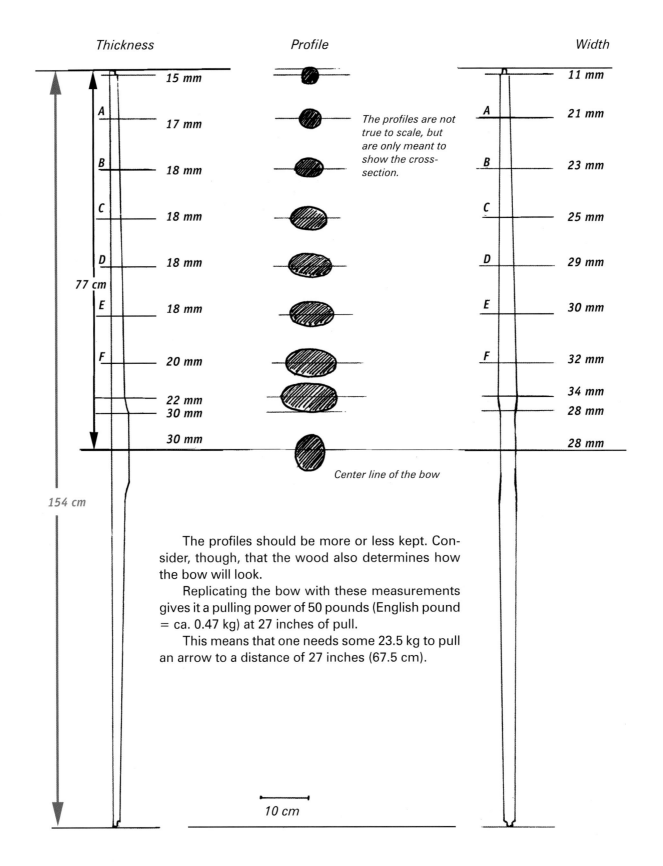

Thickness

15 mm

A — 17 mm

B — 18 mm

C — 18 mm

D — 18 mm

77 cm

E — 18 mm

F — 20 mm

22 mm
30 mm

30 mm

154 cm

Profile

The profiles are not true to scale, but are only meant to show the cross-section.

Center line of the bow

Width

11 mm

A — 21 mm

B — 23 mm

C — 25 mm

D — 29 mm

E — 30 mm

F — 32 mm

34 mm
28 mm

28 mm

10 cm

The profiles should be more or less kept. Consider, though, that the wood also determines how the bow will look.

Replicating the bow with these measurements gives it a pulling power of 50 pounds (English pound = ca. 0.47 kg) at 27 inches of pull.

This means that one needs some 23.5 kg to pull an arrow to a distance of 27 inches (67.5 cm).

THE CRUDE SHAPING OF THE TRUNK

Now we can begin to shape the bow, and the starting point is: An elm trunk, ca. 180 cm long, ca. 7-8 cm in diameter, aged at least four months without bark. For this work you will do best to use a small, very sharp hand axe.

Standing with the trunk, look and see where the back of the bow belongs. It should naturally be on the best-looking side, meaning where there are no or few (small) branches.

When you look at the cross-section, you can tell at once from the annual rings where the best wood is.

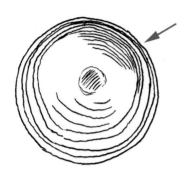

Where the annual rings are close together is the best wood. But one must often make compromises. Where the best wood is, there may be knots.

On the chosen side, lay the bow out with a pencil. Start with a center line through the bow; this makes it easier to visualize.

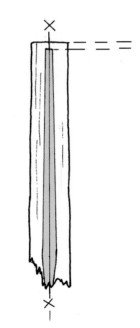

Leave a little wood at each end, so you don't damage the bow while you work on it. This will be sawed off when you finish.

X – X is the center line of the bow.

With the axe, cut wood away from the belly of the bow. As a base, use chopping blocks of various heights, two or three of them.

Always begin at the ends and work your way to the middle.
Don't cut off pieces that are too big to start, and avoid splitting pieces off, as the splits may be bigger than you planned.

Back

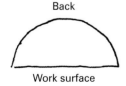

Work surface

Always cut toward the ends, never toward the grip.
The cutting can be continued calmly and pleasantly. Check often to make sure the shape is even and the cut surface is exactly parallel to the back.

Back

Belly

Stop cutting the belly when you reach the thickness of the bow plus 5 millimeters. Then cut both sides, stopping again 5 mm before the line.

The completely cut bow stave.
The bow is still marked at all the angles, and the shaft is 5 mm bigger than the bow in every direction.

The crudely cut stave is now cut down to the markings with plane and knife. The stave is still angular and should now be rounded, so that the profiles and cuts are right.

During this work, you should be careful when you get to difficult spots, so as not to use the plane too vigorously, giving the wood the tendency to split. This can also happen around **knots**.

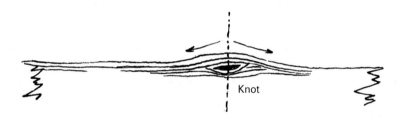

Knot

Here it is always important to cut and plane in the **direction of the arrow** in the diagram and not the opposite, since you will unavoidably tear a large chip out of the bow.

If that happens, the result can easily be a ruined bow. Knots are not catastrophic if they are not so dry that they fall out. But when they stay in place, one must be careful around them and leave some additional wood.

Using the plane, we have now shaped the bow so that its cross-section looks thus:

Back

We work with the plane and rasp until it looks thus:

The plane is used in the longi-tudinal direction of the bow, always from the grip area toward the ends. There is the common danger of the plane going too deep and getting stuck. Use the plane the other way around, and the problem is solved.

Be careful at all times to maintain the dimensions of the bow.

Where the plane slips, do the remaining work with rasp and file.

At this point it is very important that the back not be damaged!

File and rasp are used in the direction of the arrow.

Now work with rasp and file, from the center toward the nocks, while you "rock" with the tool to round the edges.

After working with the file, the whole bow should be smoothed with 80-grit sandpaper. The result is a spindle-shaped bow with a round cross-section at the nocks, and in the middle, and an oval cross-section in the limbs. The stave should be completely straight.

Enjoy it!

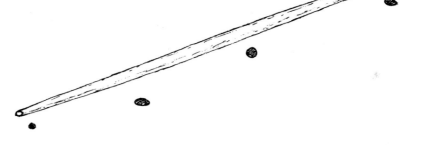

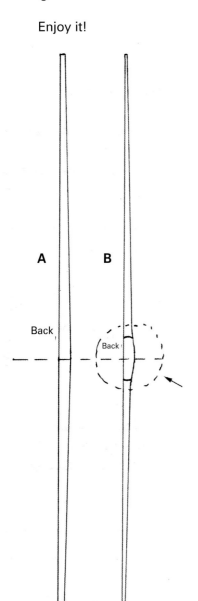

Forming the Limbs

The bow is now nicely rounded, as in A, and spindle-shaped.

Now, the belly should be smoothed down until the right dimensions are reached in the limbs.

The area within the dotted circle will be dealt with on the next page.

Check your work constantly!

GRIP AREA

Now we'll finish the grip area of the bow. To do this, find the midpoint of the shaft and use a pencil to make a light line across the back. Then measure 5 centimeters to either side and draw lines there in the same way.

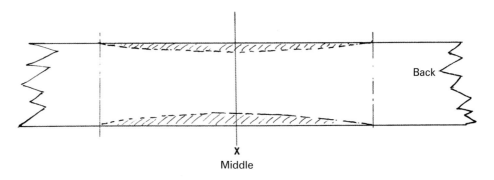

Back

X
Middle

The cross-hatched area of the shaft is now removed with knife, file, and sandpaper. Round all edges gently and smooth them with sandpaper.

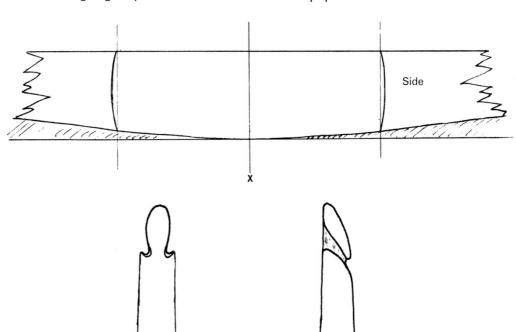

Side

X

Important:
Cut the nocks only on the sides, not on the back of the bow!

Back view   Side view

THE NOCKS

The nocks, the outermost parts of the limbs, should be cut to hold the string, as grooves.

They should be cut only on the sides, never on the back.

It is important that there be no sharp edges on the grooves, otherwise the string will be worn away and can break easily.

Use a small saw, a sharp knife, round files, and 180 sandpaper. Finally, everything should be smoothed with file (240-320) sandpaper.

TILLERING

The bow is now almost finished, but one thing is still lacking, namely the trimming or, as it is called, "tillering."

This means that the limbs of the bow match each other and bend equally in the right way at the right places.

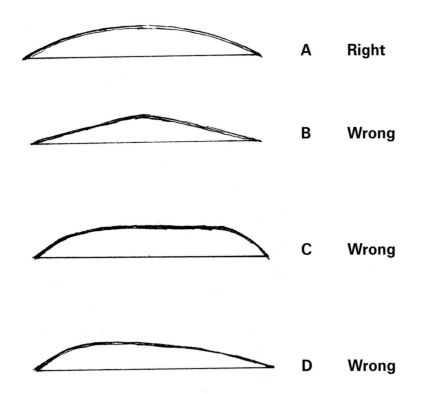

A	**Right**	
B	**Wrong**	
C	**Wrong**	
D	**Wrong**	

The bow should bend as in diagram A, with gently bent limbs.

It should appear smooth and even, with a nice balance. Harmony is the right word. But the bow should not look like that for the sake of beauty.

Why the Limbs Should Be Even and Function Evenly

Briefly stated, the bow functions as follows:

When the string is pulled, the limbs of the bow bend. When the string is held, energy and power are built up in the bow; they are active when the string is released and the arrow flies away. The arrow has transformed the energy of the bow into its flight.

In a good bow, the goal is to create maximum energy with as little use of power as possible.

The power/energy in the bow depends on how hard it is to draw, that is how many pounds one must apply to draw the bow, and how fast the bow returns to its normal position when the string is released.

The last has something to do with the materials, but also with the bow being built and trimmed correctly, so that both limbs work equally—that one of the two limbs does not "take it easy."

Thus it is very important that the bow be trimmed correctly. Take plenty of time, be critical, and work slowly.

In practice, one begins thus:

The string, in this case a test string made of strong cord with a loop on each end, is put on. Place the bow with its back on a table or similar surface, so that the string is upward.

Take a few steps backward and observe the result.

- Is the string parallel to the tabletop?
- Do the bow limbs bend the same amount at the same places?
- Does the bow look good as a whole?

On can easily measure that with a yardstick to be sure that the limbs are right. If they are not, then the limb that bends less has to have something taken off. This can be done with the bow strung. Work very carefully with a file, and check the results constantly.

Patience – Patience

Tillering a bow is a somewhat tense and laborious process. One must take plenty of time for it, for good results depend on it.

If one builds bows frequently, a tiller stick or a tiller wall is a practical aid. See also pages 153 and/or 175

FINE TRIMMING

Now only the fine smoothing with sandpaper remains. Do this longitudinally on the bow, using 180 sandpaper.

THE FINISH

For a protective finish, one can choose among shellac, linseed oil, wax, or lacquer. It is a matter of taste. I myself use linseed oil; it works well and smells wonderful.

Editor's note: There is a danger of spontaneous combustion if linseed oil soaked rags are not properly disposed of. Be careful.

WRAPPING THE GRIP

It is a matter of taste whether or not one wraps the grip with leather. I always do it, because it seems to me that it is thus more pleasant to hold. And I find that it decorates the bow.

The wrapping is done with a thin leather strip with a width of 1-1.5 cm.

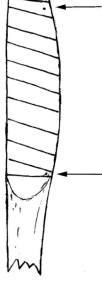

Upper Limb

The leather is attached to the side of the bow with a small nail and the wrapping is done from above to below. Let the leather overlap a few millimeters.

The end is also secured with a small nail (or you can use glue instead of nails).

Be sure that the wrapping is tight.

Congratulations, you have built a bow!

THE BOWSTRING

No traces of strings were found on the bows at the excavations. It is very likely, though, that they were made of animal matter.

They could have been made of sinew, gut, or rawhide. If the strings were made of plant material, fibers of nettle or linden bark could have been used.

The string for our finished bow can be of ready-made cord that is very strong, but not made of nylon or the like. It should be a natural material. Plastics are often too elastic and smooth for use as bowstrings; it is difficult to make firm knots in them, and they are hard to splice.

I myself make my bowstrings of linen thread used for sewing leather. One can get it in leather and fur shops; be sure that it is waxed, as it is easier to work with, and is available in rolls of various colors.

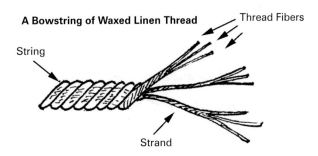

A Bowstring of Waxed Linen Thread
Thread Fibers
String
Strand

This bowstring consists of three strands, each with three (or more) fibers. And here's how it is made:

The three thread fibers (for each strand) are tied to a hook on a wall, laid out to a length of 170 cm each, and tied together with a knot at the end. With the help of a "genuine Stone Age" drill, the three pieces of thread are twisted into a single strand. When that is done, attach it somewhere, so it will not come undone.

When the three pieces are finished, they are twisted together to form a strand. If you twisted the fibers to the right, the strand should be twisted to the left. This is done by itself. The three strands are tied together and attached to the hook. Now begin carefully to twist them into the bowstring. This can get on your nerves, but be patient.

The finished bowstring should be well and thoroughly stretched, so that it "sets."

Both ends of the string should be secured with a wrapping of the same thread that was used for the string. Begin with a knot some 3 cm from the end and wrap tightly to ½ cm from the end. Close it off here with a knot.

Wrapping

The bowstring, to be sturdy, must be rubbed and impregnated with beeswax. Keep a sharp eye on it. Whenever you shoot, you should check the bowstring afterward.

Now the bowstring is finished and can be placed on the bow. For its attachment to the upper nock, we use a "Palstek" knot, the loop of which is just big enough so that it can move easily in its place. The knot is pulled tight **before** the bowstring is placed on the bow.

Bow Line

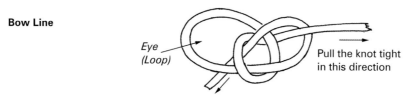

Eye (Loop)   Pull the knot tight in this direction

At the lower nock, the bowstring is secured with a so called "bowyer's knot." It is tied on the bow and then pulled tight. The bowstring is now 5-6 cm shorter than the distance between the two nocks.

Bowyer's Knot (timberhitch)

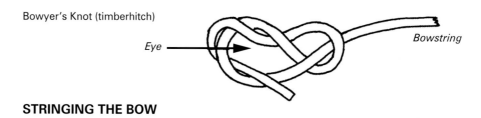

Eye ——→   *Bowstring*

STRINGING THE BOW

A wooden bow should not be under tension when it is not used.

Make a habit of only stringing the bow when it is to be shot. Unstring it as soon as it will not be used again.

Attention:
This is, of course, a very widespread method of stringing a bow, but unfortunately, it is often done incorrectly, with possibly fatal results for the bow.

Be sure to put pressure on the bow evenly, which means: pull on the upper and lower limb tips, and push only (!) on the grip area.

Step-through Method

The right hand pulls the bow toward the body.

At the same time, the left hand pushes the bowstring into place.

Behind the upper thigh.

Over the left instep

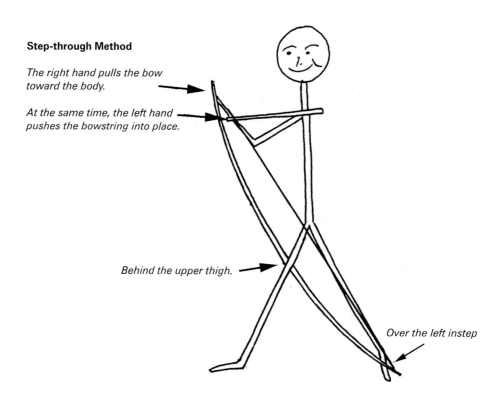

28

THE BRACING HEIGHT

After you have strung the bow, always make sure that the string is seated correctly in both nocks. Try drawing the bow a little and feel the power. Release it halfway, but not all the way. Hold the bowstring firmly and move it slowly back to the bow.

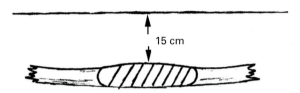

The bowstring has the right length when the distance between it and the middle of the grip is 15 cm when the bow is strung.

It is important to maintain the right distance, so that the bow can do its best. If this distance is too little, remove the string and twist it a couple times in the same direction as the strands, tightening the string.

If the distance is too great, do the opposite. If the desired effect is not achieved, one can also tie the carpenter's knot a little farther out.

The distance should be checked before every use—and also now and then during shooting.

Note well the condition of the bowstring, for a fault in it can ruin the bow. If a strand of thread is worn or torn, the bowstring must be replaced.

NOCKING POINT

So that the arrow always comes to rest at the same point on the bowstring, you should attach a marker there. You can tie a knot (of thin thread) at the spot under which the arrow is always placed.

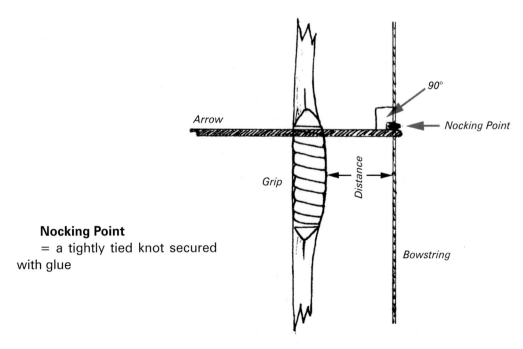

Nocking Point
= a tightly tied knot secured with glue

Editor's note: It is recommended that on wooden bows on which the back of the hand serves as a support for the arrow, you should attach the nock point 5-10 mm (or simply one arrow diameter) above the 90-degree angle.

ARROWS

A good bow is worthless with a bad arrow, for not even the best shooter can accomplish anything with it. A bad bow with a good arrow is a dangerous weapon in capable hands.

If you let care and accuracy reign in building a bow, it is doubly important for the arrows.

Building the bow is basically the hardest job, but making 10 to 12 arrows takes just as much time. So roll up your sleeves and get ready for the task.

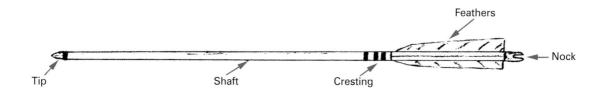

Feathers

Nock

Tip   Shaft   Cresting

Editor's tip:
This is naturally just a crude division. More precise advice, as well as suitable shafts, arrowheads, and feathers, can be ordered at bow suppliers.

The material for the **arrow shafts** can be purchased. For bows under 50 pounds, use 8 mm pine dowels; for bows over 50 pounds, 10 mm pine dowels.

Be very critical when you select them. The dowels must be straight, without knots and cracks; the annual rings (as best can be determined) should run parallel in the whole shaft. The dowels should be shortened to 28 inches or 72 centimeters.

After checking the shafts, those that are suitable should be smoothed with fine sandpaper. Make sure they are equally long.

THE BOWSTRING NOCK

For reasons of safety, it is very important that the nocks for the bowstring be made correctly—and perfectly. A weak nock is a risk for the bowman as well as his environment.

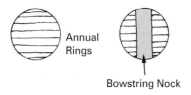

Annual Rings

Bowstring Nock

Very important:
The nock must be made perpendicular to the annual rings.

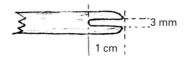

3 mm

1 cm

The nock is easiest to make with a 3-3.5 mm round file or a sawing cord.

Editor's tip:
A commercially available *flagstone saw* has the ideal width for the nocks.

Mark the middle of the nock and cut a V for the round file, so it can stay in the right place. While working with the file, the shaft should be turned often. Check the results constantly.

Finally, the nocks should be cleaned and rounded with 320 sandpaper.

There must be no sharp edges in the nock; they would damage the bowstring.

Under no circumstances may the bowstring get stuck in the nock. It should be able to slide easily and without hindrance to the base of the nock.

MOUNTING THE ARROWHEAD

The point that should be used is a training point, a field point made of steel or brass. One can buy them in various shops that stock archery equipment.

You can get arrowheads with three different diameters:
5/16 inch = ca. 8 mm
11/32 inch = ca. 9 mm
and sometimes **23/64 inch**
The arrow shafts that are worked with here are round 10 mm and 8 mm dowels, meaning that 5/16 inch can be used directly, while 10 mm shafts must be reduced to 9 mm, so that 11/32 inch will fit. (Editor's note: Or you can find 11/32 inch dowels.)

These arrowheads should cover 20 mm. This can be accomplished easily with a small hand plane and sandpaper, but check constantly to make sure the shaft remains straight.

Note: pinewood can also be somewhat tricky to work.

Finally, the shaft should be pointed so that it fits into the head. Remember to leave space for the glue. The head is glued on with two-part epoxy glue. Make sure to maintain the drying/hardening time. Remove excess glue and place the arrow vertically on its head while drying.

Handling the Arrows

It is best to lacquer the arrow shafts to preserve them. Consider how many times they will land in soil, dirt, or the like. Use a robust lacquer and give the shafts at least two coats.

If you want a **cresting** of painted-on rings, you can apply that now.

GUIDING FEATHERS OR VANES

Vane is the correct term. In the earliest days, feathers of various wild birds were used; in the Middle Ages, they were usually the wing feathers of the gray goose or peacock. Today the feathers of various birds are used: turkey, peacock, swan, and goose. The feathers we speak of here are the outermost 5 or 6 feathers of each wing.

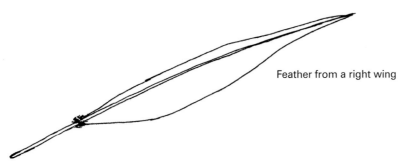

Feather from a right wing

Attention! For an arrow, only feathers from the same-side wing can be used. It does not matter whether they are from the left or right wing, but:
"Same arrow—same side."

Making Your Own Vanes

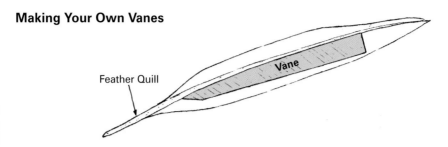

Ready-cut, full-length feathers, and those cut to shape and dyed in many colors, are available through sup-

A feather is a true wonder of nature. The cross-hatched area indicates the part of the feather that we'll use. Here the individual barbs of the feather are thickened, and the whole area is thus more stable than the rest.

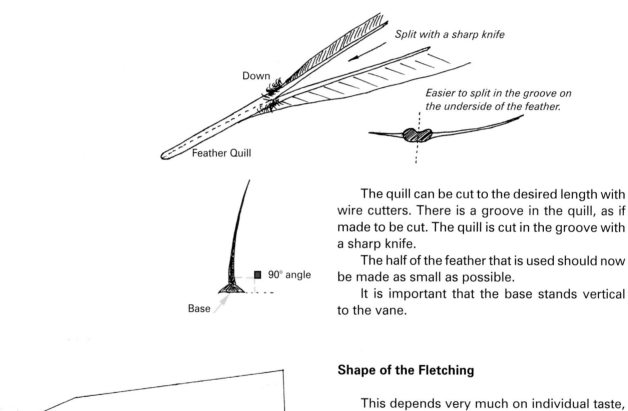

The quill can be cut to the desired length with wire cutters. There is a groove in the quill, as if made to be cut. The quill is cut in the groove with a sharp knife.

The half of the feather that is used should now be made as small as possible.

It is important that the base stands vertical to the vane.

Shape of the Fletching

This depends very much on individual taste, but a few useful guidelines will be offered here.

The length of the base should be at least 9 cm and at most 13 cm. The highest position of the fletching should be behind the midpoint of its length and should not exceed 2 cm.

Take your inspiration from literature and magazines, and create your very own shape. Draw the result twice on stiff cardboard and cut it out. Place the two cutouts on either side of the fletching. Push the lower cutout down to the base, and while you grasp it tightly, pressing the two cardboard pieces against each other, cut along the edges with sharp scissors or knife. It is very important to cut against the direction of the barbs.

After cutting, there is always some fine work to do. The underside of the base can be cleaned lightly with sandpaper. It always pays to cut and attach several fletchings at a time. The faster you do this work, the more time and enthusiasm you have for the important jobs.

two suggestions for vanes

Fletching

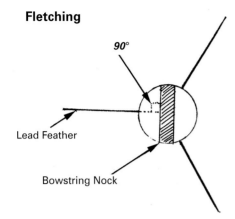

90°

Lead Feather

Bowstring Nock

The angles between the vanes should be 120 degrees.

It is a very tricky—and time-consuming—job to attach the vanes. That's why the fletching jig was invented a long time ago.

But there is also a fletching method from the good old days.

Use a good hobby glue (not water-based).

Begin with the lead feather, that should be perpendicular to the nock. Spread glue under its base and hold it on with pins until it dries. Use pins with big plastic heads, otherwise your fingers will get stabbed.

The 120 degrees between the fletchings can be determined easily by eye, or you can make a cardboard pattern.

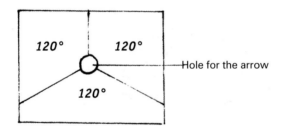

120°   120°

120°

Hole for the arrow

The fletchings will seat themselves at somewhat of an angle.

Suddenly it will become clear why one should take the feathers for an arrow from the same wing.

Let the glue dry well before you remove the pins.

The joint between vanes and shaft should be as smooth as possible. The least bit of roughness can cause a bloody cut on your index finger.

Put a spot of glue on the joint. Let it dry, then smooth it with a sharp knife and sandpaper.

If the arrow is to have identifying marks, this can by done with a so-called "cresting," a combination of various colored rings in front of the fletching.

Put your heart into this work, for nothing looks worse than rings that were painted on hastily and carelessly with a felt-tip brush.

And that's it!

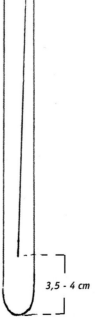

3,5 - 4 cm

Editor's tip:
A smooth, finger-sparing joint between quill and shaft can be formed by wrapping with strong thread.

ACCESSORIES

You can easily make various equipment that goes with the bow. Some of it is more important than others, but you cannot do without a finger guard. Without one, you cannot shoot more than 10 to 12 arrows—it hurts too much to do more.

Below is a finger guard, shown life-size—but the size depends on the size of the shooter's hand and fingers. It is made of smooth leather about 1.5 mm thick, the smooth side faces the bowstring. Make a few of them and keep them in a small box with talcum powder. That makes them smooth, so the string slides over them better.

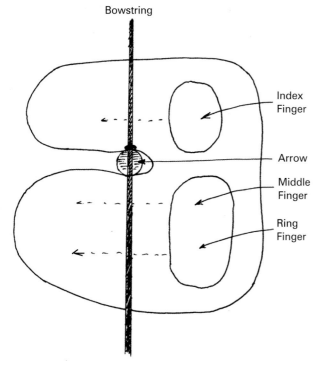

Bowstring

Index Finger

Arrow

Middle Finger

Ring Finger

The **finger guard** should lie between the fingers and the bowstring. The dotted lines show that the fingers are behind the leather.

The bow is drawn with three fingers. You pull on the bowstring and grip the arrow lightly with your index and middle fingers and pull it backward.

Many archers use an **arm guard**. This is needed only until one learns to hold the bow correctly. I myself never use an arm guard.

You can have problems caused by the bowstring striking your wrist until you are more experienced. But without an arm guard one learns faster—from bitter necessity. (As to the arm position, see the section on shooting.)

A **quiver** is also needed at times. You can buy one or make it yourself. No limits are set on your creativity, and what you choose is a matter of personal taste.

It can be either a back or side quiver, depending on where it is to be carried. A quiver should primarily provide space and protection for a number of arrows, and must therefore be made out of leather at least 2 mm thick. It should have a length that corresponds to that of the arrows, but should not cover their fetchings.

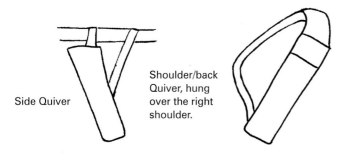

Side Quiver

Shoulder/back Quiver, hung over the right shoulder.

The bow should have a **cover** to protect it in transit. This is simply a long, narrow tube made of linen (sailcloth), which can be made quickly on a sewing machine. At home, it is best to protect the bow by placing it on a pair of wall brackets. The bow is hung on them with the back upward.

Never hang the bow over a heating unit or in a damp area. Always keep an eye on the bow and arrows and observe their condition closely.

USING THE BOW AND ARROW

Now the equipment is complete, the shooting can start, but first, here are a few guidelines:

SAFETY RULES

A bow and arrow are weapons—and absolutely not a toy. They should be used with care and respect. No matter how strong or weak the bow is, the weapon can cause serious damage. The bow and arrow are the entrance to a fantastic world of experiences, which are only good if you follow the safety rules. The rules apply to the archer and his or her environment.

1. Never shoot at animals or people.
2. You should be able to see the arrow's complete flight path, and there should be something there that will stop the arrow. This can be a target, a slope, or a row of hay or straw bundles.
3. You should be sure at all times that animals or people will not suddenly come between you and the target.
4. Your arrow stop should also be secure when you miss the target. Never use the hedge between your yard and your neighbor's.
5. Never shoot straight up in the air. Remember that the arrow comes back down.
6. Never put an arrow on the bow before you and the bow are pointed at the target.
7. Do not show off or brag with your bow.
8. Hunting and fishing with a bow are banned in Germany, Austria, and Switzerland.
9. Never lend your bow to anyone who doesn't know how to use it properly.
10. Help those who have not yet learned the safety rules.

SHOOTING

Archery, like other "sports," can be described with two concepts: technical ability and concentration. There are many ways to practice archery—the style that applies to our bow will be explained briefly here.

Shooting should be done "instinctively," which means that one does not aim, but applies body and soul, through rigorous training, so that you know where the arrow will be shot—something like throwing a ball. Instead of aiming, concentrate on the target.

There are many opinions as to how a good shooting style should look. It is a very personal matter that every archer develops on his own.

The following instructions are written for right-handed people. Left-handers simply need to switch left and right.

Editor's note to boys and girls!:

If you would like to make bows and arrows, talk it over with your parents. Win them over to your side. If they have trouble with the idea, ask them to let you enroll in a bow-building course.(Such courses are given in many places, including museums.)

Do not build a bow secretly (without your parents' knowledge), because that would be dangerous.

ARCHERY—A BRIEF INTRODUCTION

- Begin with a large target at a short distance (ca. 5-15 meters).
- Stand with slightly spread legs, so that your feet form a 45-degree angle to the target. Hold the bow in your left hand, relax your shoulders and breathe quietly.
- Naturally, you have warmed up in advance.
- Put an arrow on the bowstring and make sure the "leading feather" is perpendicular to the string, pointing away from the bow.
- Make sure the arrow is completely under the nocking point.
- The left hand should hold the bow firmly, but not too firmly. The upper side of the index finger is placed so that the arrow, when resting on it, is under the nocking point, at a 90-degree angle to the bowstring.
- So the arrow won't fall away from the bow, hold the bow at a slight angle, with the upper limb tilted a little to the right.
- The right hand, which pulls the bowstring, should be placed thus: index finger above the arrow, middle and ring fingers under the arrow.
- Only these fingers hold the bowstring.
- Hold the string with the first finger joints, and grip the arrow lightly with the index and middle fingers. Think about the finger guard.
- Concentrate on the target and nothing else. Look only at the target, not the arrow. This is called "instinctive shooting," and this is presumably how our ancestors used bows and arrows.
- While concentrating on the target, keep your back straight. The left arm is turned slightly clockwise, the left shoulder is lowered and the elbow joint is bent a very little bit.
- Thus you prevent the bowstring striking the lower arm. If that still happens, the reason is the wrong arm position, and you should try a few times until you get it right.
- Never shoot with a straight elbow; that will ruin the joint. That's why you should bend it a little.
- Lift your left arm when you draw the bow.
- The back muscles between the shoulder blades pull, and when the middle finger of your right hand reaches the corner of your mouth, relax the hand. The bowstring pulls your fingers straight, and the arrow is shot.
- Keep looking at the target until the arrow hits it, before you lower the bow.
- This is a short outline of how to shoot a bow. A great deal has been written about archery, and for further information, see the bibliography at the end of the book.
- Along with reading about shooting techniques and styles, the development of your own style is a question of training and more training.
- Don't stand too far from the target, or too many arrows will go astray.
- During shooting, it is important to see just how the arrow is positioned for every shot, so that technical errors will become clear at once.
- If you are physically or mentally tired, I advise you not to shoot a bow. You should feel strong and alert to do it.
- If you get tired, stop—take a break and think about whether you want to continue.
- On the next page I describe my own shooting style step by step.

Suggestions for a Shooting Style

1.   Take a good position.
2.   Stand with your back straight.
3.   Relax.
4.   Lower your shoulders.
5.   Breathe quietly.
6.   Hold the bow "firmly."
7.   Use only the necessary muscles.
8.   Draw the bow calmly.
9.   Anchor point (where you find it best).
10. Concentrate on the target.
11. Steady bow arm.
12. Let your fingers be pulled straight by the bowstring (passive release).
13. Follow the shot.
14. Lower the bow.
15. Breathe quietly.
16. Relax before the next shot.

Archery is a very personal and individual activity. Take what you can use from my guidelines and think of this:

"A few good shots are better than a lot of bad ones."

Good shooting.

Flemming Alrune

JORGE ZSCHIESCHANG

Jorge Zschieschang was born in Buenos Aires, Argentina in 1950. Since the early seventies he has lived in Germany, and for twenty years he has worked with wood as a material, first as a self-taught bowyer, later as a trained wood turner.

"In the formation of fine bowls and bows and arrows, there are united unique possibilities to use wood in its manifold ways. The finishing and coloring of wood, the moment in which a piece of raw material becomes a 'living' bow, or the secret of a bowl. Making all this tangible to the senses in objects that are useful is my desire."

A SIMPLE BOW

**"One takes a tree and an axe,
And cuts away all that does not look like a bow."**

That is the shortest guide of all time, but alas, not very helpful. But now let's be serious. This guide is meant for beginners, and so I'll limit myself to a simple construction and easily obtained wood. As for the latter, it can be said that I have gained very positive experience by talking to the forester at the right time of the year.

NECESSARY TOOLS
- Workbench or firmly mounted vise
- Tape measure
- Coarse and medium half-round rasps
- 4 mm diameter round file
- Drawknife or sharp knife
- Sandpaper of various grades
- Steel wool
- Hand plane

CHOOSING THE WOOD

For the "first time," my choice would be to try it with **ash**. A trunk of about 15 cm diameter is especially suitable. Ash and elm are ring-pored woods. That means the pores are concentrated in the early wood ring, which is followed by a splint wood ring with much firmer material. (See also Chapter 7, page 96)

Ash

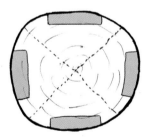

Cut surfaces of trunk and
center board

Important in the choice of wood:

If possible, take a trunk with **wide** late wood rings. This is easy to identify from the cut surface. (see drawing at left)

The gray areas show the possible positions of the bow in the trunk or the board.

The so-called **"grass ash"** found in open fields or wood edges, offers a better choice than "wood ash."

If no trunk wood can be had, try to get a center board, at least 50 mm thick, from a lumber supplier.

WORKING WITH THE TRUNK

After you have obtained a nice straight, branch-free trunk about two meters long, you should remove the bark at once. This should be done very carefully.

Since the outermost layer of wood forms the back of the bow, which is put under pressure by pulling, it absolutely can not be damaged!

It is best to take off only the roughest bark with a drawknife and then remove the rest carefully with a knife.

Splitting and Storing

From a trunk 15 cm in diameter you can, with optimal growth, make four bows. So we quarter it. To do this, drive a wedge, as wide as possible, into the middle of the heartwood (cutting edge).

Into the resulting split we drive additional wedges from the side, always alternating sides. Since ash splits very easily and smoothly, one usually gets by with two wedges. Now split the resulting halves in the same way.

Now put the quarters in the vise. One at a time, of course. Always but a piece of soft wood between the outside of the bow wood and the jaw of the vise, so as not to damage the outermost annual ring.

Now we use the drawknife to cut off the sharp angles of the triangular quarter-trunk, so that new surfaces, 2 to 3 cm wide, are formed.

Next, the ends and the heartwood surface are coated with wood glue, about 5 cm wide.

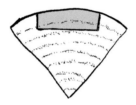

Dark gray surface shows the position of the bow in the quarter of the trunk.

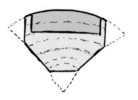

Light gray area shows the stave.

When you have stored such a stave in your home for half a year, it is generally dry enough. You can also have the dryness measured by a carpenter. The stave should have 9-11% moisture.

THE BOW

For the sake of simplicity, we'll build a flat, straight bow with a stiff grip. When the stave is dry enough, we shorten it to 1.80 meters. It is possible to build a considerably shorter bow, but in the beginning a longer type of bow is simpler.

• With a straight line from one end to the other, we now mark the longitudinal center of the stave on the outside.
• Now we mark the outlines as on the top view drawing. The grip should be placed 3/4 under and 1/4 over the middle of the stave.
• Now use the drawknife, plane and rasp to take wood off the sides of the stave, until you reach the drawn lines.

Rough Bow, seen from above

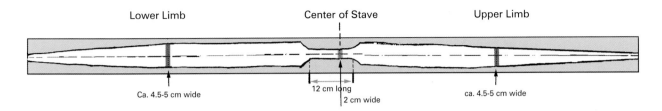

Lower Limb   Center of Stave   Upper Limb

Ca. 4.5-5 cm wide   12 cm long   ca. 4.5-5 cm wide

2 cm wide

Carefully smooth the sides with a knife, round them gently toward the back of the bow, and sand them neatly.

Always work from the grip to the end of the limb, since a cutting tool going in the opposite direction would cut into the bow.

On the resulting side surfaces, mark the profile of the bow, as in the side-view drawing.

Rough Bow, seen from the side

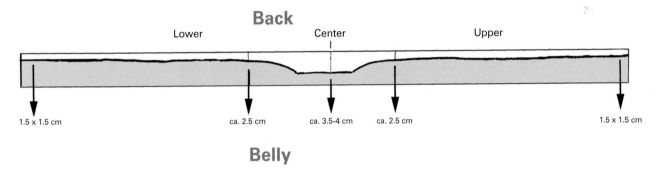

Back

Lower   Center   Upper

1.5 x 1.5 cm   ca. 2.5 cm   ca. 3.5-4 cm   ca. 2.5 cm   1.5 x 1.5 cm

Belly

Now work toward this line, in the same way, on the sides. Now we have a **rough bow,** and the real work begins.

Since wood does not grow in a straight line, it is vitally important that the inner surface of the bow, the belly, follows every irregularity of the bow's back; otherwise thicker, stiffer areas will result. The tapering toward the tips (ends of the limbs) must be absolutely even to attain a regular curve.

When that is attained, we can make the bowstring nocks at the tips, using a small round file.

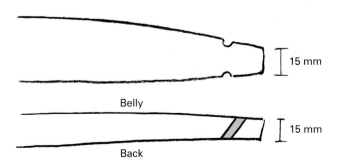

15 mm

Belly

15 mm

Back

THE HIGH ART OF TILLERING

So now the real work begins. Blood, sweat, and tears—for you, and also for me as I write, for precise directions in this realm are very difficult.

The work that the limb of the bow performs is, of course, not even. The limb should bend **evenly,** but not in an arc of a circle, but rather in an elliptical arc.

That means: The arc curves steadily more from the grip out to the tips, but the last ten centimeters should be almost straight. In addition, the limbs have a very specific unequal weight, compared to each other. The lower limb must be a little bit stiffer than the upper limb.

So that is what we want. Now, how do we get it? The stave, as it is now, will surely still be too stiff.

• Despite that, for **testing,** take the middle of a limb in your left hand and put the other end near your right foot. Take the grip in your right hand and press on the bow somewhat. Probably not much will happen, but when you slide along the limb, you may see a slight bending.

• Now turn the bow around and observe the other limb. One may feel harder than the other. If that is true, begin with the harder limb.

• With a rasp, remove some of the thickness from the inside, the front. Always do this very evenly. And conduct the pressure test again.

The bending should spread evenly along the limb, weaker by the grip, stronger farther down, stiff at the tip.

When you have the feeling—unfortunately, it cannot be expressed any more precisely—that the limb is more or less in balance, then comes the next step.

FIRST STRINGING

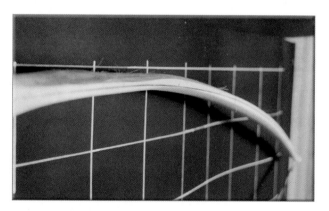

A grid makes it easier to judge the bending.
(Photo: J. Zschieschang)

• Take a bowstring that is as long as the bow, or slightly longer, and put it in the nocks.
• Now stand in front of a mirror and pull a bit while observing the bow in the mirror, or if necessary, directly.

Another possibility is to hold the bow horizontally against your body and push the bowstring away from you.

In this case, the bow should never be bent farther than the final strung distance from the grip to the string.

If irregularities (weak areas, an angle in the curvature) show up, mark them with a pencil.

Now take some wood away to the left and right of these areas—always from the belly of the bow, so that after several observations the bending is even.

Then even up the other limb.

When you think the bow is "soft" enough for its first stringing, use a bowstring that brings it to about 1/3 to 1/2 of the final strung distance (5-7 cm).

Now mark the middle of each limb.

There are now two things that must be noted. First, how do the bendings of the limbs compare with each other? Second, where is the bowstring?

Where is the Bowstring?

If the string is not centered behind the grip, you must figure out why.

To do this, run your hand over the back of the bow, to tell whether the limbs, or one of them, show a twist.

If so, that means that this limb is weaker on the side to which it bends. Then you must weaken it on its stronger side by removing wood there.

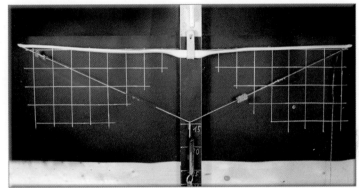

But always remember to work from the belly of the bow, and always just a little at a time.

Remember that removing material does not always solve the problem immediately, but only after one has pulled the bow a few times—in the direction in which the bowstring should move.

Naturally, you shouldn't give a hard pull here either, but only a third of the way at most.

Often it is enough to deepen the string nocks on the side that bends toward the string.

The method described above does not have to be used immediately, but in combination with the further tillering that follows.

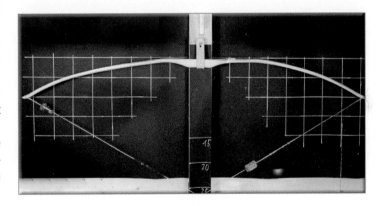

Equalizing the Limbs, Removing . . .

First of all, compare the two limbs. If one is notably stiffer than the other, take some wood off the belly of the stiffer limb.

If they are about equal, measure the distances from the middle of the limb and the bowstring.

From now on it must be kept in mind that this distance is some 5 mm greater for the upper limb. You should also check the even movement of the bending, and correct differences in the way already described.

A tillering wall allows judging the movements of the limbs. (Photo: A. Hörnig)

Now draw the bow about 1/3 of the way 15 to 20 times, observing the bending very closely, to see if stiffer or weaker areas show up.

If they appear, they must be corrected at once. And continue to check the bowstring's position.

Be careful . . .

From here on, you should work very cautiously with the rasp, just "stroking" the bow. Even better, start to scrape fine strips of wood off with the drawknife or knife. That also serves to smooth out traces of the rasp on the bow.

And always remember that taking material off does not show immediate effects, but only when you have drawn the bow a few times.

So always take material off cautiously, draw the bow, observe, measure distances, make corrections.

DRAW WEIGHT

We can also speak a little about draw weight. I do not find it so important to attain a certain level in the first bow, but rather to make sure the bow works.

Still, you should make sure never to exceed the planned weight when you draw the bow (check with a spring scale).

When the bending is even, the string distances are right and the pulling weight seems to be suitable, you can pull farther, always checking and correcting.

You can also have someone else pull, so you can observe better—if you can stand to let someone else handle your bow!

You should also take off the bowstring, to check the bow for possible string-follow, and make corrections if necessary by relaxing this position.

If the full draw (ca. 27-28 inches = 67-70 cm) is reached **at half the string distance** (about 7 cm), and the bow functions correctly so far, you should shoot a few arrows.

And then again measure, observe, make corrections.

By this time your spouse is probably yelling, the children are being noisy, the dog is whimpering in quiet despair, and your nerves are on edge. But you are not quite finished.

At the same cautious pace you still need to bring the bowstring distance, the "fistmele," to its **final height**.

THE BRACE HEIGHT

As a rule, I string my wooden bow somewhat less tightly than is customary with a modern part-fiberglass bow. This reduces stress on the bow, which can be drawn more easily, and works faster through a longer pushing path.

The disadvantage is that one must make note of the spine value of the arrow much more precisely, and releasing errors bring more emphatic results.

My recommendation is 15 cm at most for this bow.

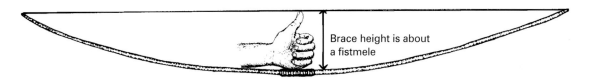

Brace height is about a fistmele

FINE SMOOTHING

Now you can begin to smooth your work of art with sandpaper and steel wool.

There must be no sharp angles, since tension concentrates in them; in addition, they are sensitive to being hit, and this can lead to damage.

In particular, everything must be rounded and smooth in the nocks for the bow-string.

A torn bowstring is almost the same as a broken bow.

Finally, there is a wide variety of good paints and oils with which to finish the bow. I generally use only several coats of linseed oil varnish.

I would not advise waxing, since waxes are very sensitive to water.

Best of luck!

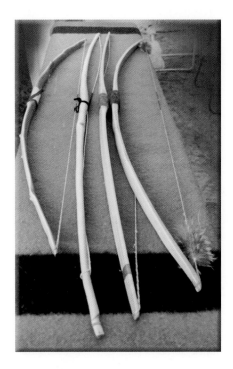

THE AUTHOR

JÜRGEN JUNKMANNS

Born in 1962, this archaeologist became a bowyer through his studies; he has written a dissertation on prehistoric bows and arrows.

He is an expert on prehistoric bows and arrows in Europe. Since 1985 he has built wooden bows, sinew-backed bows, and composite bows, as well as made reconstructions for archaeological museums and taught bow-building courses.

3

NEOLITHIC BOWS

DISCOVERIES

Neolithic bows have been found mainly in shoreline settlements in the Swiss, French, and South German lower Alpine area (the formerly so-called lake dwellings). Some were also found during turf cutting in the Northern European moors of Great Britain, the Netherlands, and Northern Germany.

The oldest Neolithic bow discoveries date approximately from the beginning of the 5th millennium B.C. Two types of Neolithic bows can be roughly differentiated: stave-shaped and "paddle-shaped" bows. Both types existed through almost all of the Neolithic era. Numerous variations of the two types exist, presumably resulting from regional or ethnic differences.

The **stave-shaped bow** is more or less straight over its entire length and has no carved-out grip section. Its greatest width is in the grip area, and the bow tapers only very gradually from there to its ends.

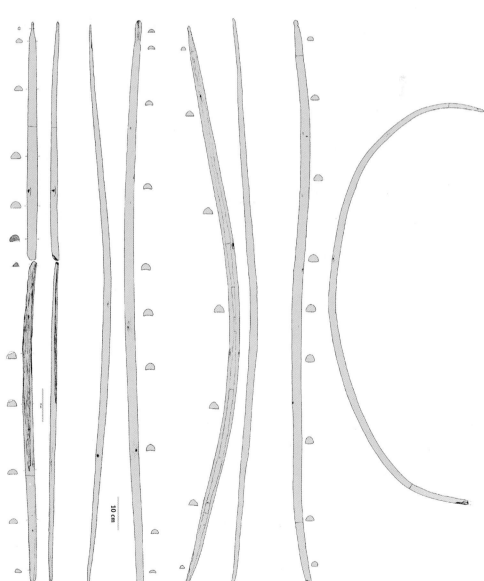

Examples of Neolithic bows of the stave-shaped type.

Figure 1.
1. **Egolzwil 4** (CH), ca. 4000-3700 B.C., original length ca. 170-175 cm, broken in ancient times.
2. **Niederwil** (CH), 3822-3584 B.C., length 171 cm.
3. **Thayngen-Weier** (CH), 3822-3584 B.C., length 170.5 cm.
4. **Robenhausen** (CH), undated, 143 cm long.

10 cm

1   2   3   4

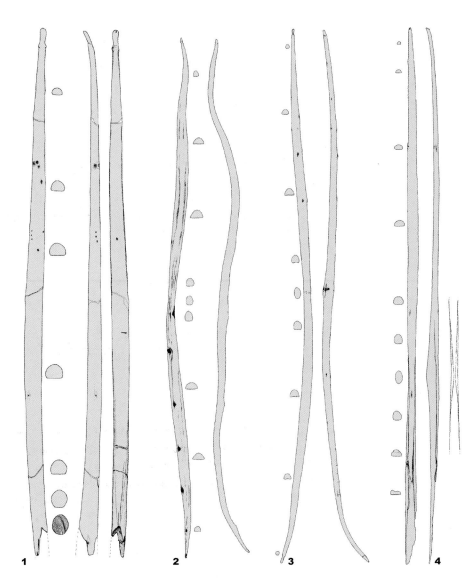

The **paddle-shaped bow** resembles a paddle when seen from the front or back.

Its greatest width is about in the middle of the limbs; from there it narrows both to the middle of the bow and to the ends. The wrapped grip section usually has a sculptured thickening on the inside of the bow, to compensate for the weaknesses of the bows, which are very narrow there.

The limbs often run to points, which saves weight on the bow ends.

Neolithic bows of the "paddle-shaped" type.

Figure 2.
1. Ashcott Heath (GB), 3650-3100 B.C., length now 84 cm, originally about 160 cm, broken in modern times.
2. Bodman (GB), undated, length 149.5 cm.
3. Robenhausen (CH), undated, length 163.5 cm.
4. Rotten Bottom (GB), 3960-3710 B.C., length now 136.5 cm, originally about 178 cm, broken in ancient times.

CROSS-SECTIONS

The cross-sections of Neolithic bows differ radically from that of the medieval longbow. While the longbows of the Middle Ages are almost flat on the outside and rounded on the inside (the side facing the shooter), thus having a lot of stability against breakage, the Neolithic cross-section is just the opposite.

Until very recently, the prevalent theory was that of the "backward"-drawn Stone Age bow found in the literature (P. Comstock: "Ancient European Bows," in J. Hamm (ed): *The Traditional Bowyer's Bible*, Volume Two, New York, 1993), because, in 1963, the British archaeologist G. D. Clark assumed, based on the cross-section of the longbow, that the prehistoric bows were oriented with their flat side to the belly (J. G. D. Clark: "Neolithic Bows from Somerset, England," and the "Prehistory of Archery in North-Western Europe," *Proceedings of the Prehistoric Society,* 29, 1963, pp. 50-98), and this was copied and believed over and over.

But the fact that sapwood is present on the arched sections of the original discoveries shows very clearly that this is a fable.

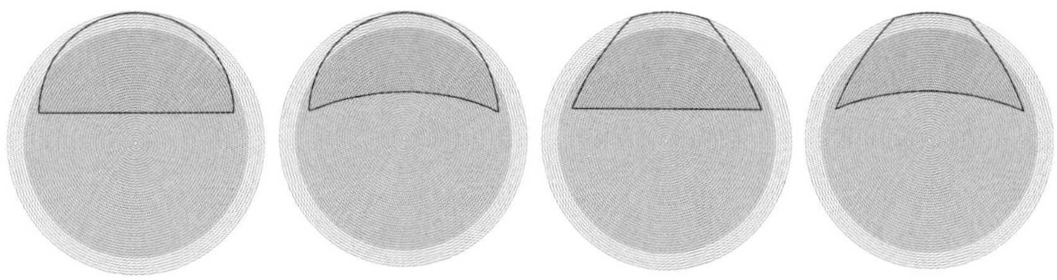

With the rounded upper side, the bowyer takes a rather large risk and places on the mostly flat inside the priority for maximum pressure resistance, which is expressed in less continued bending. This in turn works out as greater effectiveness and arrow speed.

Variants include bows with their inside hollowed out, thus concave instead of flat. What the meaning of this may be is controversial. It is clear that through the resistance to pressure, the bow's own weight is decreased. Perhaps it is not a design chosen for technical considerations, but more of a purely decorative element.

To learn more about the practical effects, several bows first had to be built with a flat inside surface and then tested thoroughly. Then the inside had to be hollowed out and the same bows tested again, so as to be able to find differences in performance.

In the last phase of the Neolithic era, roughly between 3000 and 2400 B.C., a flattening of the bow's belly to a small central strip on the unworked surface can be observed in Swiss bows. This leads to improved breakage resistance compared to the cross sections that are rounded in front.

Figure 3
Idealized cross-section of Neolithic bows, showing the relation of sapwood to heartwood. The belly of the bow is upward; not to scale.

NOCKS

A remarkable variety of differently shaped bow ends can be seen. There are cone-like, button-like, spoon-like, and notched-end pieces. Usually the nock for fastening the bowstring is so weakly made that fastening with a fixed knot, such as is the rule today, was not possible. The end of the bowstring usually must have been attached with the help of a wrapping knot or self-tightening sling.

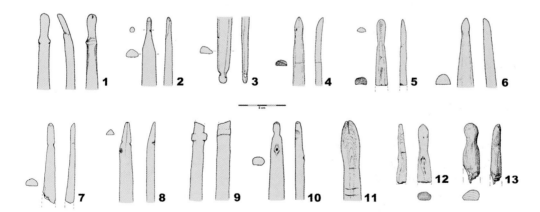

Figure 4
Various types of Neolithic bow ends.
1. Ashcott Heath (GB),
2-4. Egolzwil 4 (CH),
5. Lüscherzo (CH)
6. Thayngen-Weier (CH),
7-8. Robenhausen (CH),

9. Vrees (D),
11. Zürich-Mozartstrasse (CH),
12. Vinelz (CH),
13. Hornstaad (D),(drawn by M. Kinsky, Landesamt für Denkmalpflege, Hemmenhofen)
Scale: 1:4

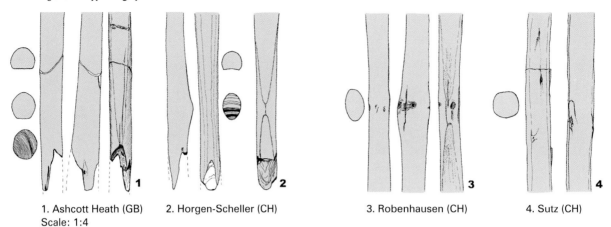

Figure 5 **Typical grips of some Neolithic bows**

1. Ashcott Heath (GB)   2. Horgen-Scheller (CH)   3. Robenhausen (CH)   4. Sutz (CH)
Scale: 1:4

GRIP SECTIONS

The grip sections of Neolithic bows also show a great deal of variation. While the grips of the staff-shaped type are usually not worked out at all and thus cannot be recognized as such except for their position in the middle of the bow, the grips of the paddle type were almost always shaped especially. In the latter, there was a technical necessity of equalizing the thinness in the middle of the bow through a thickening in this area, since the bows would break if the area were of constant thickness. This thickening on the inside could be made either rounded or rib-like, with flat central strips or two adjoining facets, etc.

In the stave-type bows, no thickening in the middle was needed, so for simplicity's sake a special shaping of the grip was avoided.

RAW MATERIALS

Yew, *Taxus baccata L.*

Since the Neolithic era, the wood of the yew tree *(Taxus baccata)* has been used almost exclusively for building bows. Only very seldom was elmwood used, the material used in North European bows of the Mesolithic era. Examples are a Neolithic bow from Northern Europe and a Swiss Bronze Age bow.

To this day, yew is regarded by bowyers as the best European bow wood. It consists of a yellowish-white layer of sapwood lying outside on the trunk and a red-brown heart inside.

As Saxton Pope was able to prove beyond a doubt through breakage tests in the twenties, yew sapwood is considerably tougher and more elastic than heartwood. The latter, though, is harder and more pressure-resistant. (S. Pope: *Hunting with the Bow and Arrow,* New York, 1925). Only by combining the two materials in the bow did the special quality of the wood for bow building result.

Since then, the sapwood has been used on the outside of the bow, while the heartwood forms the inside. The tough sapwood affects the pulling-pressured outside like a backing and improves its resistance to breakage. The hard heartwood on the inside can very well resist the pressure that occurs there, and effects a slight permanent bending, plus high efficiency and arrow speed.

Since the yew trees used then, some 5 to 15 cm thick, grew in very shadowed forests, the slow growth resulted in very thin annual rings, 0.2 mm not being rare. The sapwood part of the trunks that were used was mostly under 1 cm thick. Thus it was not necessary to reduce the sapwood area as in the present-day, when yews with very thick sapwood sections are often used. The sapwood part of Neolithic yew bows is usually between 5 and 10 mm thick.

No remains of **grip wrappings** or leather grips have been found, so it is quite likely that the Neolithic bows, like the longbows of the Middle Ages, were shot "bare," with only a wooden grip.

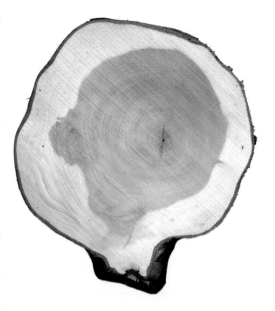

After long years of practice, one can also say that such a thing is quite unnecessary. The wood can be gripped very firmly when shooting; no problems with slipping grips have turned up. It seems, though, according to some archers, that a bow that, when shot, hits hard or causes hand shock, can be eased with a leather grip. It is probably needless to note that such things as sights and nock points were unknown.

Cross-section of a yew trunk, with the dark heartwood clearly visible, contrasting with the light sapwood.

What material was used for the **bowstring** is not clear to date for lack of discoveries. Although numerous Stone Age cords and weaves, mostly of inner bark, have been found, a recognizable bowstring has not yet been found.

Animal fibers, such as intestines or tendons, were probably not used in Europe, since these fibers have the unpleasant quality of absorbing a lot of moisture in long-term rain and humidity, and then becoming soft and slippery. This is the reason why the Native Americans of the North American plains and prairies did not hunt or make war in rainy weather. But in the continental climate prevailing there, it rains rarely or not at all.

Since in Europe, on account of the climate, there is scarcely a day in the year when the possibility of rain can be ruled out completely, a bowstring made of animal fibers would be very impractical. Among the suitable plant fibers, flax or linen is ideal for bowstring use because of its extreme resistance to tearing, and it was grown by the farmers of the Neolithic Age. The inner bark used for most of the Stone Age cords that have been found, linden and other tree material, is too weak for such a purpose.

Although proof in the form of a preserved bowstring has not yet been found, one can assume that most of them were made of flax or linen. The old technique of twisting, which is used to this day by traditional archers (in the famous "Flemish splice"), has already been confirmed by discoveries from the end of the last Ice Age.

PRODUCTION TECHNIQUES

The preserved raw bows of Neolithic Era show very clearly that the bows were shaped with a hatchet when the wood was still moist. Although it has not been proven, it must be assumed that the half-finished products could dry for a time before they were finally finished. A still-moist bow could lose much of its power through premature drawing, because still-damp, soft wood gives, and the bow would be permanently bent after being strung.

A problem in the drying of extensively pre-formed raw bows is the danger of the wood warping. When a strong sideward bending takes place, the rough bow is generally ruined. Whether and how the Neolithic bowyers handled this problem is unknown. One possibility might be greasing the raw bow as the Native Americans did.

After splitting the yew trunk, which could also be done with very thin trunks, the bow form was worked out very precisely with a stone hatchet, or, possibly, with a kind of ripping chisel, or other bone or stone tools. Smoothing the bow was presumably done with sharp-edged pieces of quartz or filed boar tusks. The final smoothing, which cannot be described as anything but perfect in many preserved Neolithic bows, could have been done at first with fine sandstone, then with sections of horsetail grass, which are still used today for polishing in instrument building.

Flint knife

BENDING PROCEDURES

Some of the Neolithic bows, as far as can be determined from the width and thickness of the discoveries, were not perfectly tillered. One can thus assume that some specimens were bent fairly unevenly when fully drawn. It is no wonder, for, as far as we know, the tiller board of the medieval and modern bowyer was still unknown then. Presumably the bows were tillered by making sure that the limbs bent symmetrically when drawn. Surely a helper would also have bent the bow to test it. Places that were too stiff could then be noted or marked with charcoal and then reduced in thickness. In this way a satisfactory symmetry of the limbs, though by no means perfect by present standards, could have been achieved.

Neolithic bows are certainly symmetrical longitudinally, meaning that the two limbs are more or less equally long and the grip is located in the middle. Thus the arrow is in shooting position (on the knuckles of the bow hand) 2 to 3 cm over the symmetrical middle of the bow. A difference in shooting qualities in comparison with the asymmetrical bows of the Late Middle Ages, which had upper limbs a few centimeters longer than the lower ones, has not been found to date.

REPLICATING THE BODMAN BOW

In 1995 a replica of a bow found at the lake shore settlement near Bodman on Lake Constance was made. Since the original was found in the previous century during unsystematic excavation, nothing is known, unfortunately, as to its layer and conditions, and exact dating is not possible. On the basis of its cross-section shape and the small button-like tip, the bow probably belongs to the period of 4000 to 3000 B.C. The original, kept at the Rosgarten Museum in Constance, is very strongly warped by the drying of the wood, and looks more like a snake than a bow.

The length of the complete bow is only 149.5 centimeters, which may well have been a man's height at that time. On the front, a strip of light sapwood some 0.5 to 1 cm wide can be seen clearly. The thickness of the sapwood is only 5-6 mm.

Very fine-grained yew wood with 20 to 30 annual rings per centimeter was used, and the trunk was, according to the warping of the rings, at least 5 cm thick. The cross-section is curved on the outside, while the inside is completely flat. Its maximum width of 3.7 cm is reached about in the middle of its limbs. The thickness decreases rather irregularly from the center to the ends.

Knots on the belly were worked out very well, so as to strengthen these potential breaking points and thus minimize the danger of breakage. The grip area is not noticeably thickened on the inside, which constitutes an exception in the paddle-shaped bows. Yet there is a thickening on the belly because of the presence of several strong knots in the grip area.

BODMAN (ORIGINAL)		Total length: 149.5 cm Effective length 147.5 cm			Wood: yew		
cm	place	width	thickness	cm	place	width	thickness
75,0	Bow end under	--	--	-74,5	Bow end under	--	--
73,0	string nock	0,90	1,00	-72,5	string nock	0,80	0,80
65,0		1,60	1,50	-65,0		1,75	1,45
55,0		2,30	1,40	-55,0	Branch	2,90	1,65
45,0		3,00	1,80	-45,0		3,30	1,75
35,0		3,60	2,10	-35,0		3,60	1,70
25,0		3,70	2,25	-25,0		3,40	1,75
15,0	Branch	3,20	2,40	-15,0		3,10	2,10
5,0		2,30	2,20	-5,0	Branch	2,25	2,85
0,0	Middle (branch)	2,50	2,45				

Figure 6
Dimensions of the original Bodman bow

BODMAN TYPE (built 8/95)		Total length: 151 cm effective length: 149 cm		Sustained bending: 2.8 % Wood: Yew		Draw weight: 53 lb/70 cm	
cm	place	width	thickness	cm	place	width	thickness
76,0	Bow end under	--	--	-76,0	Bow end under	--	--
74,0	string nock	0,95	0,98	-74,0	string nock	0,95	0,96
70,0		1,37	1,25	-70,0		1,34	1,14
60,0		2,23	1,42	-60,0		2,15	1,40
50,0		2,90	1,53	-50,0		2,93	1,49
40,0		3,50	1,57	-40,0		3,33	1,60
30,0		3,84	1,64	-30,0		3,71	1,62
20,0		3,65	1,78	-20,0		3,47	1,77
10,0		3,00	2,10	-10,0		2,86	2,25
0,0	Middle	2,40	2,70				

Figure 7
Dimensions of the replica

53

CHARACTERISTICS OF THE REPLICA

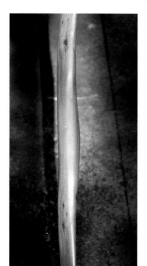

Bodman bow replica, lower end of the grip, inside. (Photos: J. Junkmanns; see also color plate 1)

Bodman bow replica, lower end inside.

A less finely grained yew wood than that of the original was used for the replica. The yew trunk, some 7 cm thick, had been seasoned for three years before being put to use in 1995.

While the sapwood had grown slowly (ca. 20 rings per centimeter), the heartwood shows rings up to 2.5 centimeters wide. The sapwood was reduced to 5-10 mm.

On the basis of the different growth rates, the dimensions of the original could not be taken over unchanged for the new bow. The original bow was very thick in some place, mainly because of knots.

The replica has somewhat smaller dimensions than limb 2 of the original. Since knots were missing in that area, the grip was thickened on the inside.

The small, button-like ends do not allow the use of a firm bowstring loop; thus the string was made of flax and given a tightening loop for attachment at each end. The carefully tillered replica, with a draw length of 70 cm (the measured distance between the inner edge of the bow and the string), attained a draw weight of 50 pounds or 23 kilograms.

The bow bends over its entire length and is not stiff in the grip area. The chart line, remarkably, runs straight up to 60 cm of draw (gaining 2 kg every 5 cm); then the draw weight increases by 3 kg to 70 cm every 5 cm. Thus in the end phase of being drawn, the bow becomes slightly "hard" (in the English literature this behavior is called *stacking).*

If it were longer, then the curve would be completely straight and a little "softer" when drawn. For such a short bow, this behavior is very straight-lined, and the stacking is very meager.

This is attributable to the positive qualities of the cross-section, which is flat on the inside, and to the fact that the bow also bends in the grip area. The flat inside is very resistant to pressure and tends to bend only a little.

This string follow amounts to 2.8% of the effective length (derived from the departure of both ends from a straight line in an unstrung condition).

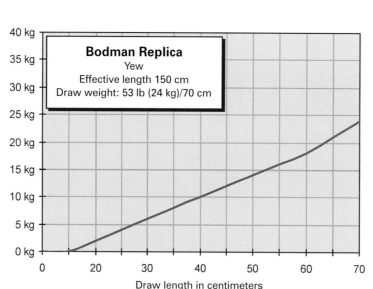

Bodman Replica
Yew
Effective length 150 cm
Draw weight: 53 lb (24 kg)/70 cm

Draw length in centimeters

Figure 8
Chart curve (power track diagram) and arrow speed measurement for the replica of the Bodman bow. The chart line is based on the draw weight of the bow being 3 pounds more than in the speed measurements.

The arrow speeds achieved by the bow using various arrow weights show that the bow is better suited for use with lighter arrows.

The attained speed of 182 kph with a 20-gram arrow show the high achievement potential of this prehistoric bow.

Because of the great differences in wood firmness (not only within the *Taxus baccata* type) and other immeasurables (tillering, draw length of the original users), one must avoid simply equating the replica with the original. Only a determination of the potential performance of this bow type can be derived in this way.

In cautious conclusions, a very high range of variations must be included in the calculations: the original of this Neolithic bow from Bodman could have had a draw weight between 40 and 60 pounds and corresponding performance data.

Such a bow would have been sufficiently powerful for most of the wild animals existing at that time.

Figure 9
The author testing the Bodman replica.

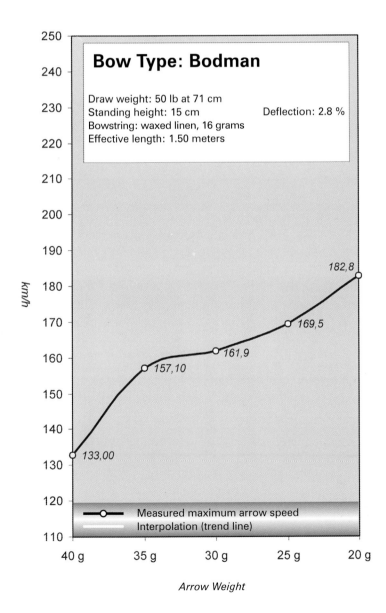

Bow Type: Bodman

Draw weight: 50 lb at 71 cm
Standing height: 15 cm   Deflection: 2.8 %
Bowstring: waxed linen, 16 grams
Effective length: 1.50 meters

km/h

182,8

169,5

161,9

157,10

133,00

— Measured maximum arrow speed
— Interpolation (trend line)

40 g   35 g   30 g   25 g   20 g

Arrow Weight

PREHISTORIC ARROWS

In principle, the arrow is a further development of the throwing spear of ancient times, which was thrown only with the hand for a very long time. The oldest spears of *Homo erectus* that have been found to date are some 400,000 years old. Only in the last third of the last Ice Age, some twenty to thirty thousand years ago, was a device invented with which the spear's performance could be increased significantly: the spear-thrower. The power transmission from the thrower to the spear generally took place through a barbed hook that had a counterpart in a small groove at the rear end of the spear. This groove can be seen as the forerunner of the nock in the arrow. Just when the bow and arrow were invented is as yet unknown; but in any case, it was in the Paleolithic Age.

The oldest direct evidence of the bow weapon consists of the arrows from **Stellmoor** near Hamburg. The perfectly worked arrows, equipped with changeable foreshafts, date from the end of the last Ice Age, about 8000 B.C. Their nocks show that they were definitely arrows that were shot from a bow. It is thought that the bow weapon is actually much older than the Stellmoor arrows, although proof has not yet been found.

Of the great numbers of prehistoric arrows that were used for more than 10,000 years in prehistoric Europe, only a handful exist today. That is because the wooden shafts can only remain for long periods of time under especially favorable conditions. Organic materials such as wood must spend the whole time shut off from air, for example, in the constantly wet ground of lake shores or moors, sometimes also in the sediments of spring shafts; otherwise they will soon succumb to bacterial rotting.

The discovery of the fully armed glacier-man Ötzi has shown that ideal conditions for the preservation of organic objects exist in the ice of high-mountain glaciers. There are probably other "Ötzis" waiting to be discovered.

In extremely tropical areas, such as the Atacama Desert of Peru, organic materials can indeed survive without being closed off from air, but in Europe such dry areas do not exist. Almost all of Europe's surviving prehistoric arrows thus come from shore settlements (such as the well-known lake dwellings) or villages in turf bogs.

Figure 2
Complete arrow shaft from Stellmoor; at left, the main shaft (73 cm long); above, the foreshaft, beside it the finder's pocket knife.

RAW MATERIAL

Arrow shafts were made in two basically different types.

For one, one- to two-year **shoots** of certain kinds of shrubs were used; for the other, split lengths of large tree trunks. Both types had to be straightened or directed using heat.

Many different types of wood were used to make arrows. The most important qualities were hardness and elasticity, and, for split wood, good splitting qualities; for shoots, even growth. Shafts of viburnum, dogwood (*Cornus*), hazel, and burning bush (*Euonymus*) were generally made from shoots; as for other woods, such as pine, ash, or birch, they were made of split wood.

Shafts from shoots are considerably tougher than split-wood shafts. They break only under extreme pressure, but also bend very easily and must then be straightened anew. Another disadvantage is the weight, which varies strongly from shoot to shoot, even in the same type of shrub with the same diameter, which depends on the varying thickness of the hollow inner channel. Shafts made of split wood break more easily, but remain relatively straight even in humid weather.

Pine dominates among older arrows, probably because of the limited availability of warmth-loving types of wood shortly after the end of the last Ice Age. Only with the gradual spread of warmth-loving types of wood was a greater variety of wood types available.

PINE	VIBURNUM	BIRCH	ASH	DOGWOOD	HAZEL	HONEYSUCKLE	ALDER	LARCH	WILLOW	BURNING BUSH	LOCALITY	DATE
		●									Haithabu (D)	ca. 800 A.D.
			●	●	●						Altdorf-St. Martin (CH)	660–680 A.D.
	●	●									Oberflacht (D)	ca. 450–550 A.D.
●											Nydam (D)	4th century A.D.
	●			●	●			●	●		Hochdorf (D)	500–550 B.C.
	●										Fiave/ (I)	ca. 1500 B.C.
							●				Gortrea (Ireland)	Neolithic Era/Bronze Age
					●						Tankardsgarden (Ireland)	Neolithic Era/Bronze Age
	●										Fyvie (Ireland)	Neolithic Era/Bronze Age
	●			●							Ötzi (I)	ca. 3200 B.C.
	●			●							Arbon-Bleiche 3 (CH)	3400 B.C.
						●					Zug-Geissboden (CH)	Neolithic Era
	●										Thayngen-Weier (CH)	3800–3400 B.C.
					●						Egolzwil 4 (CH)	ca. 3800 B.C.
	●										Magleby Long (DK)	Neolithic Era
			●								Muldbjerg (DK)	ca. 4000–3000 B.C.
				●							Bregentwedt (D)	ca. 4500–3500 B.C.
			●								Kückhoven (D)	5090–5065 B.C.
●	●	●									Holmegård (DK)	ca. 6500 B.C.
●											Vinkel (DK)	ca. 7000–6000 B.C.
●											Fippenborg (DK)	ca. 7000–6500 B.C.
●											Lilla Loshult (S)	ca. 7000 B.C.
●											Stellmoor (D)	ca. 8800 B.C.

Arrowheads were generally made of flint or similarly hard and brittle types of stone, or of antler or bone. Often the heads were simply carved from the wood, whether as points or clubs. The stone arrowheads were very fragile and almost always had to be changed, sharpened, or repaired if a shot missed or hit a bone.

A tar distilled from birch bark, known as birch pitch, was used as glue. With it, both arrowheads and, at times, feathers were attached. At normal temperatures, birch pitch is very hard, but it liquefies with heat and can then be applied and brushed very easily. For wrappings, strings of animal sinews or plant fibers were used.

CHARACTERISTICS

Prehistoric arrows are very long. As a rule their length exceeds 80 centimeters and can, as the arrow from Vinkel (Denmark) shows, measure even more than a meter. Their diameter is usually between 8 and 9 mm, and in the very long pine shafts can even reach a centimeter. Naturally, such long arrows could not be drawn to their full length with the simple wooden bows, mostly only 145 to 165 cm long, used then, as the bows certainly would have broken. The intention of such long arrows was probably to increase the penetrating power by the greater weight of longer arrows. Lighter arrows, of course, fly faster and have a flatter trajectory, which means that, at a greater range, the shooter does not have to shoot so far above the target. In target shooting today, it becomes clear that shorter and thus lighter, faster arrows have the advantage. To bow hunters, though, the greater penetrating power of heavier arrows is valued more highly. Their ability to fly more cleanly and forgive shooting errors more easily also leads to heavier arrows being used for hunting.

Lengths of some Prehistoric Arrows

Locality	Date	Wood	Length
Stellmoor (D)	8800 B.C.	Pine	ca. 83.5-98 cm
Lilla Loshult (S)	7500 B.C.	Pine	92 cm
Holmegård	6500 B.C.	Pine	over 86 cm*
Vinkel (DK)	6000 B.C.	Pine	102 cm
Förstermoor (D)	ca. 5000 B.C.	Dogwood	over 74.5 cm*
Thayngen/ Weier (CH)	3820-3584 B.C.	Viburnum	ca. 68 cm
Ötzi (I)	3400-3200 B.C.	Viburnum	84-87 cm
			* incomplete

The penetrating power of an arrow is determined chiefly by its inherent motive energy and the cutting or striking effect of the arrowhead. The kinetic energy of a body depends on its speed and weight. For calculation, the formula $E^{kin} = 1/2\ m\ v^2$ is used.

Although by this formula the speed theoretically should have a much greater influence on the kinetic energy of an arrow, in practice, the weight has considerably more importance.

The reasons for this are that a heavier arrow can take up much more of the energy stored in the bow, and also the air resistance increases significantly at higher speed, and light, fast arrows are braked very quickly.

The prehistoric points were as effective as present-day arrowheads. Modern tests showed that, for example, small animals like goats could be shot without problems by simple wooden bows with some 50 pounds of pulling pressure, using flint-tipped replicas of prehistoric arrows, as long as bones were not hit. Of course the arrowheads have to be fresh, for their very sharp edges are dulled very quickly from use. Larger animals with thicker hides, such as wild boars, can be shot only with absolutely fresh, razor-sharp flint arrowheads.

Penetrating Weights of Shafts of various Wood Types

Wood type	Penetrating Weight	Deviation to
Viburnum	47 grams	29%
Dogwood	45 grams	33%
Burning bush	37 grams	31%
Pine	28 grams	10%

Raw shafts ca. 90 cm long and 8 to 9 mm thick

Weight of some Reconstructed Arrowheads

Type	Date	Material	Weight
Cross-cutter	Mesolithic	Flint	> 1 gram
Microlith	Mesolithic	Flint	> 1 gram
Triangular point	Neolithic	Flint	4 grams
Scythian triple*	ca. 500 B.C.	Bronze	4 grams
Armor-piercer	Medieval	Iron	18 grams
Modern field point	Current	Iron	6.5-8 grams

* original three-winged arrowhead

Whether stone, antler, or bone is used for the arrowhead, the influence of the head on the total weight remains meager. An arrowhead of antler or bone weighs, as a rule, no more than 2 to 3 grams.

Flint arrowheads can be somewhat heavier, of course, but in most cases they weigh under 6 grams, since the specific gravity of flint quartz is not as high as that of metal, and they would otherwise be so large that the air resistance could greatly affect the arrow's flight.

Early arrowhead types like the Mesolithic Era microliths weigh much less, mostly below one gram.

The Neolithic arrowheads are an exception, as they are fitted with a coating of birch pitch and thus move the arrow's center of gravity toward the point. To attain higher arrow speeds, the shaft itself had to be made heavier, longer than really necessary. Stone Age arrows, depending on their length and wood type, weighed 30 to 60 grams.

The fletching is important to stabilize an arrow, although it, more or less, flies without feathers when the main weight of the arrow is in its forward third. Its effect depends on two factors: the braking effect of the feathers at the rear prevents the arrow from turning sideways or lengthwise, with the rear to the front, and the curved natural shape of the feathers makes the arrow rotate on its long axis, which stabilizes straight flight.

Fletching can be done in various ways; for example, parallel, radial, or spiral fletching. Fletching can be preserved underground only under almost unbelievably good conditions. The only case in which a prehistoric arrow found in Europe still had its fletching was that of the glacier man Ötzi, whose two finished arrows each had three radial fletchings. This type of fletching remains unchanged as the most successful and popular type to this day.

PREHISTORIC ARROW FORMS

For their various uses, such as hunting various mammals, birds and fish, but also for wartime use, many forms of arrows were used over the course of time. The array present here makes no claim to completeness. It notes the most important and most commonly used forms, on the basis of selected examples, and should, above all, make the variety of the many types and their various uses apparent.

PALEOLITHIC AGE
16,000 B.C.   Arrowheads or Spear Points?

When the discoveries from the cave at Parpallø, a hunting camp of Late Ice Age antelope hunters near Valencia, were made public in the 1940s, doubts arose as to whether the quartz points with barbs and tangs, dating from about 16,000 B.C., could really be that old. In terms of form and size, they were very reminiscent of Copper Age arrowheads more than 13,000 years newer.

Figure 1
Projectile points from Par-pallø (Museo de Prehistoria, Valencia, Spain), see also color plate 2.

Meanwhile, though, similar discoveries from further Spanish and Portuguese sites became known, and their great age is no longer in dispute. The tangs of the points from Parpallø are only some 6-7 mm wide, and thus are much too narrow for direct installation on spears for the spear-thrower. Since the points are often barbed, the tang diameter cannot be much greater than the width of the arrows, for otherwise the barbs would have been useless.

Even if one considers their use on the foreshafts of spears, these tangs must have been so thin that they would have broken every time they hit anything. Spear points that were demonstrably thrown with a spear thrower are notably larger and heavier. The Parpallø points are thus very probably a very early indication of bows and arrows on the Iberian peninsula.

8800 B.C.   *Assembled Hunting Arrows with Flint Heads and*
Simply Pointed Wooden Arrows

105 fragments of pine arrows were found in an excavation, also in the 1940s, at Stellmoor near Hamburg.

This was a hunting site at which the Late Ice Age reindeer hunters of the so-called *Ahrensburg Culture* lay in wait for the yearly migration of the reindeer herds as they crossed a stream. The animals were presumably shot while they were in the water, for hundreds of arrows, which were probably carried downstream by the current and finally sank, were found there.

Dated at some 8800 years B.C. by using the Carbon 14 method, the Stellmoor shafts are the world's oldest sure proof of bows and arrows. Since the shafts are nocked, it is certain that they were shot from bows.

Figure 3
The brilliant joint
of main shaft and
foreshaft of the
Stellmoor arrows.
The joint must
not have been
glued, but only
wrapped with
sinew, and should
have come apart
easily.

The nicely worked and perfectly smoothed arrows were brilliantly made of two parts (main shaft and foreshaft), and were generally about 90 cm long. The split trunkwood of large pines was used. Nothing remains of any fletching. Simple pointed flints were used as heads. Two fragments of used arrowheads were found sticking in reindeer vertebrae.

Many of the Stellmoor arrows were simply pointed. That such arrows were also used for hunting is shown by an arrow fragment with a simply pointed wooden end, which was found sticking in a wolf's bone.

MESOLITHIC AGE
7.500 B.C.   Micropoints, Blunt Points, and presumed "Bird Arrows"

After the end of the last Ice Age, arrows with very small, extremely sharp points and side-cutters of flint were used for hunting larger and more dangerous animals such as bears or aurochs. With its high cutting effect, this type of arrow is a highly effective hunting weapon, which can penetrate an animal's body very easily, even through a thick hide. The smallness and simplicity of these points and blades, known as *microliths,* and glued on with birch pitch, are striking.

Traces of wrappings at the rear end of a found arrow shaft show that the fletching was attached only with binding and not with pitch. The fact that some of the early pine arrows, such as those from Lilla Loshult and Vinkel, have barrel-shaped shafts, is noteworthy, for it means that their diameter is greatest in the middle and tapers toward both ends.

A good example of this type of arrow comes from the Lilla Loshult bog in southern Sweden; it is also one of the very few completely preserved prehistoric arrows (Figure 4, left).

It dates from the early Mesolithic era, about 7500 B.C. The arrow, 92 cm long over-

Figure 4
Arrow from Lilla Loshult (Lund University Museum, Sweden).

all, is made of split pine and perfectly smoothed. At its front end are two *microliths*, one as the point and the other as a side cutter, attached with a gleaming black material, very probably birch pitch. The fact that the adhesive has been so well preserved at the head but none is to be seen at the other end of the arrow means that the fletching was not attached with birch pitch. The V-shaped nock is cut perpendicular to the growth rings.

The **side-cutter** is an interesting special form of microlithic arrowhead, although the unlikely little artifacts seem at first glance to have little to do with an arrowhead. Yet the thin, razor-sharp blade of a fresh side-cutter, standing at a right angle to the long axis of the shaft, has an extraordinary cutting effect. Its production is very quick and uncomplicated, for a side-cutter can be installed in a matter of seconds.

An arrow fragment from Vissenbjerg (Denmark) shows that the straight flint blade is set in a small slit across the shaft, fixed with an adhesive (birch pitch?), and secured with a binding of animal sinew or plant fibers.

Figure 5
Straight-cutting arrow fragment from Vissebjerg (National Museum, Copenhagen, Denmark).

Blunt heads, arrows with a club-like head carved from the front end, were presumably used to hunt small animals whose fur or feathers were to be damaged as little as possible.

The effect of these club heads should not be underestimated. Archers report that such arrows can kill small animals purely from shock. Even larger animals can suffer serious injuries, such as broken bones or skulls. Harm Paulsen, an experimental archaeologist from Schleswig, happily demonstrates this by shooting holes in two-centimeter wooden plates with blunt, club-tipped arrows.

Relics of many arrows, including pieces of two club-tipped ones, were found near a complete bow and a large fragment of another, both made of elm, in the excavation of a Mesolithic settlement site in the Holmegård Moor in southern Denmark. They date from about 6500 B.C. and are the oldest known arrows of this type. Both club arrows have long cylindrical thickenings that are formed into stubby conical points at their front ends. The larger cone is 5.6 cm long and 1.6 cm thick; the shaft itself has a diameter of about 9 mm. The second arrow has a somewhat shorter point. Both arrows are said to be made of birch wood. At least one of them is clearly made from a shoot.

Figure 6
Blunt arrow from Holmegård (National Museum, Copenhagen. Denmark). After C. J. Becker, 1945.

"Bird arrows"—In Northern Europe, a special form of arrowhead made of bone was quite often used during the Mesolithic era. These were formerly known as bird arrows. A bone point, some 5 to 15 centimeters long, had a long row of flint blades inset on one or both sides, and were attached to the wooden shaft with a thin peg. These razor-sharp flint blades, made in a special way and unworked, were set in grooves with birch pitch. Thus shooting at birds really amounted to shooting at sparrows with cannons. . . .

A hint at the actual purpose of this type of points came from the discovery of such points between the bones of brown bears in the Medvedia cave in eastern Slovakia. Two brown bears were presumably fatally injured in the vicinity, very probably with just one shot each, and died in the cave.

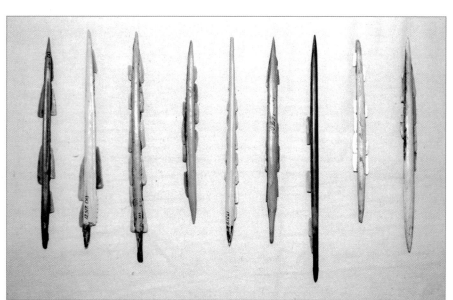

Figure 7: Bone arrowheads with flint blades (National Museum, Copenhagen. Denmark)

63

NEOLITHIC AGE
3500 B.C.   Arrowheads with Birch Pitch Coatings

Figure 8
Arrow from Burgäschi-
see (Historical Museum,
Bern, Switzerland), after
H.-J. Müller-Beck, 1965

In the Neolithic era, laboriously worked, aesthetic arrowheads with a triangular basic form were preferred. Any modern man is capable of recognizing them as arrowheads, without any previous knowledge.

Despite the laborious preparation, taking up to an hour, their pure cutting effect was no better than that of the older types, but rather worse. Perhaps these arrowheads had become status symbols somehow. It is at least striking that some heads were worked very much more laboriously than pure functionality required. Along with very "beautiful" works of art, there are also many badly or hastily worked pieces, which were made either in a hurry or by less talented artisans. Ugly arrowheads were, of course, used along with beautiful ones, and were just as effective as the latter. In the Neolithic Era this type of arrowhead was always attached to the shaft with a coating of the universal adhesive, birch pitch. The covering usually formed a streamlined thickening, out of which only the cutting side edges and the actual point projected. This coating presumably served two purposes: first, it added weight to the front end of the arrow, and second, it protected the very breakable flint arrowheads.

"Ötzi," the man who died while crossing the Alps around 3200 B.C., and was found with all his clothing and equipment, carried not only a not yet finished rough bow of yew, but also a filled leather quiver. In it there were found, along with other pieces of equipment, 12 raw shafts of viburnum and two ready-to-use arrows of the same wood, 85 and 87 cm long.

The assertion that the two arrows were not ready to shoot because they had been broken is not accurate. It can be determined that the transverse breaks visible on these arrows, with completely smooth broken surfaces, could not have happened during Ötzi's lifetime, but only after they had spent a long time in the ice and their wooden structure was already partly destroyed. Viburnum and dogwood shoots with intact wood structure show completely different breakage behavior: they split longitudinally and break with fanlike fibers.

The three-pointed, shafted quartz arrowheads are attached with birch pitch. One of the arrows has a foreshaft 10 cm long, made of dogwood (*Cornus*), which is set into the main shaft with a thin peg. The connection area is bound. It must be a repair, for both woods are about equally hard and heavy, so that there is no advantage over a one-piece arrow.

Figure 9
Upper and lower ends of two arrows from "Ötzi."
After M. Egg & K. Spindler, 1993

The survival of the entire fletching, which could never before be examined on Stone Age arrows, is unique. The three feather vanes, each 14 cm long, were attached by a very thin layer of birch pitch covering this distance, and spirally wrapped with a very thin string of plant fibers. The shafts were even thinned slightly in the area of the birch-pitch covering, to avoid making them thicker there. The nocks, barely 2 cm long and some 3 mm wide, are sharp-edged and form right angles. They were split out of the shaft end.

An arrow fragment with a surviving quartz point, displayed at the Museum of Ancient History in Zug, Switzerland, is a complementary example of the way these arrows were produced. To be able to make an accurate reconstruction of the arrow, the relics were subjected to a careful study.

The shaft, some 9 mm thick, consists of a honeysuckle (*Lonicera*) shoot. The last two centimeters of the shaft were flattened on two sides. To make a nock in which to insert the head, a flint cutter was used to saw a V-shaped groove, 9 mm deep and 4 mm wide. First a long cut was made from either side; this was then widened into a groove. With much drying, the groove has become much more deeply split today. Directly under the groove are remains of a binding that was meant to prevent the shaft from splitting in a hard hit.

In a test by the Zürich Police, it was determined that on the basis of its structure, it cannot be plant fibers. Viewing it through a magnifying glass shows flat, shining fibers, which are very probably bundled animal sinews. A closer look shows several black spots under the groove in the area of the binding; under the loupe, they show a wrinkled, shining black surface, as is typical of birch pitch. These are remains of a former coating of birch pitch. The relatively small arrowhead, 2.6 cm long, 1.2 cm wide, and 5 mm thick is made of white quartz of unknown origin.

Blunt arrows have also been found from the Neolithic era, though of different form, and usually with a mounted club of antler. Presumably this material was used to make the club easier to hold. Sections of deer antlers of appropriate size were used, bored out to the diameter of the arrow shaft. Sometimes the shaft was wedged with a small piece of wood after the club was put on. In the lake shore settlement of Arbon-Bleiche on the Swiss shore of Lake Constance, from about the same time as Ötzi the glacier man, hundreds of fragments of these clubbed arrows were found, but so were numerous ordinary three-edged arrowheads.

Figure 10: Arrow from Zugerberg (Museum of Ancient History, Zug, Switzerland. Photo: Museum of Ancient History

Figure 11
Antler sleeve of a blunt arrow from Schreckensee, Oberschwaben (Landesdenkmalamt Baden-Württemberg). After H. Schlichterle & E. Wahlster, 1986

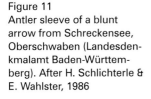

Figure 12
Arrows found at Egolzwil 4. After R. Wyss, 1983 (right)

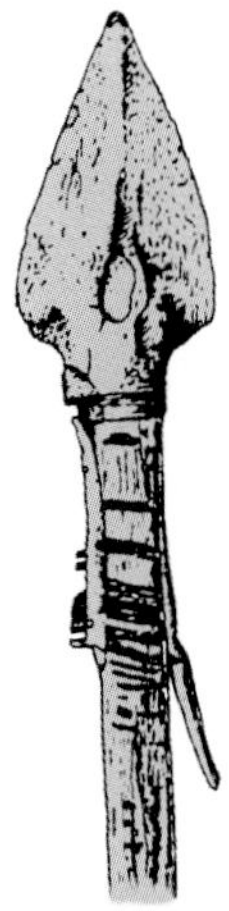

Figure 13
Bronze Age arrow from
Behringersdorf. After H. J.
Hundt, 1974-75

BRONZE AGE
1200 B.C.   Barbed Hooks and Thorns

The arrowheads from the Mesolithic era and later are very clearly no longer simple hunting devices. In the Bronze Age, stylized forms with long, thin barbs were developed. The barb points, made out of both quartz and bronze, were fitted additionally with spine-like thorns, often blackthorns that broke off easily, and were obviously meant to cause painful wounds and prolong or prevent the wound's healing. Such thorns were useless in hunting, for their effect would take place only if the animal could escape and survive the wound. They are probably war arrows that were used to put enemies who were not killed out of action for long periods because of lasting wounds.

In a Late Bronze Age warrior's burial, dated about 1200 B.C. at Behringersdorf near Nuremberg, a fragment of a quiver made of wood covered with birch bark was found. There were still seven arrowheads in it, with remains of wooden shafts still attached. Five arrows were each equipped with a pair of fine wooden thorns attached by a binding. One of the bronze points had a fine cast bronze thorn instead. Because of the fine thorns and a black pitch-like material that coated the binding, this type of arrow was called a poison arrow. But if poison were used, this elaborate construction would have been fully unnecessary, for then even a small cut on the skin would have sufficed to transmit the poison. Poisoned arrows of the Kalahari Bushmen, for example, are often fitted with just a pointed piece of feather quill.

REPLICATING A NEOLITHIC ARROW

The manufacturing technique described here will be based on that of a Neolithic arrow made of a shoot and fitted with a three-cornered flint arrowhead mounted in birch pitch. The techniques are derived from traces of workmanship on original discoveries and results of experimental archaeology.

The described methods can be applied to other Stone Age or prehistoric arrow types without problems. The accurate replication of a Neolithic arrow can, if you want, be made out of only appropriate raw materials and done with Stone Age tools and aids. To save time, though, modern means can also be used.

MATERIALS AND TOOLS

1. A shoot of viburnum, dogwood (*Cornus*), burning bush (*Euonymus*), or honeysuckle (*Lonicera*), about 90 cm long, with bark one centimeter thick, branch-free and grown as straight as possible. The shoot must already be dry. The curing time is some two to three weeks without bark, or two to three months with bark.

2. Birch pitch to attach the arrowhead and the feather vanes. Birch pitch is distilled out of the outer bark of the white birch at great heat in the absence of oxygen. It can be made relatively simply either in the so-called one-pot process, in which the pitch remains behind as a residue, or in a two-pot process, in which the pitch flows out of a small pot through a hole in the bottom into a bigger pot and collects there. A third method consists of burying the bark in lime, lighting a fire over it, and letting the pitch flow through a gutter into a container in a pit nearby. In the last two methods, the fairly liquid end product must be cooked for a long time and thus thickened. As a substitute, asphalt or strongly thickened wood tar can be used. But these materials smear quite a bit and never become as firm as birch pitch. Real birch pitch can be recognized by the very delicate, aromatic smell that it gives off when warmed.

Figure 15
Neolithic flint knife with
poplar-bark handle.

3. Three right or left wing feathers of a large bird, such as a gray goose, swan, etc.

4. Animal sinew, such as the back or leg sinew of cattle, for the wrapping under half of the arrowhead. One gets them by talking nicely to butchers.

5. Plant fiber string for binding the feathering. One can use self-twisted cord, such as nettle or flax fibers, but also very thin, purchased flax or hemp cord.

6. A fragment of flint for making arrowheads. Flint is found, for example, at some places on the Baltic Sea. You should look for good quality, so that you do not find out at home that the flint is totally useless, being internally cracked and worn.

You get a fragment by breaking it off a larger piece. To do this you need a striking stone, which can be any round, fist-sized stone made of tough rock, such as quartzite or granite. To make an arrowhead, the flint should be of regular shape, about 6 cm long, and not thicker than one centimeter.

7. A large unworked piece of flint for removing bark. You can also use it later when you want to make arrowheads.

8. A Neolithic knife with a scraper, with a deer's-antler striking tool made of a piece of flint, for planing the shaft as well as sawing and rasping. Such a tool can be made only by an experienced flint worker, so non-specialists use modern planes, knives, or files.

9. A drawknife of flint with a right-angled working edge (such as a transversely broken piece), or a sharp knife blade for scraping and smoothing.

Figure 17
A flat piece of flint suitable for making arrowheads.

10. Charcoal as a source of heat, to straighten or align the arrow shaft (alternatively, a candle or a tea light may be used).

11. Several pieces of horsetail for smoothing. Horsetail is still used today in violin making. If none should be available, you can also use sandpaper.

12. A pair of arrow-shaft smoothers made of sandstone. If you have none, use sandpaper or steel wool.

13. A particularly sharp flint blade for cutting the feathers (or a very sharp knife/scissors).

14. A heated stone for smoothing the birch pitch (or an old copper soldering iron or a modern electric soldering iron).

15. A pushing stick for making arrowheads. It consists of a wooden handle, about a hand long, with an inserted working point of antler, copper, or iron.

Figure 16
A pushing stick for use in making stone tools, such as the glacier man Ötzi had. Linden wood and antler shavings.

Figure 18: Removing bark

REMOVING BARK

First of all, the raw shaft, grown as straight as possible and free of branches, must have its bark removed. With a flint tool or a sharp knife, the dry bark can be scraped off relatively easily. Don't cut, but scrape, otherwise you will cut into the substance of the wood. The thin upper end of the shaft should become the rear end of the arrow. If the shaft is longer than the finished arrow will be, you should cut it to the desired length only later, because possible bends right on the shaft ends are hard to straighten.

Thick spots (knots) in the shaft can be scraped down or planed gently, but should not be removed altogether, since the wood structure will otherwise be weakened at these points.

Figure 19. Straightening

STRAIGHTENING

The debarked shaft can be straightened with the help of heat. This method is based on the characteristic of almost every kind of wood to become soft at a certain temperature.

Only dry raw shafts can be straightened; a still-green shaft goes right back to its original shape.

Any source of heat can be used. The heat of a candle is fully sufficient. You hold each bent area of the stem, one at a time, over the source of heat and bend it against the bend with your free hand as soon as the wood begins to get soft.

If you bend the shaft slightly with both hands, you will notice very clearly when the wood begins to give way. Extreme bends can be straightened by pressing the hot shaft down on a hot stone or your knee.

A so-called *holed staff* of antler is also practical here. You stick the shaft into the hole bored in the end of the staff and use it as a lever. Unfortunately, unsightly dents are made in the wood, so the holed staff should be used only when nothing else will work.

To determine whether and where there are still bent places in the shaft, you can hold one end right in front of your eye and sight along it, turning the shaft slowly. Such naturally grown shafts never can be made 100% straight, but you can come close, so that the small bends still present balance each other out and the shaft as a whole appears straight.

The straightening process must be repeated from time to time, since these arrow shafts sometimes bend back again, especially if they get wet. Now the shaft can be cut to the desired length.

SMOOTHING

Smoothing the surface can be done very well with a draw knife (a traditional carpenter's tool, available in good hardware stores), a pocket knife, or a flint blade with a right-angled edge. With one of these three types of blades, you scrape, with the edge held at a slight angle to the work, in an even pull over the surface of the shaft. Very fine scrapings can be removed that way.

Sometimes washboard-like grooves result, which can be removed through frequent changes in the working direction. With some practice, you are able to produce a very smooth surface.

Figure 20: Smoothing

SANDING

Horsetails are an authentic means of sanding. Alternatively, you can use sharkskin if you want. Fine sandpaper (150-200 grit) will naturally work as well.

POLISHING

To bring the shaft to a high polish, use a pair of so-called shaft polishers made of sandstone. These devices date back to the Stone Age; each has a groove, corresponding to half the diameter of the arrow, on a flat surface. They are held together so that the arrow shaft is placed in the two opposite grooves, and the shaft is pushed back and forth. The harder the sandstone is, the finer and more polished the shaft is; soft sandstone wears itself out quickly and has more of a filing effect. A modern substitute might be steel wool.

Oiling with linseed oil or the like gives somewhat effective protection, for a time, against dampness. In principle, though, all oils and fats are suitable. The effect wears off quickly, though, and thus the oiling must be repeated, especially before shooting in damp weather.

Figure 21: Polishing with sandstone

CUTTING THE NOCK

The nock for the bowstring can be made in various ways. An interesting and surprisingly simple way can be seen in Ötzi's two arrows. The nocks, about 1 to 1.5 cm long and 3 mm wide, were split out of the shaft, making use of the fact that shoots are more or less hollow thanks to their hollow interior channel.

First, a wrapping must be put on 1 to 1.5 cm from the thinner shaft end, so as to prevent the shaft from splitting farther than you want it to. Then split it with a sharp object, such as a flint or modern blade, making two parallel splits at the right distance from each other, in the end of the arrow.

The two pieces to be removed must now be nocked directly over the binding. This is done with a flint blade or pocket knife.

Figure 22
Wrapping with sinew
under the nock.

With a pointed object, you can now break the excess pieces of the hollow interior of the shaft off to the outside. The insides of the nocks should still be smoothed down, so that the bowstring will not be cut by sharp edges.

The nock for mounting the flint arrowhead need only be 5 to 10 mm deep, since the attachment of the head is chiefly the job of the coating of birch pitch. It is simplest to saw it with the slightly toothed flint blade or cut it with a pocket-knife. The nock should be V-shaped, since the flint head comes to an edge underneath. To prevent the sharp lower edge of the arrowhead from splitting the wood when it hits, another binding is made under the nock. A binding of either plant fibers (such as flax) or animal sinews is authentic.

The sinew must be dried and can be drawn very finely by hand—leg sinews after plenty of beating with a hammer or the like, if necessary (the fibers should not be thicker than one millimeter). You take such a fiber in your mouth and chew it to soften it, then wrap it around the shaft.

When it dries, the sinew contracts and becomes relatively hard.

FLETCHING

Figure 23
Pulling off the feather
flags.

Since the sticking power of the birch pitch is not strong enough to attach the hard, bending feather quills sufficiently, it is advisable to pull the vanes off the hard quills. This is true only for fairly large and strong feathers, especially goose or swan feathers. You grasp the far end of the feather vane with the fingers of your right hand and begin to pull them off the quill very carefully, downward to the right. The quill is held between the index finger and thumb of your left hand (naturally, left-handed people do it the opposite way). It is important always to grasp it as near or short as possible, to avoid tearing the skin to which the feather flag is attached. After some practice, tearing off the veins will not present a problem. The individual fletching can now by rolled up gently, which is normal and creates no problem in attaching them.

Even if you don't use a flint knife to cut the fletching to the right size, you should do it before attaching them, since the spiral binding of the fletching can be applied much more easily.

When you use flint, the feathers can be cut down on a surface relatively easily.

The knife you use must have a really sharp blade. Now the feathers must be cut to a uniform length. Ten to fifteen centimeters is advisable.

Now the length of the feathers on the shaft is coated with a thin layer of birch pitch, onto which the feathers are to be stuck. The layer should be only one-half to one millimeter thick.

A relatively soft pitch is especially good for attachment. It can be applied in spots, by forming a roll of the pitch through repeated warming, by which the head of the roll liquefies by being near the flame and gradually gives off drops.

If the pitch is extremely soft, this method is not suitable, and it can be warmed better in a pot and applied with a piece of wood or a brush. A hot stone or soldering iron is very well suited for applying the pitch evenly and smoothing it.

Before gluing, the rear end of the shaft will be heated again until the pitch is almost liquid. Now you can stick the three feather vanes on quickly, one after another. The arrangement of the feathers as a so-called triple radial feathering is just the same as in present-day archery.

The first feather is stuck onto the shaft longitudinally, perpendicular to the nock, some four to five centimeters from the end; the other two feathers are applied at equal distances around the shaft. The feathers are put on straight, parallel to the shaft. Mounting them at an angle is not necessary because the feathers are rather large and thus have a greater steering effect than the small plastic vanes used in modern archery.

The feathers will probably not adhere very well at first, but this is not a problem, since they will be immediately bound with a spiral of very thin thread. You begin at the forward end of the feathers, wrap around the shaft several times, and begin to wrap in spiral form to the end of the arrow. The filaments of the feathers must always be separated carefully at equal intervals to let the thread pass through. Don't worry if the feathers slip in the process. A false position of a feather can still be corrected before the pitch hardens, which, depending on the nature of the pitch, can take a few minutes to several days. Finally, all the bindings on the rear end of the shaft are coated with pitch again, and this is smoothed with a hot stone. The smoother the coatings become, the less likely it is that the back of your hand will be scratched when shooting.

Figure 24
Applying the coating of birch pitch

Figure 25
Smoothing the birch pitch with a hot stone

Figure 26
Applying the fletching

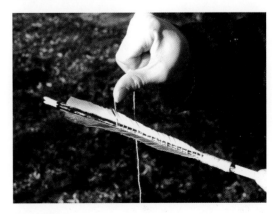
Figure 27
Binding the fletching

FLINT ARROWHEADS

Arrowheads of flint or similar hard, glassy materials are best attached by the so-called pressure technique. These arrowheads can be very sharp, depending on the quality of their production and the type of stone, but have one major disadvantage compared with metal heads: just as easily as they can be split when you want them to in preparation, they can shatter when you don't want them to on hitting hard material, and usually the head is then destroyed. But since making them is quite uncomplicated, it is always possible to carry a supply of replacements with you.

To make a Neolithic arrowhead, one needs a regularly shaped flint fragment some 6 centimeters long. A fragment can be broken off a chunk of flint with a striking stone, antler, or hardwood mallet.

Figure 28
Making the arrowhead
with a pressure stick

There are a few rules to obey in doing this, the most important being a correct striking angle of 75 to 80 degrees and a good preparation of the surface to be struck.

To turn this fragment into an arrowhead, one needs an instrument for chipping the angles, a so-called pressing stick. It has a head of bone, antler, or metal (for example, a soft iron nail or strong copper wire), usually set into a wooden staff (see figure 16, page 67). This tool can be a hand to a lower arm in length.

A tapering pointed end of a deer antler will also do. Your left hand, in which the piece of flint lies, must be protected with a piece of leather, for the chipped slivers of flint are very sharp.

The tool is held in the palm of your hand, which is open upward, by your fingertips, in order to chip off the side angles with the tool. Here too, the right pressure angle is important. It should be between 35 and 45 degrees.

You move along the edge with the pressure stick and chip small fragments off in a row, at short intervals.

Figure 30
The finished arrowhead

From time to time you turn the flint over, so that it can be worked above and below from all sides. Ideally, the chipped-off spots extend about to the middle of the surface of the flint, and their hollows finally cover the whole arrowhead.

The shape is more or less triangular.

At the lower end, a handle can be formed, but most Neolithic arrowheads are simply straight on the base or somewhat concave.

All edges, including the lower one, are sharp.

ATTACHING THE ARROWHEAD

In order to attach the arrowhead to the shaft, you need birch pitch. The preparation of birch pitch was already described briefly.

First, you heat some pitch and smear it in the nock at the forward end of the arrow shaft. The base of the flint arrowhead is pressed into the still-warm pitch until it is set deep in the nock. Then more pitch must be heated and applied to the head and the forward part of the shaft with the binding.

It works very well if you form several thin rolls first, which then can be warmed and pressed onto the arrowhead. To shape the pitch permanently, you then carefully warm the arrowhead area and shape it with dampened fingers.

Be careful, for the hot pitch can cause unpleasant burns if you don't moisten your fingers before you touch it. The surface of the pitch coating is completely smooth and without grooves. This keeps the air resistance as low as possible and also causes no needless resistance when it enters the animal's body. On the original Stone Age arrowheads, the pitch forms a voluminous, drop-shaped covering, which often leaves only the tip of the arrowhead and the cutting side edges uncovered.

An arrow of this type has its center of gravity toward the front because of the weight of the birch pitch on the arrowhead, which makes its trajectory very stable. The high total weight, on the other hand, makes it relatively slow and shortens its range considerably.

Figure 32
Attaching the arrowhead with birch pitch

Figure 33
Coating the arrowhead with birch pitch

Figure 34
The finished arrow

THE AUTHOR

WULF HEIN

Born in 1959, Wulf Hein is a trained carpenter. After his training he specialized in the reconstruction of prehistoric discoveries from bone needles to a full-size model house. He has been active for more than ten years in the practice-oriented preparation of archaeological contents, various projects in the realm of experimental archaeology, archaeological open-air museums, films, radio and television, expositions, specialist books, and much more.

5

SHAFT MATERIAL:
Wayfaring Tree Viburnum

The wood of the wayfaring tree viburnum shrub (*Viburnum lantana*), along with hazel, dogwood, split ash and pine wood, alder, birch and yew, was a popular material for arrow-shaft making in prehistoric times (Beckhoff 1965, Fischer 1985, Paulsen 1994, Stodiek & Paulsen 1996). The man from Hauslabjoch filled his quiver with twelve shoots, before or while he hiked into the high mountains one last time.

Is this wood remarkably well suited to making arrows, and what must be noted thereby? To answer these questions, numerous arrows of various woods were made and shot over the years. The results gained thereby are given here as a temporary experience report.

Figure 1
Wayfaring tree viburnum,
(*Viburnum lantana*), in
April

TYPES

In all, there are some 120 different varieties of viburnum, the most important of which will be presented briefly here.

Wayfaring tree viburnum, *Viburnum lantana,* is a deciduous shrub that bears rounded white flowers in the spring (Fig. 1), hence its other common name **wooly snowball.** The cylindrical berries are first green, later reddish (Fig. 2), then bright red in the autumn, and finally turn blue-black.

The leaves are heart-shaped and pointed, thick, wrinkled and firm, and thickly white-haired on the light-colored underside. Their edges finely toothed (Fig. 3). The bark of young shoots is brown and smooth, light green at the buds and covered with white powder. On older branches it is rough and torn.

The dull, musty aroma can become unpleasant.

The wayfaring tree loves sunny slopes with chalk-rich soil, which is why it is found more commonly in Southern Europe and Asia Minor. In Germany it often occurs south of the Main River, but lone examples are also found along roads in the north.

The arrow shafts in "Ötzi's" quiver came from this shrub.

Figure 2
Wayfaring tree viburnum,
end of July

Figure 4 Leatherleaf Viburnum,
Viburnum rhytidiophyllum

Leatherleaf viburnum, *Viburnum rhytidophyllum* (wrinkeled snowball), resembles the wayfaring tree but is evergreen and has insignificant blossoms, and is found as a decorative shrub in gardens and parks.

It was not used for making prehistoric arrows, as its homeland is China.

European cranberry viburnum, *Viburnum opulus* (common viburnum), likewise with white cymes, but with red berries and three-lobed leaves, the lobes irregularly toothed, shining light silvery bark. Arrows made of this wood have been found at the Danish sites of Magleby Long and Holmegärd IV, the last dating from the Mesolithic era.

In special cases, the wayfaring tree can grow to a height of five meters; then it bears "arrow-straight" thin shoots up to two meters long before they branch. The wood smells like latex, is white, and when it is a few years old is quite hard but extremely elastic.

It "stands" very well, meaning that it bends little and can be straightened easily. All of this makes it of interest to the archer.

HARVEST

By my experience, the best harvest time is the late autumn and winter. The plants are very easy to recognize then, since they bear their leaves fairly long, and one can see straight growths more easily then. The sap is in the plants then, an advantage in drying the wood. Shafts cut in summer dry much more slowly and are very prone to breaking during straightening. You

Figure 5 European cranberry viburnum, *Viburnum opulus*, end of May

should carefully choose practically straight shoots. "Crooked dogs" can be forced into shape with some trouble, using a hot stone or steam from water, but incline toward disadvantageous warping, especially if they are not lacquered but only oiled or greased.

You should leave the rough stems a good deal longer than usual, so as to make straightening easier. Small leaf attachments at the knots are no trouble, but if the stem already has side branches, it is usually useless as a shaft. Then the knots become so thick that too much material must be removed in cutting them down—resulting in heightened danger of breakage.

The bark should be thoroughly brown and rough and bark-like, no longer smooth and greenish. This is especially important for shafts of larger bows, since the shoots, when they are still young, show a central channel up by the blossoms, and it can be half the diameter of the shoot in width. This decreases the stability very much, especially in straightening.

DRYING

After cutting, it is advisable to dry the shafts outdoors under a roof, with bark on, for four weeks, to avoid splitting at the ends.

During drying, the shafts should be straightened every evening, for a fully straight shoot is rarely found. Wayfaring tree tends to grow somewhat wavy at the branch knots (nodes). These waves, though, can be straightened through repeated bending the other way, on account of their extraordinarily great elasticity, if the bending is not too sharp. Later, if a shaft still shows gentle "snake lines," this will not detract from its flight performance as long as the arrow is not completely bent in its longitudinal axis. If the inner channel is relatively thick, the shaft will crease very easily before breaking when being bent. Such shafts are unusable, as are those that crack when being bent.

Often you only see the break when the bark is carefully removed after some four weeks. After that, the ends of the shaft (upper and lower cut surfaces) should be dipped in wax or grease, so as to avoid overly fast drying and resulting cracking.

STRAIGHTENING

The shafts can best be straightened after removing the bark. Now they no longer bend back to their old shape, but remain straight.

After four or five days, though, they very quickly become hard and inflexible. What is still not straight now, never will be! Similar observations on arrow making are found in R. Bohr's book on the bows and arrows of the North American Indians (Bohr 1997).

Now the shafts can be brought inside. It is good to let them dry another 4 to 6 weeks before removing the branch knots. Since wayfaring tree viburnum wood is so long-fibered, the slight thickenings that are always present on the nodes are hard to remove from fresh wood. There is great danger that one will run the knife deep into the wood. In this case, dry wood is easier to work. You should always move the blade toward the branch and not over it. Now you can only bundle the shafts and let them rest until they attain a balanced state of moisture.

ÖTZI'S ARROWS

Whether "Ötzi" spent so much time on his arrows is hard to say, but in view of the conditions under which he probably had to climb into the mountains, it is unlikely.

First he cut the shaft nocks before he completely cut off the nodes or polished the shafts. That suggests quick work under pressure of necessity.

Slitting the shafts also means that the wood will not split so easily, as the tangential splitting is interrupted. A first work step, usable in terms of wood technique, took place when the glacier man removed the bark immediately, so as to let the shafts dry more quickly.

Maybe his next step would have been to finish building the bow, in order to smooth the shafts, attach arrowheads, cut nocks, and feather the arrows "in peace and quiet," doing all twelve simultaneously, because this way of working is sensible and practical. One does not have to change tools so often, and is more likely to achieve the same results (see also Spindler, 1993, 146).

Then, too, the arrows are made after the bow, because their elasticity has to depend on the pulling weight of the bow. As to the chosen thickness of the shafts, a bow of some 60 pounds can be chosen, according to my experience, at which figure the bow was already estimated. To be sure, the spine value is very dependent on the growth conditions of the wood. Not all thick shafts have a high spine; thin shafts with much narrower annual rings can be very stiff and thus suitable for a heavy bow.

There is a way to measure this value exactly (Beckhoff 1965), but I do not believe that such a process was used in the Stone Age. Once one has cut several shafts and then finished and shot them, one gets a feeling for what is well suited in terms of elasticity and hardness.

The damage to the two intact arrows can, I believe, be attributed to breaks that took place before the man went into the ice. If these "ready-to-shoot" arrows were broken in the quiver, then the twelve fresh shoots should also have been damaged (see Spindler 1993, 146). Later damage during recovery can also be ruled out for this reason.

And even in intense cold, wayfaring tree viburnum breaks like an explosion with typically fibrous structure (Fig. 7), which requires a goodly amount of power, as several experiments with, among others, deeply cooled woods have shown. Naturally, the great age and the resulting much-decreased firmness of the originals must be considered, but a clean break, by my experience, takes place mainly at the cut-off nodal points (Fig. 8) or at the cuts where the narrowing for the feathers begins.

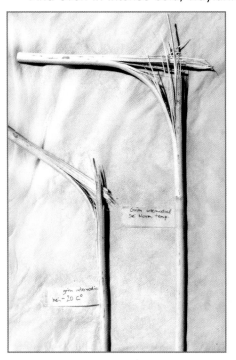

Figure 7
Typical internodal breakage, at left at -20 degrees C, at right at normal temperature (+ 20 degrees C)

Finally, releasing errors or bowstrings sticking in the nocks (or coldness) are often the causes of other breaks, with missed or grazing shots, above all, being caused by them.

I can imagine that "Ötzi" had shot all his arrows. For which reason he collected two pieces (his own or another hunter's?) that were lying around (perhaps mainly for the arrowheads, but maybe for the feathers as well?), and wanted to make new equipment on his way into the mountains.

On this subject, Harm Paulsen indicates that the two "usable" arrows were very probably built by different makers, because of their being made for right- and left-handers in terms of feathering, for one has Z-type and other S-type binding.

The discolored spots, sometimes called "camouflage," thus put on for the sake of disguise, could also have resulted from either using a shaft already dried on the bush or drying too long with bark on.

Either could cause such discoloration, which is fairly common on wayfaring tree viburnum, especially from bark damage through the chemical processes it causes.

In comparison with other plants, the **wayfarin tree viburnum** is best for arrow making, from practical experience. Almost as good results come from **dogwood** *(Cornus sanguinea)* and **hazel** *(Corylus avellana)*, with dogwood shoots being straightest. To be sure, they are nowhere near as easy to straighten, as they are less elastic and tend to become brittle in time.

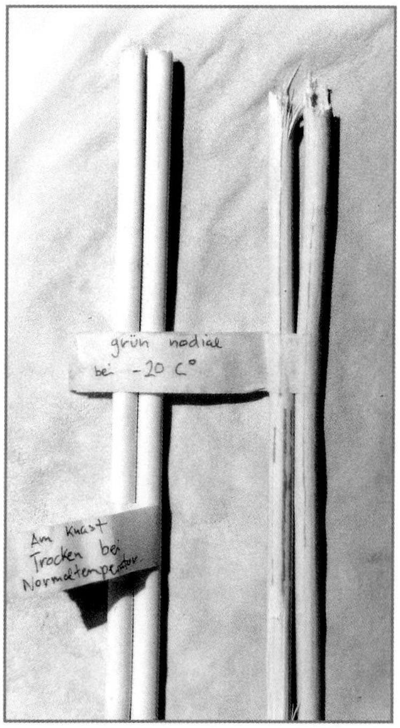

A wayfaring tree arrow is also extremely flexible after years, while a dogwood or hazel shaft would break under the same flexing. But the wood of the wayfaring tree viburnum is also the heaviest.

The **European cranberry viburnum,** *Viburnum opulus,* is just as suitable, but it is less flexible. For bows with high pulling weights, shafts of this wood would need much greater diameters, which would worsen the flight performance of the arrow. To be sure, the specific gravity of *Viburnum opulus* is lower than that of *Viburnum lantana*, so that a thicker arrow does not necessarily have to be heavier.

Figure 8
Nodal breaks, at left, at normal temperature, at right, at -20 degrees C.

I consider the process mentioned by Beckhoff (1965) of making shafts of split European cranberry to be fairly impracticable. Stems with the given diameter, branch-free, and straight for a meter, are extremely hard to find, judging from my experience, on both the woolly and common snowball. Since only the European cranberry viburnum was found in the prehistoric North, it makes sense to split such a piece of wood, when one has found one, into four or more good arrows. But with the tools of those times, it would mean, by my experience, a much greater expenditure of time to make a splitter and do the work than to turn a shoot into one arrow shaft.

But who knows what role time played then? In any case, it is technically easier and not at all primitive to blend the higher surficial stability of a tube with the resulting saving of weight (thanks to the pith channel). Nor is it provable that this process should be impractical because, with their different qualities, one cannot tell heart- and sapwood apart (Mertens 1993), for all the wood types used in the form of shoots are bark or splint wood.

In addition, the center of gravity is improved, for a shoot's thicker, lower end forms the point of the arrow, thus *tapering* is also needless. Because of the pith channel, the arrow becomes lighter and lighter toward the back, an advantage with the usually lightweight stone arrowheads used in Mesolithic and Neolithic times.

Of course the rear section becomes more and more unstable as the sidewalls become thinner, which is also a reason for slitting the raw shafts at the lower end to avoid cracking and thus to be able to use the fully stable length.

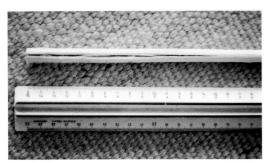

Figure 11
Drying crack

The shafts must be nocked later anyway to take the arrowheads. Tests have shown that shoots freshly cut and immediately debarked on sunny, dry autumn days, though stored outdoors, sometimes crack more than 10 cm on their lower ends (Fig. 11), but those already nocked, like those of "Ötzi," do not.

Along with that, I have found that shaft nocks can be cut more easily into a hollow shoot with quartz tools than into full wood.

Sapwood was probably used when nothing else was to be had, such as pine in the arrows from Stellmoor.

It would also be possible that extra wood was not cut for making arrows, but that naturally split wood was used, perhaps from a tree broken by wind or snow. From such a stump, meter-long thin bundles of fibers often project into the air, and can very easily be cut and planed or scraped round.

Only with the advent of metallurgy and the resulting improved woodworking did it become easier to produce series of arrow shafts with the same qualities, by cutting trees to suitable lengths and splitting the wood.

For a long time after, almost all arrows were made of solid wood, but new materials like carbon fiber, fiberglass, and aluminum make it possible today to make arrows again out of light, stable, and thin tubes.

Bibliography

Aichele-Schwegler 1976: *Welcher Baum ist das?* Bäume, Sträucher, Ziergehölze, Kosmos-Naturführer, Stuttgart 1976.

Beckhoff, K. 1965: *Eignung und Verwendung einheimischer Holzarten für prähistorische Pfeilschäfte.* Die kunde NF 16, 51-61.

Bohr, R. 1997: *Pfeil und Bogen der Plains- und Prärieindianer Nordamerikas.* Wyk auf Föhr 1997, 73-76.

Egg, M. e.a. 1993: *Die Gletschermumie vom Ende der Steinzeit aus den Ötztalerc Alpen.* Jahrbuch des Römisch-Germanischen Zentralmuseums 39, Mainz 1993, 38-49.

Fischer, A. 1985: *På jagt med stenalder-våben.* Forsøg med fortiden 3, Historisk-Arkaeologisk Forsøgcenter Leijre 1985, 6.

Mertens, E.-M. 1993: *Pflanzliche Ressourcen des Mesolithikums in Dänemark und Schleswig-Holstein*, Dipl.-Arbeit Universität Kiel 1993, 62-68.

Paulsen, H. 1994: Der querschneidige Pfeil vom Petersfehner Moor. Archäologische Mitteilungen aus Nordwestdeutschland 17, 1994, Oldenburg 1994, 5-14.

Spindler, K. 1993: *Der Mann im Eis.* München 1993, 142-151.

Stodiek, U. & Paulsen, H. 1996: "Mit dem Pfeil, dem Bogen…" *Technik der steinzeitlichen Jagd.* Oldenburg 1996, 37-52.

pp. 53-55, photos: J. Junkmanns

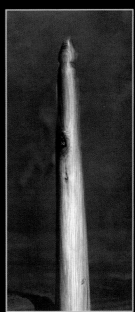

Upper end of bow from front (bow back) and inside (bow front)

Replica of Bodman Bow
Full views from front and side.

Lower end of bow from inside

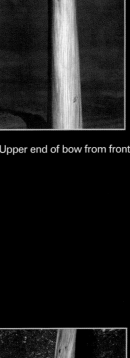

Grip, seen from the side

Fig. 1. Flint arrowheads from Parpallo (Museo de Prehistoria, Valencia)

Fig. 10. Arrow from Zugerberg. Photo: Museum für Urgeschichte(n) Zug

Fig. 15. Flint knife   Fig. 17. Flint fragment   Fig. 30. Arrowhead

Fig. 20. Smoothing

Fig. 23. Tearing off feather flags

Fig. 25. Smoothing the birch pitch

Fig. 33. Arrowhead with birch. Pitch coating (replica)

Figure 2. Wayfaring tree viburnum (wooly snowball), end of July

Figure 1 Wayfaring tree viburnum,
Viburnum lantana, in April

Wayfaring tree viburnum in late
summer. Photo: J. Junkmanns

Figure 5 European cranberry
viburnum (common snowball),
Viburnum opulus, end of May
Photos: Figures 1, 2, 5 Wulf Hein

Reconstructed Neolithic arrowheads by Wulf Hein

Ahrensburger arrowhead by Wulf Hein

Variations of flint quartz (photo: W. Hein)

"Modern" arrowheads of various materials, by Frank Stevens, USA. (photo: V. Alles)

6

ARROWHEADS MADE OF FLINT

What archer has not already admired them during a museum visit: flint arrowheads from the Stone Age. Their shape was retained almost unchanged for millennia into our times; even in the ensuing metal ages, flint was held to be the true material, until our ancestors began to cast bronze in molds, forge iron, and thus simplify and normalize the production process.

Because these arrowheads sometimes appear to be surface chippings from the Neolithic era, and their production seems quite simple, there is a general tendency to shrug off prehistoric (the word itself embodies it, *before* history, as if the millions of years before the invention of writing did not belong to human history) tools and weapons as primitive. But whoever has tried to make such an arrowhead "just once" will soon "use up all his Latin" when chipping a good flint blade, which is the starting point of nearly every prehistoric projectile. And whoever has watched a practiced stone chipper at work will understand that although it looks so easy, a lot of experience and practice goes into it, and Stone Age "flinters" were truly masters of their art.

Thus this article is not meant to be a hasty introduction after the motto of "stone chipping made easy," but a short, informative overview of history, material, and production, describing my own experiences and perhaps giving those people who have tried it and not succeeded a little help.

In addition, the working of flint is quite dangerous (and not just for the inexperienced), as we shall see in what follows.

HISTORY

The perhaps 4.5 million years of man's developmental history from their origins in East Africa to the beginnings of metalwork some 5,000 years ago (in Northern Europe) are named the **Stone Age** after their preferred material. In addition, our ancestors have used all kinds of other materials on an everyday basis, such as wood, antlers, or bones, but for cutting or scraping tools, projectiles, etc., stone was most suitable. The very first tools were the "choppers" (illustrated), which were made with a little, but powerful striking of another stone, giving them a sharp edge. With these tools it was possible to dissect an animal or sharpen a stick that could be used as a digger or lance.

2 cm

Choppers

Surely the "fallen-off" pieces of this process were also used for cutting, since they often had sharper edges than the big tool.

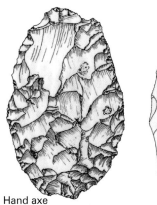

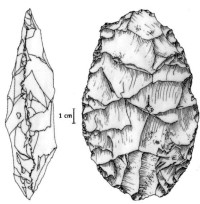

Hand axe

In time, the early people learned to perfect these stone implements that were made by deliberately removing material from a piece of stone, a development that proceeded beyond the hand axe (left) to thin, sharp "leaf points" (right).

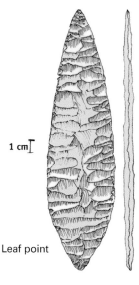

Leaf point

These apparent lance points could only be made of flint, a raw material that the Stone Age toolmakers very soon learned to value for its good splitting and extraordinary hardness. Where it was not available, local stones with similar qualities, such as quartzite, were used, or flint was obtained elsewhere, on migrations or in trade. Flint or other types of quartz exist in practically all parts of the world, often enough in small occurrences.

QUALITIES

Flint or firestone, Latin *silex,* as many know it from vacationing on the Baltic Sea, originated some 80 million years ago in the deposits of a warm sea, in which countless large and small living creatures lived, that then covered Northern Europe.

After they died, the organisms sank to the bottom, where their skeletons formed chalk and calcium deposits. According to the most current theories, the silicon dioxide—SiO_2—in their bodies came out as a gel and, under the pressure of the ever-growing deposits above them and the heat from inside the earth, finally turned to hard stone that formed lumps or layers in the surrounding bedrock. Thus flint almost always has a more or less thick outer "bark" (Latin *cortex*), and inside one often sees large and small petrifications (picture), such as whole sea urchins, which could cause trouble for the flinter, as they decreased the splitting quality of the stone and often strongly repel aimed strikes.

Flint is almost as hard as diamond (hardness 7 on the Mohs scale), but unusually brittle and not the same in every direction, but very easy to split, similarly to glass.

Petrifications in flint

Minerals with similar qualities are hornstone, jasper, chalcedony, opal, quartz schist, quartzite, radiolarite, and obsidian. Flint exists in many different colors and shapes, but not all variations are equally well suited to its various uses.

From different granulation it acquired not only chalk but also water molecules that were stuck between the individual, invisible (cryptocrystalline) crystals and produced flint's good splitting qualities—through the effects of frost or heat, they expand and break the stone from inside, forming many tiny hairline cracks that one often sees only after chipping the stone.

A sign of quality is the good sound when a piece is struck lightly, an indication that the flint is homogeneous and of undisturbed structure. (Taking away beach stones, at least in large quantities, is, by the way, illegal in Schleswig-Holstein, so don't take "hol Stein" (fetch stone) too literally, although the large supply is tempting. During the Ice Age, the mighty glaciers plowed off the rock covering Scandinavia and dumped countless chunks of flint at our doorstep.

When the Neanderthal men disappeared some 30,000 years ago, the stone tools used until then also faded into the background—for *Homo sapiens sapiens*, who was to "rule the earth" from then on, had refined and improved toolmaking considerably by inventing new production techniques. By the controlled striking of long thin "blades" of well-prepared stones, the supply of sharp edges from a lump of flint was vastly increased. These blades served as raw materials for the production of various tools which were needed then.

Now man was in a situation where he could make relatively small, light but sharp-pointed projectiles. In **Aurignacia**, some 35,000 years ago, there appeared the first arrowheads made from blades, which were very good for equipping spears. The backed knives found at Gravettia and Magdalenia were made to set on or in arrowheads of wood, bone, or antler. Flint projectiles fitted with shaft tongues occur only at the end of the New Paleolithic era; they include the Hamburg points, which were made from blades by side chipping and breaking in the notch.

The somewhat newer Ahrensburg arrowheads (see picture below) were made of thin pointed blades, which were simply attached to the end of spear.

At this time, some 11,000 years ago, came the first signs of the use of bows, in the form of about 100 arrow shafts and a few pieces of bows that were found on the edge of an Ice Age lake, now a bog, near Hamburg.

The times of the great reindeer heard moving across the open tundra were past, and Northern Europe began to grow forests that followed the retreating ice.

And thus the spear-thrower had served its time; what was needed was a soundless, fast weapon for hunting individual animals from cover, and material for building bows was now available in ever-growing quantities.

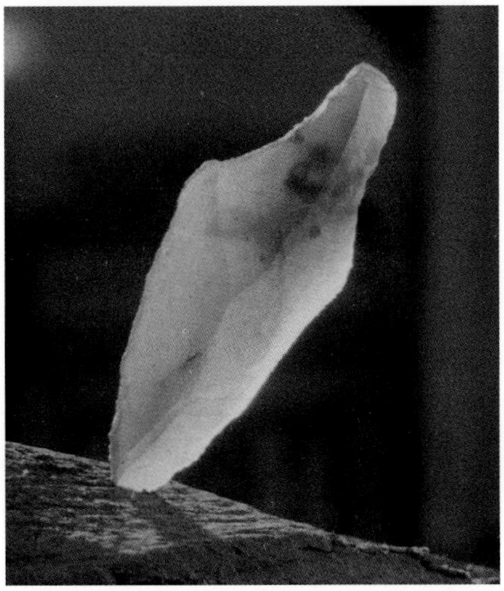

Years & Eras

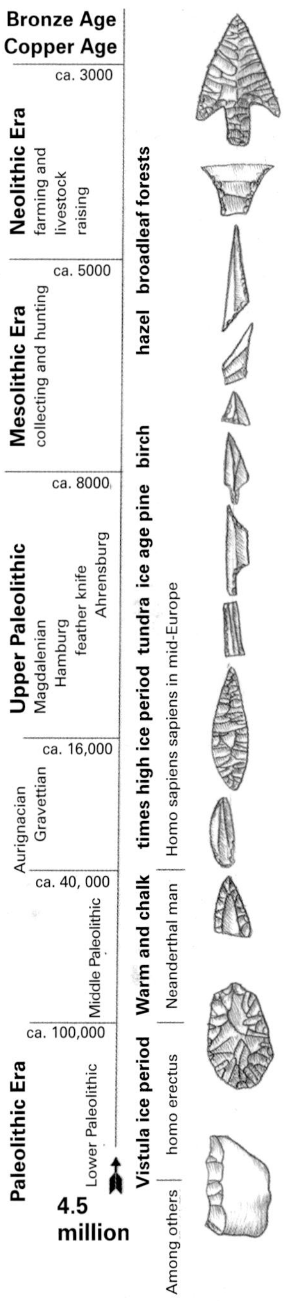
Bronze Age
Copper Age
ca. 3000
Neolithic Era
farming and livestock raising
ca. 5000
Mesolithic Era
collecting and hunting
ca. 8000
Upper Paleolithic
Magdalenian
Hamburg
feather knife
Ahrensburg
ca. 16,000
Aurignacian
Gravettian
ca. 40, 000
Middle Paleolithic
ca. 100,000
Paleolithic Era
Lower Paleolithic
4.5 million
Vistula ice period
Warm and chalk
times high ice period
tundra
ice age
pine
birch
hazel
broadleaf forests
Among others
homo erectus
Neanderthal man
Homo sapiens sapiens in mid-Europe

TIMELINE (simplified)

Microliths

Straight cutters

In the **Mesolithic Age,** the bow was the decisive hunting weapon; of course the appearance of the arrowheads changed; there was a tendency toward making them smaller; the time of microliths (Greek mikros = small & lithos = stone) began. Perhaps usable flint was no longer readily available because of the growing ground cover after the Ice Age, or was needed for other tools such as the axes that appeared at that time, or sparing weight may have played a role, so that they turned from small chunks to tiny blades.

At first, simple triangles were used for projectiles, but, later, geometrical forms like long, thin triangles, trapezoids or segments appeared.

Through the whole Mesolithic era and into the Bronze Age, we find the so-called straight cutters, which were made by notching and breaking blades into small pieces.

Finally, in the Neolithic Age the people remembered a technique that was known in the Paleolithic Age and had been lost—the surface chipping or production of a stable, thin, sharp projectile by chipping tiny bits off the surface of a raw stone or blade by using a special antler tool. So it was possible to produce specially formed arrowheads, such as those with barbs or shaft tongues.

TECHNIQUES

If I strike downward on a flint piece with a stone, a so-called Hertzian cone break occurs under the surface (Figure A).

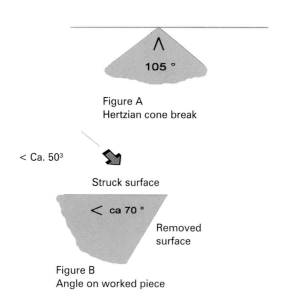

Figure A
Hertzian cone break

Figure B
Angle on worked piece

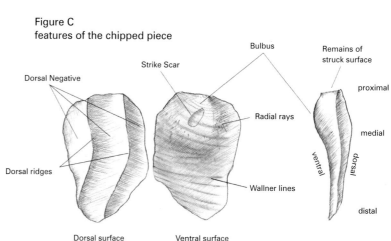

Figure C
features of the chipped piece

If I strike instead at an angle of some 70 degrees (Figure B), I separate a piece of the cone: the result is a chip that on its back has a bit of this cone, the so-called strike bulge or Latin *bulbus.*

The broken surface is conchoidal and often shows (on the bulbus) a so-called strike scar, plus radiating cracks and Wallner lines (Figure C).

The striking energy rushes through the stone at about 2 kilometers per second, the separating process occurs in millionths of a second. The angles of this fragment are often remarkably sharp, flint breaks on a crystalline plane, obsidian even on a molecular one. This is why, in the most modern medical operation technology, knives of this stone are being used. Fine long blades (which, unlike the fragments, are more than twice as long as wide), though, cannot be produced with this so-called "direct hard" technique. The most important methods of working flint will be portrayed here:

1. DIRECT HARD TECHNIQUE

With a striking stone of light or heavy weight, as needed, the piece being worked is struck directly at flat angle (Figure D, right).

Depending on how much or little material is to be taken off, the striking point is correspondingly far from the edge of the striking surface.

This technique is used to break or separate large chunks crudely.

a

Figure D
Leading ridge through a negative edge

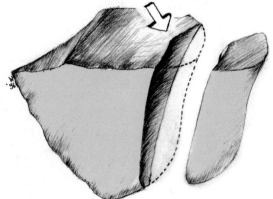

2. DIRECT SOFT TECHNIQUE

It functions as above, but instead of a stone, a piece of antler, bone, or hardwood is used as a striking instrument (Figure E, right).

This technique has the advantage that the striking energy is "softer," meaning that it is transmitted to the stone in a more measurable and apportioned way. The fragments are thinner and straighter, the bulbus is usually not so prominent as with the hard strike.

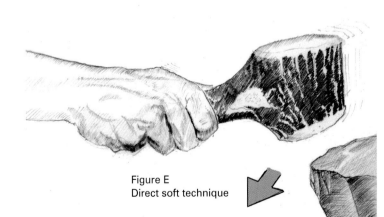

Figure E
Direct soft technique

Thus, with some practice, very usable blades are made, though under two conditions: the blade must run off along a ridge, and the striking surface angle must be reduced.

LEADING RIDGE AND ANGLE REDUCTION

In order to reduce a chunk of flint to sharp blades, it must first be broken up. This is done by a strong blow with a big heavy stone, the direct hard technique, which works best with a soft surface under it, like grassy ground, or a leather bag full of sand is very suitable.

For the direct soft technique, we need an angle between the striking surface and breaking surface of about 70 degrees; if this cannot be found on the stone after turning and checking it, then several hits may be needed until two surfaces of this angle appear.

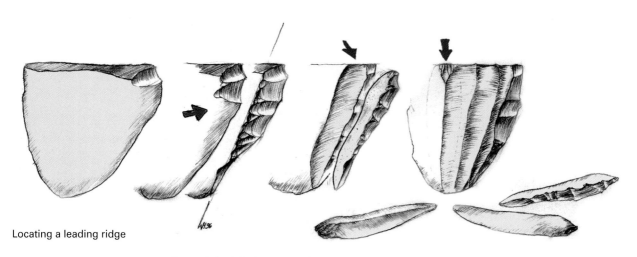

Locating a leading ridge

A straight blade can only exist on one ridge; if such a ridge is not already present on the surface from striking it, then it must be created. This can be done by a direct hard strike on the striking surface; a large fragment is created, and angle of its negative forms the desired ridge (Figure D), or the breaking-off surface is worked in a very flat angle with a large striking stone. Fragments come off, and the negative of their proximal ends under each other now form the basic angle (drawing above).

If I now struck over the ridge directly outside on the striking-surface angle with the antler hammer, I would get one small fragment at best. At the end of the striking bulge, the fragment surface would again be reached, there would be an insecure zone, the energy could not spread further downward in the stone (drawing at right).

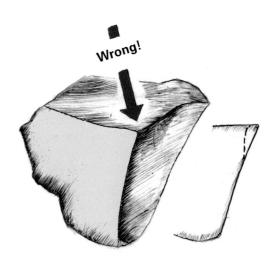

Wrong!

To make this happen, I must move the bulbus farther inside the stone, and thus I reduce the striking edge by first removing tiny fragments or even almost blades from the leading ridge, working very carefully with a small striking stone, and in this way I create a small overhang (drawing at right). Then I go over the edge and the striking surface with a rough stone, to make it handier for the antler hammer. Now apply the stone loosely to the left upper shank, the left hand holds the striking stone . . .

BUT STOP!

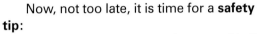

Now, not too late, it is time for a **safety tip**:

For everyone who experiments with flint, and especially for beginners, I consider the following equipment to be vital!!

• Safety goggles

• Large apron of fairly thick soft leather; separated old crack-leather ones, such as many of us used to have, are quite suitable.

• Gloves; longshoremen's gloves are very suitable, at least for rougher work, as they are made completely of leather (available from marine outfitters).

• Keep your entire body covered; no bare feet or legs, etc.

• Never work in closed spaces!! If you can't help it...

• Provide good ventilation, wear a mask, and change clothes afterward.

• Don't work alone if you can help it. But spectators should keep a safe distance of at least three meters.

This good advice has its reasons, as I and others have had to learn on our own bodies. The safety goggles are vital, at least when breaking large pieces, because fragments don't necessarily fly in the direction they should—with good luck, the odd ones just whistle past your ear, and with bad luck . . . Gloves and clothing for the same reason, unless you like to show scars.

Breathing protection is especially important. Very fine dust particles result from working on flint; they are very aggressive, as they have sharp edges (!), and they settle in your lungs. The result is **SILICOSIS** or miner's disease, certainly nothing nice.

The "flint-knappers" who produced "flintstones" professionally in past centuries as replacements for gun ignition stones, did not live to be particularly old!!

Thus outfitted, you can now seize the stone with your left hand, so that the blade, when it comes off, will fall directly into your hand, and strike away from yourself with the antler hammer, at a fairly acute angle (ca. 50 degrees) on the overhang you made on the striking surface, short and dry and with medium power (Figure E).

Did it work? If not, why not? If only a small piece is broken off, the angle was too acute or the blow did not strike right (Figure F.1).

If a too big of a piece was broken off, the blow was too hard or struck too far in, and if the blow stopped halfway, the angle was too steep or the blow too soft; the same is true of step breaks.

F. 1 Failed blow

F. 2 Too far

F. 3 Step break

F. 4 Angled break

Errors and their causes

Important: The striking surface of the antler hammer must always be nice and round, so that the striking energy can be passed on punctually; otherwise the results will be a lot of noise and a lot of shards.

A hidden crack can also be the cause here; angled breaks often occur on breaking surfaces that are too flat; these should be as convex as possible; or the angle was too steep (Figures F2-4).

This all sounds quite theoretical, but when you try it, you gain practice and a feeling for the stone in time, for the right angle, the right blow, or you get instruction. Above all—even if you turn out a real "masterpiece," you don't necessarily sit there a quarter hour later in a heap of masterpieces. Just the avoidance of blows gone astray and similar mistakes call for patience, experience and ability, for "flint doesn't forgive much."

G.1 Removing a tablet

G.2 Removing the foot of the stone from below

Trimming the stone

In an ideal case I have one stone with two ridges that I can use for the next two blades, thus working around the stone. But the striking surface must be prepared carefully each time.

At some time the next difficulty will turn up: since not all blades run through to the bottom of the stone, and more material is taken off on top through the bulbus, the angle between the striking surface and breaking surface decreases more and more, until further breaking of edges is impossible. There are several possible ways to be able to make a new start here.

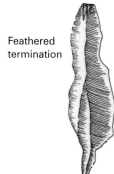
Feathered termination

Either you take off a so-called tablet with a blow of the big striking stone on the side (or back) upward (Figure G.1), or you try with one powerful, deliberately somewhat overly steep blow of the antler hammer or striking stone, to remove the projecting foot of the stone (Figure F.2).

Sometimes it is also possible to take this off from below (Figure G.2) or from the side, thus returning to about 70 degrees.

But even blades made with the direct soft technique very seldom have parallel lines, because they tend toward *feathered termination* (drawing at left), meaning that the blade edges become irregular at the end, and so it becomes harder and harder to find a good ridge for the next process.

In order to produce a series of thin, regular parallel edges, we need a different procedure:

3. INDIRECT SOFT TECHNIQUE

or *punching.* This English term originates from the tool used here, as opposed to the other processes, where you strike directly on the worked stone with a striking instrument; here you use a *punch,* a chisel-like tool of bone, antler, or hardwood, which is put on as an intermediate piece when striking.

Figure H

This has several advantages: the angle between the striking and breaking surfaces can be up to 90 degrees, the striking angle is precisely controllable on the ridge, the blows fall exactly on the place where the blade is to be separated, and the striking energy is given off in proper doses through the elastic intermediate piece, meaning that the tension produced in the stone by the blow, which leads in the end to the breaking off of the blade, is exact, controlled, and built up slowly.

Thus practiced stone strikers are able to create blades with desired, predictable sizes and qualities, since it is not possible to set up the individual parameters by any other procedure. These blades are very thin, straight, parallel, and usually have a very small, flat bulbus.

The punch should be about 15-20 cm long and have a pointed conical shape. The most suitable material is antler, because of its elasticity and toughness; roe deer antlers are very suitable, as they are very sturdy. Antler points are formed of two layers; outside is the hard *compacta*, inside, as in hollow bones, a spongy soft material, the *spongiosa.*

Roebuck or chamois points consist almost completely of compacta and can thus be used thoroughly, while the roe or elk points will strike diagonally when the original point is worn away, so that the chisel point remains in the compacta.

You can also use a hardwood punch, made, for example, of beech, burning bush, or lilac, though their occurrence during the Ice Age is fairly unlikely.

Now you must first prepare and trim another stone, whereby, as stated, the angle between the striking and breaking surfaces can go up to 90 degrees.

A nice ridge is important, as is a careful reproduction of the striking-surface edges with strong over-smoothing of the edge and roughening of the striking surface, so that the punch grips more firmly and doesn't slide. This is now placed on a direct lengthening of the ridge in the striking surface, directly over the ridge, as far as possible toward the edge, then tilted about ten degrees toward the striking surface, and receives a short, dry blow from the hammer, whereby a blade is broken off.

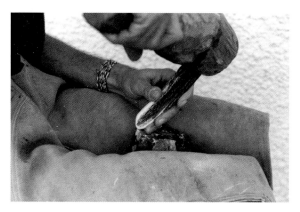

Figure I

I use a wooden mallet made of white beech and weighing about 900 grams, letting it fall from 30 to 40 centimeters above, more or less, just onto the punch.

You can also use a stone as a hammer, but the striking tool may not be too light, for you must otherwise use a certain power that you cannot always dole out as precisely as when you simply let the weight do the job.

The body position when punching is different for all the stone strikers I know. You can

a) sit in the cutter's seat, hold the stone with your feet, and strike toward yourself (H)

b) kneel or sit with the stone between your knees, and strike toward yourself (I)

c) hold the stone as in a) or b) but strike away from yourself, or

d) put the breaking surface on one upper thigh; the cut-off blades will then fall between the stone and your leg (J)

e) kneel on one knee and hold the stone under the other foot

f) build yourself a device in which the stone can be held.

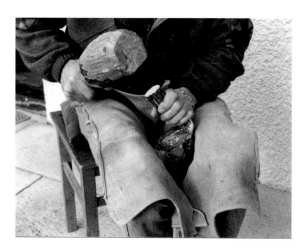

Figure J

In any case, it is important to provide sufficient protection for your legs. I use a big apron of very thick, soft leather, which reaches from my navel to my knees. On principle, observers should keep a distance of at least three meters, and particularly when you are striking toward or away from yourself. Normally the blades are caught by the leather apron, but it can happen that they fly a meter away.

In addition, you must be careful when the stone is lying on the ground that the surface below is soft and absorbs the blows, grass or a leather bag of sand will do.

You should also choose the striking place with care, for if the children's wading pool stands on a flint workplace in summer, or the kids run barefoot over it, they're going to scream! And anyone who cares and makes his first attempts on the beach, should do it like the professionals, please. First dig a pit some 40-50 cm deep, into which all the junk can fall, then put a big stone over it, and fill it all with sand again. The swimmers will thank you!

If you hold the stone between your knees, you must hold it firmly so that it can't tip when struck, which could ruin the striking geometry. For punching, the transparent, glassy black flint is not so suitable, because the blades swing sharply in the breaking process, then collapse and break into fragments. Grainy, streaky, opaque flint is better, even with many small inclusions.

4. SHAPING

Now that we have, after some practice and with many bandages and ice bags, made our first nice blade, we can go on to turn it into a simple arrowhead. This process is called shaping and known in the literature as *Retusche.* Shaping can be done with a quartzite chipper or a bone or antler tool, and it is usually carried out from the ventral side of the blade, though sometimes on both sides on an anvil of wood or antler.

If we want to make a so-called "Hamburg notched point" (the folk of the "Hamburg Culture" were deer hunters and lived about 14,000 years ago in the North German area), then we need only form the blade on the acute angle in front. Many small splinters of flint will be chipped off, until the point is straight. Then the blade is chipped farther back on one side and broken at the notch—and the point is finished.

Figure K
Making a notched point

It is not clear whether this projectile was used as an arrowhead or on a throwing spear; maybe both.

The only definite arrowheads to date, proved by arrow fragments, belong to the so-called "Ahrensburg Culture," whose users traversed this same area about 11,000 years ago. These "stick points" were made similarly to notched points; the rough piece was a small blade. If it does not run to a point on the distal end, it is straightened here on one or both sides, and on the proximal end a shaft is shaped—finished. It can be mounted in a (fore)shaft only with birch pitch or resin-wax adhesive.

The "straight cutters," known since the Mesolithic era, but still used in later times and feared for their effect, are likewise very simple and quick to make. They start with very regular parallel blades, with two or more dorsal ridges if possible. These are broken (by shaping) into several sections, which are again shaped on the sides. In Mesolithic days, they were made very angled and asymmetrical, and later trapezoidal.

Microliths

To produce microliths, which were popular in the Mesolithic era, one needs just such blades, but of much smaller size, some 5-8 mm wide and 3-5 cm long. From the raw stones, these very small, often geometric "stonelets" were made by the shaping technique and set one behind another in an arrow shaft, again with pitch or glue.

And now to the **arrowheads of the Neolithic era,** and for them we must take more time. For now not only the angles of the blades were shaped, but also the whole surface, and that is a bit more complex.

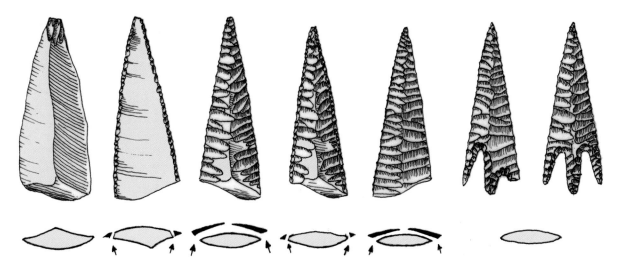

Figure L
Ideal process of making
an arrowhead

First, we knock out a suitable rough piece; these include proximal fragments of medium-thick wide blades or pointed oval fragments. The proximal end with the bulbus and the remaining striking surface forms the point, the barbs (I call them *Flunken)* go on the distal end, and here we also start shaping.

First, the edges are given very small, not too steep shapings, from the side where we next want to remove excessive material.

The edge and the shaping are smoothed on a fine sandstone, and now the pushing staff can come into action.

I usually use a nice long, slightly curved antler point that fits into my hand well and is not too rough (giving blisters), plus a piece of thick, hard leather with a thumbhole as a base and hand guard (see photo on opposite page).

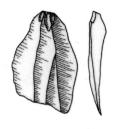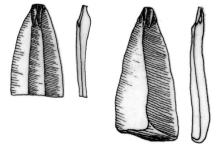

Rough pieces for surface shaping

As "pressers," bones and hardwood can also be used; "Ötzi" had a clever shaper with him: a piece of antler had been set into a wooden staff like a pencil (see page 67, figure 16). If you have a hard time getting antlers, you can also drive 5-6 mm thick copper wire into a piece of wood; it works fine.

The surface shaping is best done toward the point, that is, we lay the raw stone on the pad, hold it firmly with our thumb, set the presser on the edge and slowly, steadily build up a strong pressure, until a dry cracking is heard—a "microblade" has broken loose from the surface (photo).

Now set the presser directly on the ridge that the angle of the negative of the just-loosened blade forms. Repeat the process and so on to the point, then work the other angle—one side is finished. The other side is done just the same: first the fine straight shaping, over-polishing, pressing beginning from the back, etc.

The over-polishing is tremendously important, for it guarantees that the chipped-off pieces run out over the middle, thus reducing the thickness of the stone and giving it a flat-oval cross-section (Figure L). Otherwise the angle of the edge would become greater and greater, and the result would be a dull piece with a rhombic cross-section.

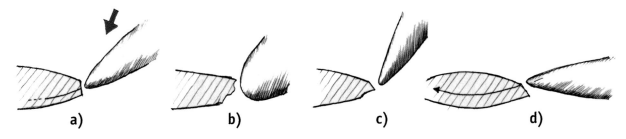

Surface retouching with the presser

ERRORS AND THEIR CAUSES

Here, too, no master has ever fallen from heaven; they are made through lots of practice. The first attempts are almost always accompanied by sudden expressions of displeasure and worse. So what can go wrong, and what causes it?

a). Nothing happens when you press, or the chips to be removed stay in place.
The edge shaping is too steep. Reshape more obliquely and cleanly. Try to remove the sagging by a long chip from the opposite side.

b). On pressing, the edge breaks in a big way, and no chips are removed.
The presser is not pointed enough. Sharpen the presser.

c). Only small bits are pressed off, or the chips remain in place.
The angle between the presser and surface is not right. Use the presser more steeply, work more cleanly, build up pressure slowly.

d). Half of the arrowhead is removed at once.
The working angle was too steep. The pressure point was to far in, so that the breaking surface ran through the whole stone. Use the presser less steeply, aim more cleanly.

e).The arrowhead breaks.
Where raw strength would be senseless . . . make sure the piece to be worked is not lying hollow, work cautiously. Maybe the stone was too thin or had weak zones.

a)   b)   c)   d)

Flint is as hard as it is brittle and reacts to pressure very sensitively. That means, be especially careful when working on the barbs. If the arrowhead is to be made with a barb, one begins pressing back in the middle and works steadily forward and sideward.

One does this alternately: the just-pressed surface forms the edge from which the shaping goes to the other side, and one must be very careful that the angle of this edge does not become too steep. If the stone is too thick here, one can start the shaping on a base of wood or antler; then it goes more easily. But be careful to place the stone solidly, otherwise it may break!

If the arrowhead is to have a shaft tongue, one begins right and left with an inward curve, from which one proceeds alternately.

For this work process, the presser must be very pointed and perhaps even a bit curved. Great care is called for, so as not to overstress the stone.

Closing Thoughts about Flint Knapping and Advice from My Own Experience

Arrowheads of flint are basically not suitable for daily use, since they usually break under the slightest pressure, such as a missed shot that hits a tree or stone. That would be bad!

Important (and it cannot be noted often enough) for beginners: obey the safety rules.

Injuries while working flint also happen to experienced workers and can be very dangerous: slivers in eyes, cut sinews, etc. I've been there, done that.

And thus very important: **Keep fingers away from the stone** if the head is not free.

Business or personal stress, pressure of time, false ambition, and above all, impatience are factors that take your mind off your work. The results will be flints made with a lot of care and then senselessly ruined.

Naturally, a beginner will use up more material, but that too can be handled if you go to work with calmness, thought, and, above all, relaxation.

In general, this is true of stone working: precise instructions for certain work processes are hard to give in writing or in theory, because for the most part we work on the basis of experience, and we get that only . . . by trying.

I wish you lots of joy and good success,

Wulf Hein

Bibliography

Bokelmann, K., and Paulsen, H. (1973). "Die Steinzeit in Schleswig-Holstein, 1 Teil: Flint-bearbeitungstechnik," in *Die Heimat 80*, pp. 110-116, Neumünster.

Bokelmann, K. and Paulsen, H. (1974). "Die Steinzeit in Schleswig-Holstein. 2 Teil: Die Weitverarbeitung der Klingen und Abschläge," in *Die Heimat 81,* No. 4, pp. 81-84, Neumünster.

Deutsches Bergbau-Museum Bochum (1999). *5,000 Jahre Feuersteinbergbau. Die Suche nach dem Stahl der Steinzeit,* Bochum.

Hahn, J. (1993). *Erkennen und Bestimmen von Stein- und Knochenartefakten—Einführung in die Artefaktmorphologie,* Tübingen.

Müller-Beck, H/ (ed)(1983). *Urgeschichte in Baden-Württemberg,* Stuttgart.

Paulsen, H. (1991). "Die Herstellung von oberflächenretuschierten Dolchen und Pfeil-spitzen," in Fansa, M. (ed) *Experimentelle Archäologie in Deutschland, Archäologis-che Mitteilungen aus Nordwestdeutschland*, Beiheft 4, pp. 279-282, Oldenburg.

Paulsen, H. (1991). "Schussversuche mit einem Nachbau des Bogens von Koldingen, Ldkr. Hannover," in Fansa, M. (ed), *Experimentelle Archäologie in Deutschland, Archäolo-gische Mitteilungen aus Nordwestdeutschland,* Beiheft 4, pp. 279-282, Oldenburg.

Petersen, P. V. (1993). *Flint fra Danmark oldtid,* Kobenhavn.

Rind, M. (1987). "Feuerstein: Rohstoff der Steinzeit—Bergbau und Bearbeitungstechnik," in *Museumsheft 3*, Arch. Museum der Stadt Kehlheim, Buch am Erlbach.

Spindler, K. (1993). *Der Mann im Eis*, pp. 119-12, München.

Waldorf, D. C. (1984). *The Art of Flintknapping*, 3rd Edition, Branson MO.

Weiner, J. (1987). "Techniken und Methoden der intentionellen Herstellung von Steingeräten (mit Bibliographie)," in *Museumsheft 3*, Arch. Museum der Stadt Ke-hlheim, Buch am Erlbach.

Wetzel, O. (1987). *Feuerstein—der Stein der Steine,* Neumünster.

A short, very readable description of arrowhead making in found in *GEO 10/1996* in the article "Gletschermumie."

THE AUTHOR

KONRAD VÖGELE

Born in Ummendorf, Oberschwaben, 1959.

Since 1994 I have been wrapped up in the wooden bow. The simplicity of the bow and the work with the organic material, wood, with its many typical qualities, fascinate me most. In this type of bow building it is a matter of putting the offered power to use without working against the bow. My favorite bow is a flat one with slight recurves and extremely slim ends, made of Osage orange.

Since many would like to build their own bows, I pass on my knowledge and experience in bow-building courses. Along with finished bows, I also offer selected woods, equipment, and tools for bow building.

WOODS FOR BOW BUILDING

When archery experienced a new popularity in America at the beginning of the 20th century, the opinion prevailed among the archers, most of whom then made their own bows, that there were only two suitable woods for bows, namely the yew, historically well known to Europeans, and the Osage orange, an American wood. At that time a somewhat different form of the English longbow was used.

Only later, especially in the 1980s, various bow builders experimented with various other woods and bow forms. The Californian bow builder Tim Baker in particular, with his almost scientific work, is to be thanked for the astonishing results from which we benefit today.

These bow builders determined that, with a changed bow shape, high-performance bows could also be made of so-called low-value woods. As soon as the limbs were made wider and flatter, these woods also provided the power in the bow, and the result is a bow that performs well and is comfortable. As you will see, a broad array of various woods is available.

SUITABLE WOODS

I would like to present some of the suitable woods here. In general, I have no interest in available pressure tables of various woods. These tables give either average values of the woods, or the value of a single tested piece of wood. In terms of experience, the quality of a type of wood varies from unsuitable to very good.

Since in an all-wooden bows the material is under pressure just shy of its breaking point, only the best wood can be used. Thus it depends more on the construction of the raw bow than on the type of wood.

This means that *a good ash is better than a bad yew.*

The structure of the wood, which I shall discuss later, is decisive here.

In presenting the various types of wood, I shall thus avoid pressure values and evaluations.

For the sake of conciseness, the list is organized by families:

Coniferous:
Toxaceae
Yew (*Taxus baccata*)

Capressaceae
Juniper (*Juniperus communis*)

Hickory (Carya)

Red beech

Elsberry

Locust

Osage orange

Deciduous:

Juglandaceae	Walnut (*Juglans regia*)
Betulaceae	European hornbeam (*Carpinus betulus*)
	European white birch (*Betula pendula*)
	Moor birch (*Betula pubescens*)
	Hazel (*Corylus avellana*)
Fagaceae	European beech (*Fagus silvatica*)
	English oak (*Quercus robur*)
Ulmaceae	Mountain elm (*Ulmus scabra*)
	Field elm (*Ulmus campestris*)
Leguminosae	Black locust (*Robinia pseudoacacia*)
Caprifoliaceae	Black elder (*Sambuccus niger*)
Rosaceae	European mountain-ash (*Sorbus acuparia*)
	Elsberry (*Sorbus torminalis*)
	Mealberry (*Sorbus aria*)
	Whitethorn (*Cartageus oxyacantha*)
	Apple (*Malus sp.*)
	Pear (*Pirus sp.*)
	Cherry (*Prunus avium*)
	Plum (*Prunus sp.*)
Aceraceae	Planetree maple (*Acer pseudoplatanus*)
	Norway maple (*Acer platanoides*)
	Field maple (*Acer campestre*)
Cornaceae	Dogwood (*Cornus sangrinea*)
	Cornel (*Cornus mas*)
Oleaceae	Ash (*Fraxinus excelsior*)
Moraceae	Osage orange (*Maclura pomifera*)

Other than hickory and Osage orange, both important bow woods, I have deliberately listed only native German woods. Other than these tried and true types, there are numerous other usable wood types. Thus I can only advise experimenting.

For a good-performance bow, the flexibility of the wood is only important to the extent that the bow does not break; the decisive factor is the power with which the limbs snap back to their starting points.

Thus I prefer hard, heavy woods, since experience shows that they have a higher returning power than soft, flexible woods such as willow.

CRITERIA FOR WOOD CHOICE

1. FORMS OF GROWTH

Above all, a symmetrical shape is helpful for the raw bow.

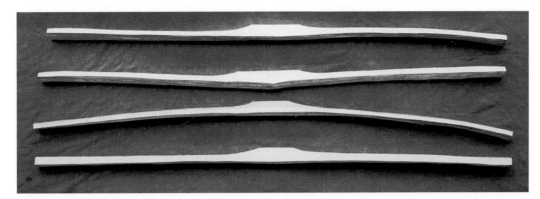

Various growth forms

Uneven (left straight, right reflex)

Deflex

Reflex

Straight

Straight Growth

This shape is the simplest to work, since, for example, drawing the bow profile is no problem. The bending is also easy to judge later.

Shape Bent Forward (Reflex)

By using a reflex raw bow, one can decrease the permanent misshaping (stringfollow) and thus improve the bow's performance. A problem, though, is the exact drawing and working of the bow's shape. Often the bow lies on one side when being strung, that is, the bowstring does not run centrally. The pressure on the wood is much greater here, since the limb becomes bent more strongly. Thus small errors of workmanship can lead to overstraining the bow. A reflex of up to 5% is relatively easy to handle.

Shape Bent Backward (Deflex)

Through natural curving in the direction of its bending, the pressure on the limbs is not so great, that is, the bow does not perform as well but is less likely to break. Straight profiling of the bow is also somewhat problematic.

These symmetrical shapes, despite their difficulties, are safe to work, since the evenness of bending of the limbs can be equalized well. Working becomes difficult with an asymmetrical piece, such as with one limb straight and one reflex. Here balancing the bow (tillering) requires more sensitive handling.

Twisted Growth

Twisting

The raw bow should have as little twisting as possible in it. With major twisting, the limb does not bend straight backward, but a somewhat to the outside. Thus the bowstring does not run through the middle of the bow. If the bow can be drawn straight even so, this is no problem. But such bows incline to twist when drawn. Major twists should therefore be straightened over steam.

2. WOODEN STRUCTURE

Yew

If you examine the cross-sections of various tree trunks, most woods will show a two-colored pattern. Trees of this type are called **heartwood trees.** Some examples are yew, locust, ash, elm, and hickory.

The dark inner heartwood has greater hardness than the lighter outer sapwood. This difference in hardness is variable.

While there is a greater difference in the locust, the difference scarcely matters in the ash.

Ring-wood trees are only sap-colored in the wood, although they have heartwood and sapwood, which differ only in hardness. Examples: field maple, beech, and pear.

The third group, the **sapwood trees,** have only sapwood. Thus they have one color and equal hardness. They include, among others, Norway maple, sycamore, hornbeam, and birch.

Late Wood Portion

Elm

Let us turn now to a very important criterion for the suitability of bow wood.

If you look at the annual rings, such as those of an ash, you will find that one ring is composed of two layers: the thin, dark line represents the end of the growth year, the winter rest.

In the active growth prevailing in spring, light wood with large pores, the so-called early wood, is formed. These pores serve mainly to transport food. During the summer the maturing process sets in, the wood thickens and forms under other lignin, a substance that gives the wood hardness. This thick wood has a darker color and is called late wood.

The thick, stable late wood is decisively better for use in bows. The wood you use should thus show as much late wood as possible.

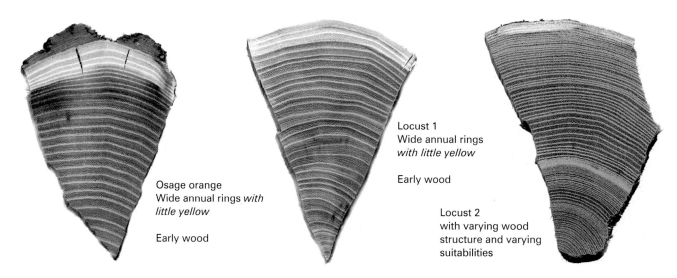

Osage orange
Wide annual rings *with little yellow*

Early wood

Locust 1
Wide annual rings
with little yellow

Early wood

Locust 2
with varying wood
structure and varying
suitabilities

In these cross-sections you can see the differences in the suitability of bow woods.

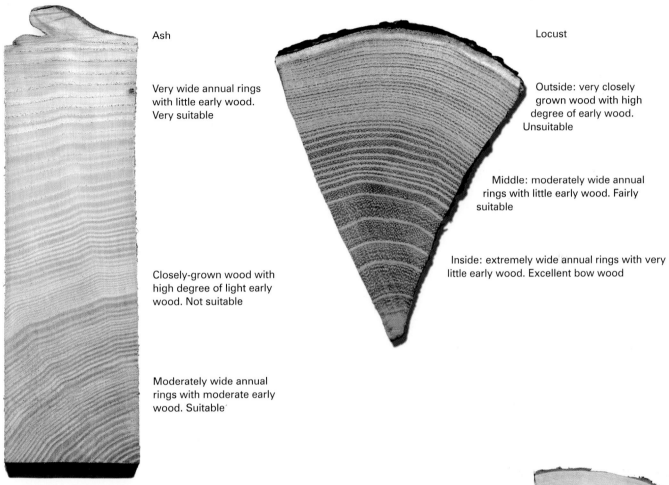

Ash

Very wide annual rings with little early wood. Very suitable

Closely-grown wood with high degree of light early wood. Not suitable

Moderately wide annual rings with moderate early wood. Suitable

Locust

Outside: very closely grown wood with high degree of early wood. Unsuitable

Middle: moderately wide annual rings with little early wood. Fairly suitable

Inside: extremely wide annual rings with very little early wood. Excellent bow wood

From the beginnings of bow building and shooting, it has always been believed that as finely grained wood as possible should be used.

Naturally, there are also narrow year rings with a good percentage of late wood, but these are rare and hard to recognize. In almost all woods, pieces with wide annual rings have a higher degree of late wood than those with narrow rings.

In yew as well, wood with wide annual rings gives better shooting qualities than narrow rings. These wood types are referred to as ring-pored, since the porous early wood appears as clearly visible rings.

Other types of wood show their yearly rings only unclearly. In these woods, the pores are almost equally large and are spread over the whole cross-section. These woods are described as scattered-pored (photo at right).

They are hard to judge. Based on experience, there are no very great differences in their suitability as bow wood, since these woods are more evenly structured.

Norway Maple
Sapwood tree, scattered-pored wood with annual rings hard to recognize.

101

Photo 1

Photo 2

Photo 3

CUTTING THE WOOD

Every bow builder would like, sooner or later, to build his bow from scratch, from the tree to the finished bow. In that case I recommend that you talk with the nearest forest ranger. Usually he/she will listen and find you a suitable tree.

The time from the end of November to mid-February is especially suitable for felling the tree, for then a fully formed annual ring is there to be used as the back of the bow. Also, the wood is drier during the pause in its growth. Cutting the wood in the growing period should be avoided, and if it can't, then cut only wood in which the outer annual ring is not used.

It is also a good idea to note the moon phase and constellations of stars. In various books (such as *Vom richtigen Zeitpunkt*), days are named on which the tree shows very special characteristics, such as not burning or not breaking.

I use the phase of the waning moon for felling; the wood is then drier and more resistant. Considering the stars is very interesting, but one should not make dogma out of it.

WORKING THE WOOD

After felling, I saw the suitable parts of the tree to between 1.80 meter to, at most, 2 meter lengths. After that, the trunk, regardless of its diameter, must be split at least once. The trunks that cannot be split reliably can be sawn with a band saw. Otherwise the trunks are split with the help of wedges.

To split the trunk reliably, put the axe on the end, through the pith, and strike the axe with a large hammer until the trunk begins to split. (Photo 1)

Then drive an iron, aluminum, or wooden wedge into the resulting crack. By inserting further wedges, the trunk splits throughout its length. (Photo 2) But if you put the wedges on the outside and drive them in, the trunk usually won't split in the middle, but along the side.

Most kinds of wood should be debarked as soon as possible. Debarking prevents parasite attacks, and drying becomes easier. (Photo 3)

Since the capillaries run longitudinally in the wood, it dries more on the cut ends, often causing deep cracks.

This can be avoided by sealing the ends. Any kind of paint, glue or wax is suitable.

Yew, Osage orange, and locust are best aged with their bark on.

Since wood often warps when drying, it is recommended that the split pieces be left as thick as possible. Through its larger mass, the wood will keep its shape better. An airy and shady place is best for drying and storing.

DRYING AND STORING

For a beginning bow builder it is very difficult to be patient for two or three years until the split piece is dry.

For impatient people, the process can be sped up: You work a raw bow out of the fresh wood a little bigger than the later bow will be. Don't taper the end yet, if possible, to prevent possible side splitting. Then reduce the thickness of the limbs enough so that the wood can be bent a little. The raw bow now has a width of 5 to 6 cm, and a thickness of about 1.5 cm on the limbs.

Photo 4
An airy, roofed place is best suited to drying.

This small amount of wood naturally dries very quickly, and stepping up the drying temperature is advantageous. For example, one week each in the hall, the living room, and then in the furnace room. By this method you have a well-dried raw bow in 4 to 5 weeks.

In locust and Osage orange, generally only the dark heartwood is used for bow building. Should one of these woods be dried, it is recommended that the corresponding annual ring to be used as the back of the bow be exposed. These woods, though, tend to form longitudinal cracks (drying cracks) when dried quickly. This can be avoided by sealing the exposed annual ring with clear lacquer. Then the wood will dry only on the front and sides.

Photo 5
Device for measuring moisture in wood

Photos 1, 3, 4: K. Vögele
Photos 2, 5: V. Alles

I dry yew carefully and slowly in its bark. When the wood is dry, I remove the bark and, if necessary, part of the sapwood to a thickness of about 5 mm. The dryness of the wood is very decisive for the bow's performance. Moist wood is elastic, to be sure, but has little returning power and warps strongly (great stringfollow).

Pictures from:
Bäume, 4th Edition, 1970,
Delphin Verlag, Stuttgart

The drier the wood becomes, the less it warps, and the more quick power it then provides. But it also becomes more and more brittle. At a wood humidity of 10%, the brittleness is not yet very great, but the wood has enough power for a high-performance bow.

Wood that was dried in an airy, unheated place shows a moisture level of 14% to 18% water, depending on the weather. If such wood is used for bow building, the results are not satisfactory. It is thus shown that any wood can be dried artificially. If you keep a worked, air-dried raw bow in a warm place one or two more weeks before tillering, the wood generally has the right dryness.

If these various points are considered in choosing bow wood, a major step to a high-performance, durable wooden bow has already been made.

AUTHOR

HOLGER RIESCH

The Merovingian era forms the focus of interest for Holger Riesch, who studies this epoch in his practical research on the subject of bows and arrows.

He has published on this subject in the journals *Technikgeschichte, Journal of the SAA*, and *Archäologisches Korrespondenzblatt*, and contributed to, among others, *Instinctive Archer Magazine* and *Traditionell Bogenschiessen.*

In 1997 he reconstructed a bow and arrow from Oberflacht for the "Die Alamannen" exposition of the State of Baden-Württemberg.

8

ALEMANNIC BOWS AND ARROWS

The Oberflacht Graveyard
A Foreword by Dr. D. Quast

Insights into the daily life of the Alemannic people are gained only by archaeological excavation and its evaluation, for the written remains from the Merovingian times (ca. 450-751 A.D.) are insufficient. The main evidence in archaeological source material comes from the graveyards, which, because of the regular arrangement of the graves, are known as linear cemeteries. The dead were buried with objects. Along with containers and various utensils (such as combs, knives, shears), weapons are often found in men's graves and jewelry in women's. Normally, the organic materials rot in the ground in a short time. Thus in the excavations, mainly only metal, ceramics, glass, and bones can be salvaged. For example, if a man was buried with a bow and arrows, only the remaining arrowheads attest to it.

In light of this background, the uniqueness of the graveyard of Oberflacht (community of Seitingen, county of Tuttlingen, in the southwest of Germany) becomes clear. Through the special geological features of the site, especially good conditions existed for the preservation of the organic materials. The graveyard lies in the brown Jura alpha, the soil of which (opaline stone) is damp, cold, badly ventilated and acidic. Thus the graves were always thoroughly damp, so that wood, leather, textiles, and foods were preserved. On the other hand, the acidic soil obviously reacted aggressively on metal. Since 1809, Merovingian graves have been found repeatedly while digging lime for a tile works. Especially significant were the investigations carried out in 1846 by Ferdinand von Dürrich and Wolfgang Menzel. An exemplary publication, for those times, on this first excavation of an Alemannic graveyard in Württemberg was published by them in the following year. Until the last excavations in 1933–34, the site was excavated "privately" again and again, for it had meanwhile become known in the field far beyond the borders of Württemberg.

The excavation report of Baron von Ow-Wachendorf, published in 1893 in the first volume of *Fundberichte aus Schwaben,* gives a good impression of the extraordinary preservation conditions: "The tree coffin of the first grave contained a feminine skeleton, still complete and in its original position, dressed in a long garment well preserved in the moist mud, with the entire texture of the fine linen cloth and its folds could be seen. A leather belt around the hips held the garment together, and a nicely ornamented bronze, probably gilded clasp was found on it. Outside the coffin were a large turned wooden bowl and a three-legged stool, and the usual hazel wands, which probably had a symbolic meaning, were not missing either. At the woman's feet were a small decorative pail, a big wooden bowl, and a very delicate small bowl, filled with fruits of all kinds, hazel nuts, walnuts, zirbel nuts, cherries, and even completely preserved apples ... the decorative, sandal-like leather shoes ... were especially well preserved."

The graveyard included about 20 graves and was used as a burial place from about 530 to 650 A.D. This implies a contemporaneous living settlement of about 55 people. It is much harder to judge whether these are especially lavishly outfitted graves, for this is usually judged on the basis of the metal and glass objects.

In Oberflacht, though—presumably because of the acidic soil—only relatively few metal objects remained. On the other hand, wooden objects were found in large numbers. Numerous pieces of furniture (beds, chests, chairs, tables) were found in the graves, as well as lyres, saddles, game boards, containers of all kinds, and even lamps and candles. The objects show the high level of Alemannic wood handicrafts and a precise knowledge of the different types of wood. Many of the objects dug from the graves in the 19th century have already crumbled or been made unrecognizable by the drying process. Only since the end of the 19th century is it possible to conserve wood successfully. Three bows, though, have remained in excellent condition nevertheless.

Experimental archaeology can offer important results in their evaluation.

1. ALEMANNIC BOW SHOOTING

In this work, the completely wooden bows found at the Württembergish village of Oberflacht at the foot of Mount Lupfen will be documented, and the arrows also found there in 19th century excavations will be reconstructed.

In the process, objects still available in museums, plus objects found in 1846 but no longer preserved, will be discussed. Aspects of handicraft work and experimental results will be included, and should allow traditional bow builders to produce functioning reproductions. Important archaeological objects from other Merovingian sites will be given a thorough description to enrich the Oberflach situation. Thus a many-faceted picture of bow shooting in the early Middle Ages will be made.

2. THE LONGBOWS OF OBERFLACHT

The three yew bows, found in graves 7, 8, and 21 in Oberflacht and essentially fully preserved, are the only long-range weapons of the Merovingian era (Figure 1, Color Plate 7) that have survived in this quality. Despite their uniqueness, these objects, which are stored at the Württembergisches Landesmuseum (WLM) in Stuttgart, have been publicized only in basic terms in the realm of inclusive specialty literature. (6.1-3, 6.5-6, 6.10) A special discussion of them in terms of bow knowledge has been lacking, and will be provided, now that the author has, thanks to the friendly permission of the Landesmuseum, been able to examine the originals on the spot. First, the working of materials and design will be studied in depth, after which authentic replicas of the bow from grave no. 21 will be tested, with the measurements cited in detail in the addenda.

2.1 DESCRIPTION OF THE MATERIALS

The outsides of the bows are mostly of a single brown color, so that when seen in profile no clear difference between the characteristic light sapwood and dark heart area of the yew wood can be seen. That it is actually made of *Taxus baccata* wood is shown not only by the presence of prominent spiral thickenings and lack of heart channels, but by the excellent state of preservation. The material shows neither bulges nor noteworthy contractions. Also noticeable is the good quality of workmanship of the pieces, which show accurately formed angles and roundings, plus smoothed surfaces, and give the picture of a careful means of production (Fig. 2).

A coating of clear lacquer applied to the objects from Grave No. 7 and No. 21 after excavation strengthens the positive impression of condition and building technique. In the more recent past, doubts were even raised by archaeologists as to its authenticity, but they were refuted in the early 1990s by analyses of the wood. (6.6, a)

The small scratches on the bow can be attributed only to lengthy microbacterial destruction in moist surroundings, and rule out the possibility of modern replicas.

Figure 2. Grip end and limb of the Grave 21 bow (Photo: H. Riesch).

The Grave 7 Bow

The specimen from Grave No. 7 is a straight longbow, in the center of which we find a light reflex placed there on purpose.

The yew stave is 1,691 mm long overall and 1,592 mm between the nocks. The measurement is taken on the top, made in the middle of each bowstring notch. Within an incision (recently made for analysis) in the last third of the upper limb (see 2.2), one growth ring appears per millimeter, parallel to the arching of the upper side and at right angles to the shooting direction. The outer radius angles suggest that a yew trunk of some 90 mm diameter was used to build it. The splint section extends 3.5 to 4 mm into the incision, with lighter coloring in the upper area.

Several small dead branches, which do not penetrate the back of the bow, are found in the grip zone. An especially wide branch is in the upper limb and caused a greater bending pressure of the wood there. This situation may have caused two crosswise cracks in the sapwood, which probably occurred only after excavation. A previously occurring break, obviously making the weapon functionally useless, would not match the otherwise typical condition of the Oberflacht finds. Probably the bow was buried strung, so that a compensation in the form of crack formations resulted. Previous use cannot be proved. Bowstring marks, which normally occur in the area of the notch, or arrow-sliding marks, as would have been left on the grip from intensive practical use, are missing.

The Grave 8 Bow

The specimen from Grave No. 8, in poorer condition than the other two that were found, has an effective length of 1,584 mm over the upper side and 1,701 mm between the ends. The yew stave still has its original length, but shows major losses in wood substance on its upper side. These weatherings give a sapwood portion of 2.6 to 3.4 mm in all. With 3.5 to 5 annual rings per millimeter, measured at the bow ends, the wood can be characterized as finely grained. Again the annual rings are parallel in profile to the arched back and at right angles to the shooting direction. Since the pith channel stands out in places on the undersides of the limbs, and only the bark was taken off above, meaning that no growth wood was removed in production, the debarked diameter of the used yew trunk was only about 60 mm. The strong arching of the profile, reaching far to the middle, also points to this.

Scattered over the entire length are about a dozen branches, 3 to 5 mm wide, growing out; they influence the outward appearance of the bow, but are uncritical for shooting conditions in growth wood left standing. Dense annual rings and a small amount of sapwood have really produced a fine long-distance weapon, which was made with comparatively flat limbs causing meager stress on material.

Thin impressions located right by the oval bowstring nocks point to the existence of a string loop. Unfortunately, no traces of arrow sliding, which would indicate actual use, can be found on the damaged grip any more. In all, the specimen from Grave No. 8, what with the noted characteristics, gives the most practice-oriented impression of the three examined bows.

The Grave 21 Bow

The once-straight yew stave from Grave No. 21, 1,842 mm long overall and 1,712 mm in effective length, has a reflex shape today. This condition, appearing by chance in discovered yew bows, can be traced to stronger decomposition processes in the soft growth wood than in the hard heartwood, which warped the limbs over their upper sides. The only larger branch was cleverly located in the zone of least pressure, the grip, when the bow was made. In general, just a few unproblematic dead branches are present. A modern incision for wood analysis is in about the middle of the lower limb. Here lighter coloring shows a splint 3 to 4 mm thick. Because of the angle of the outer annual-ring radii, whose position in the bow corresponds to that noted above, the yew stem used for the bow must have been about 200 mm thick. The flat arching of the upper side also shows that it was a comparatively massive piece of work. At the end of the lower limb, three or four growth rings appear per millimeter, at the upper one five. The acute-angled bowstring nocks below are cracked—an indication that the bow was strung. Frequent shooting, though, can be ruled out. The string pressure would otherwise have split the grooves completely.

There are also no traces of arrow sliding in the grip area, which would indicate practical use as a shooting weapon. This feature corresponds to the results gained from experiments with the replica of the Grave 21 bow (see 3.2 below).

2.2 THE OBERFLACHT DESIGN: CONSTRUCTION FEATURES

The findings from Oberflacht have a design that is unique in the developmental history of bows and arrows, and which will be examined more closely in this section.

Most prominent here is the conception of the functional aspects common to all bows. Special measurements will be found documented in tables in the addenda. There is an addition for traditional bow builders, who may want to build authentic replicas, with selected photographic as well as written documentation of the Oberflacht bows, in the publications of W. Veek and S. Schiek from 1932 to 1991 (6.3, 6.6 a, f).

Grip Areas

Each of the Oberflacht bows has a strengthened grip zone. Centrally located, slight asymmetrical forms can go out from it on the limbs, but they have no practical function in shooting. The grip reinforcements are constant and fitted to the wood structure; the width always decreases continually to the middle of the bow. Becoming slimmer in hand-ergonomic terms, on the specimens from Graves No. 7 and 8 the profile ends in oval shapes, and on the Grave 21 bow in a flat-triangular shape (Figure 4).

The grips are set off in steps from the limbs. The distance to the adjoining underside of the Grave 7 bow is greatest; that of the Grave 21 bow is less marked. In the latter, this being a very low step, the ends are narrowly separated from the limbs (Figure 2). On the other hand, the specimen from Grave No. 8, and especially that from Grave 7, whose limb profiles are clearly smaller where they adjoin the grips, are fitted with curved and slightly decreasing transitions (Figure 3).

It should be stressed that the strengthened middle includes 15.8% of the effective length of the Grave 7 bow, 14.9% of the Grave 8 bow and 18.5% of the Grave 21 bow. To date, no other pre-historic or historic full-wood bows are known to have such long extensions of the grip. They are more strongly bent when drawn than a short grip that simply serves hand action, which heightens the stiffness of the spring that every bow represents mechanically.

In addition, an extended center shortens the active length of the limbs. Short limbs, compared with longer and heavier ones, need less energy for their own acceleration. Thus the weapon gains a higher degree of effectiveness. At the same time, the long grip extensions reduce "hand shock."

Figure 3: Grip end and limb of the Grave 7 bow (Photo: H. Riesch)

The Limbs

From the arched upper sides, the edges of the bow limbs are slightly angled inward, as a rule. They bend at least at half limb strength, but usually in the last third, toward the middle and run together to a triangle on the underside. This formation begins (except the Grave 21 bow) at the grip ends and remains until the bowstring nocks. (Fig. 4)

What are the advantages of such a laborious formation? To answer this question, within the framework of a thesis written by a student at the machinery section of the Fachhochschule Bingen (University of Applied Sciences), static and dynamic calculations of different types of archeologically documented full-wood bows were carried out. (6.10)

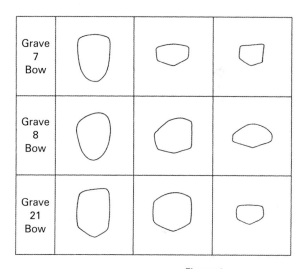

It was shown that the pentagonal cross-section is capable of giving off more energy when shooting than round, oval, or D-shaped types can.

Besides that, the mostly high-profiled limbs cause lower amplitudes of unwanted swinging behavior in comparison to flat bows. But these advantages go together with greater mechanical pressure during the drawing of the bowstring. Along with the extended grip zones, stronger material stress was taken in the bargain for the Oberflacht bows in favor of a more optimal release of energy and smoother shot qualities.

Potential danger of breaking was diminished by extending the greatest width of the limbs behind the grips, after one third of their effective length. The width then decreases only slowly in the working zone. Nearer to the string nock, a more obvious decrease takes place until the end of the limb.

The bows, which also become slimmer toward the middle, thus take on a visually "paddle-shaped" appearance, whereby the shorter examples from Graves 7 and 8 were given somewhat wider limbs than the longer one from Grave 21.

Figure 4:
Grave 7 bow: center of grip, lower limb, end part.
Grave 8 bow: center of grip, upper limb, lower limb.
Grave 21 bow: center of grip, upper limb, end part (6.6 a)

Figure 5
Upper ends of the Grave 7 (left) and Grave 8 bows. (Photos: H. Riesch)

Figure 6
Upper ends of the Grave 21 (right) and Grave 7 bows. (Photos: H. Riesch)

Bowstring Nocks and End Areas

The string attachments are about 50 mm from the limb ends in all the bows. One-sided and opposite nocks are typical of them. One-sided nocking basically provides better absorbing ability of the drawing weight than two-sided, which doubly decreases the mass of the wood structure.

The diameters of the nocks indicate a thickness of 3 to 4 mm of the bowstrings, of which, unfortunately, none remain at Oberflacht. Linen yarn is usable as a material, although other fibrous plants besides flax, such as inner bark, are also possible. For the reconstruction, a comparison piece from the Swiss town of Altdorf can be referred to, where a three-ply twine bowstring of S-twine (material structure not examined more closely) was found (6.8).

The limb profiles of the Oberflacht bows generally increase again slightly before the nocks. In the specimen from Grave No. 7, they run out in gradual narrowing; in the others, the bow end is very rectangular. (Figure 5)

Profile enlarging or stagnation in the nock areas in turn serves to oppose sufficient material to the bow-drawing at these critical areas. Long and extended ends, on the other hand, have no technical shooting uses. They should rather be avoided, so as not to make the limb heavier in its inactive zone and bring on unwanted "hand shock." The areas beyond the nocks, or their shaping, thus have purely decorative functions. This also makes the shortness of the effective limb appear to have been desired by the bow builder; otherwise the potentially usable active length would not have been "squandered."

Bowstring Holders

A further mark of differentiation between the bows from Graves 8 and 21 in comparison to that from Grave 7 is a small hole, bored only in the first of them above one of the string nocks from the top or the side through the bow's long axis. (Figures 5, 6)

Since its diameter in the Grave 8 bow is so small that it could not possibly hold the bowstring, its purpose may have been to hold a bowstring holder (string-keeper). This is a cord that, on one end, is knotted to the loop in the string, and, on the other end, is fixed above one of the notches to prevent an unwanted excessive sliding of the loop on the upper limb when the bow is not strung.

The weapon can quickly be made ready to shoot when needed. It follows that the string was attached permanently to the opposite, lower end by a knot.

Attaching the bowstring to the lower end of the unstrung bow is also iconographically confirmed for the early Middle Ages. (Figure 7)

The bow from Grave 7, instead of a bored hole, has two opposite nocks, which likewise may have served to hold a string-keeper. (Figures 5, 6)

In this respect, the old discovery of 1846, which shows the Grave 7 bow with a hole in the opposite limb end, is of interest. The corresponding part is, alas, broken off and lost today. Since two "string-keepers" would make just as much sense as one attachment of the string in the slim double nocks, this may be an artistic addition to the already damaged bow, which originally had no hole. (Figures 11, 1)

Figure 7: Bowstring attachment on the lower half of the bow ("Stuttgarter Bilderpsalter," fol. 146 r)

2.3. OTHER BOW FRAGMENTS FROM OBERFLACHT

There exist, sometimes not attributed to a grave, a few other artifacts from Oberflacht that can be seen as remains of shooting weapons. They will be noted briefly here.

One wooden object stored at the WLM in Stuttgart, very weathered and wrinkled, has a triangular profile, is 1,170 mm long, and is called a bow in the literature (6.6, d)—probably because at one end it has a spur made in steps, which (very unusual for the Oberflacht building style) could have served as a bowstring attachment. From the author's point of view, the interpretation of this very unrecognizable piece of no-longer exactly-identifiable-wood-type as a long-range weapon is questionable.

A five-sided but strongly compacted piece of elm, 1,120 mm long, can be identified more surely as a former bow, though the ends are missing, for an extended "grip zone" with offset angles can be recognized. (6.6, e) Unlike these rather vaguely identifiable objects, there is a broken piece of yew, 204 mm long, in the Landesmuseum which, on the basis of its clearly worked pentagonal cross-section, is clearly identifiable as a part of a limb of an Oberflacht bow (6.6, f)

Finally, the Museum für Vor- und Frühgeschichte in Berlin-Charlottenburg also has a copy, presently not available and, in terms of its authenticity, not unproblematic, of a yew bow about 1,500 mm long, from Grave No. 84, known as the "minstrel's grave" because there was also a six-stringed lyre buried there. (6.6 g)

3. THE PRACTICAL REPLICA

If you would like to gain information on the shooting qualities of the Oberflacht bows, in addition to visual evaluation and mechanical calculation of the originals, there is also the possibility of testing functioning replicas. (Figure 8)

Bow-building authenticity thus depends on the sharing of vital construction features, which are summed up again here among handcrafted aspects. In the framework of practical tests to determine the maximum performance, the author has experimented with several replicas of the largest remaining bow, that from Grave No. 21. The resulting data allow an interesting insight into the original use spectrum of the bow as not only a burial object but also a usable long-range weapon.

3.1 DATA FOR BOW BUILDERS

In order to be authentic, bows of the Oberflacht type must:
• first, show a strengthened and lengthened grip zone,
• second, have pentagonal limbs, and,
• third, be slightly "paddle-shaped" when seen from above.

The grip extensions vary in relation to their effective length between some 15% of the 1,600 mm short to 19% of the 1,800 mm long bow. The first also have somewhat wider limbs in their maximum extent, which also decreases the danger of breakage in shooting. Grooves for holding the bowstring are always one-sided, some 50 mm from the end of the limb, and should have an oval shape underneath, so that the string cannot cut into the wood.

There are alternatives, both for attaching a string-keeper and for the whole design of the end sections as well.

The material-stressing bow design always demands very good workmanship on the materials. Small trunks only 60 to 90 mm in diameter can be used in this case. If you compare the quality of modern yew with the antique wood, with an average of 2 to 4 annual rings per millimeter, the relation of sapwood to heartwood through the whole length is about 1:3. In view of the handiwork it should be noted that the edges of the pentagonal profile, as in the examples, were formed clearly and without being rounded. (Figure 9)

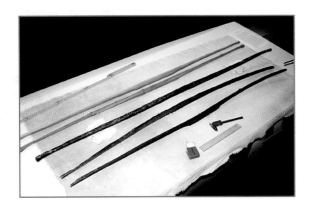

Figure 8: Grave 21 replicas (above) and originals in the WLM, Stuttgart. (Photo: H. Riesch)

Yew (*Taxus baccata*)

Ash (*Fraxinus excelsior*)

Locust (*Robinia pseudoacacia*)

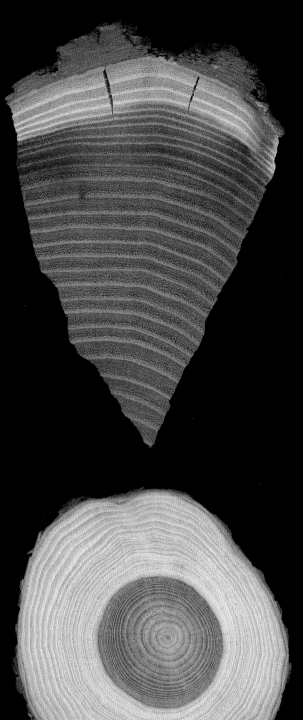

Osage Orange (*Maclura pomifera*)

Norway Maple (*Acer platanoides*)

Elm (*Ulmus campestris*)

Figure 1
LONGBOW AND ROUND SHIELD FROM OBERFLACHT. (Photo H. Zwietasch-P. Frankenstein, WLM, Stuttgart)

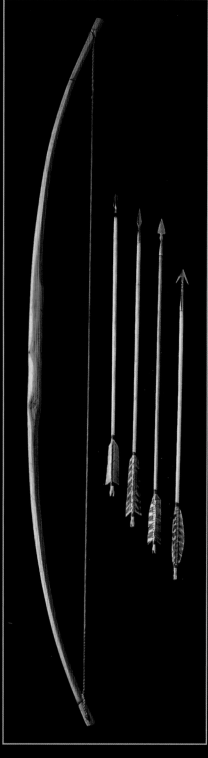

Figure 9
ALEMANNIC BOW AND ARROWS (Photo: H. Zwietasch-P. Frankenstein, WLM, Stuttgart. Replicas: H. Riesch)

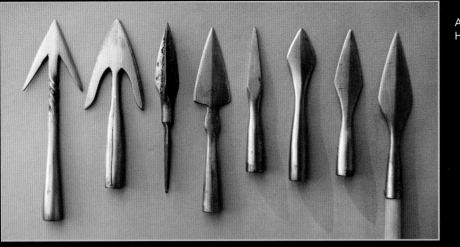

Alemannic Arrowheads (Photo:
H. Riesch, Replicas: U. Stehli)

Oberflacht Bow and Arrows
(Photo and Replicas: U. Stehli)

Figure 17: Quiver Reconstruction after Altdorf model (Photo and Replica: H. Riesch)

Figure 23 Archer with hunting arrow ("Stuttgarter Bilderpsalter," fol.
69 r)

3.2 TESTING THE BOW FROM GRAVE 21

Accurate Replicas

After adequate yew staffs had been chosen, suited to the measurements of the models and tillered, three reproductions of the grave 21 bow were available for practical tests (Figure 9, Color plates 7 and 8).

From the beginning, their extreme stiffness was noticeable, which made it possible to draw the bows only under considerable manual exertion. To measure the pulling weights, the bows were then put on the "tiller staff" again. The linen bowstrings, in each case 135 mm above the grips, were at first pulled out to 200 mm. The power used for that, tending to increase, amounted to about 5 kg per 50 mm up to a holding power of 22 kg.

Opposed to this value, the critical stress area was already beginning; from some 250 to 300 mm of draw, overstressing of material and bow breakage unavoidably set in. The meager flexibility thus resulted less from the long grip zone than from the too-highly profiled limbs within the first two quarters after the grip edges.

This experimental result strongly questions the practical use value of the original bow, for reconstructed arrow shafts from Oberflacht (see 4.1 below) need a drawing length of at least 400 mm. With the replicas, appropriate arrows could not be shot effectively when drawn only 200 mm. The Grave 21 bow with the existing dimensions was thus unusable as a long-range weapon.

Considerations as to Degree of Finish

Was the Grave 21 bow badly made, or was it simply a faulty design model? To answer this question, help could come from the fact that a bowstring was indeed strung on the unusable original. Worn nocks like those here (Figure 6) also appeared on some replicas because of the huge pull of the string when the bow was strung. More practical weights would have been attainable in terms of bow building by removing an adequate amount of heartwood on the upper parts of the limbs. Since the flexibility needed for shooting was not attained, but the bow was only built to stretch a bowstring, the opportunity and need for a final work process in terms of tillering were probably lacking.

Perhaps the bow was used merely as a grave item that did not need any real functioning ability. It is possible that for burial purposes only the representation of an visually intact specimen was needed and the bowyer thus did not go to the trouble of doing a finished job.

If the Oberflacht bows in general were deposited with applied bowstrings, then the level of workmanship still would have been enough to indicate an apparently complete weapon. Compared with the usually good useful quality of the other finds in the grave-yard, this hypothesis describes a rare exception, but would explain the high quality of work that was applied to forming the wooden corpus and the simultaneously incomplete condition of the bow from Grave 21.

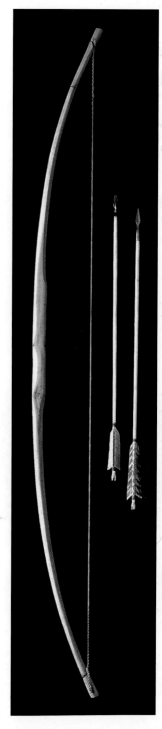

Figure 9: Alemannic bow and arrows (Photo H. Zwietasch-P. Frankenstein, WLM Stuttgart; replica: H. Riesch)

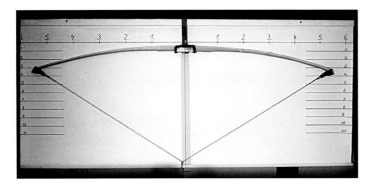

Figure 10: Bow replica during tillering (photo and replica H. Reisch)

Reconstructible Shooting Qualities

A decrease of the upper limb profile by some 3 to 4 mm put the replicas into a usable condition. Unlike the original, the greater distance between grip and adjoining limbs requires the formation of smoother steps (as in the Grave 7 and 8 bows) instead of angular edges, so as to create an unburdened connection between the grip and the working parts of the bow. (Figure 10)

Maintaining, otherwise completely, the original lengths and widths, the yew staffs allow a drawing distance of about 400 mm and have maximum pulling weights between 30 and 35 kg. On the basis of their strengthened grip extensions, they are pleasant to shoot, meaning without disturbing subsequent swinging, but because of the lesser drawing distance and material-straining design, they require a suitably dynamic shooting style with short "anchor time." Also characteristic is a high initial velocity of the arrow with optimal effectiveness developing at point-blank range.

At longer distances, on the other hand, projectiles shot from medieval longbows of comparable performance have more power. With round or D-shaped profiles and without lengthened grip zones, they are of course slower, but offer more pulling area and less danger of breaking. With this alternative design model in mind, also used by Alemannic bow builders of the Merovingian times (see 5.1 below), one could pointedly call the Oberflacht bows "long-range weapons for close ranges." Probably their unusual design was based on special practical requirements.

Figure 11: Oberflacht bow and arrow from Grave 7 in the 1846 documentation (6.1 a-c)

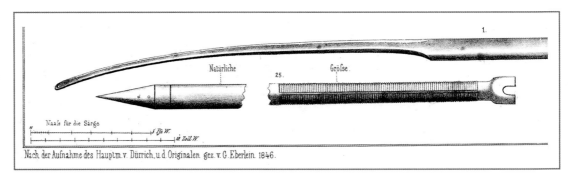

4. THE OBERFLACHT ARROWS

"The arrows were the same in all coffins, two feet long, thicker above than below, made for a fast arrow flight. Below, one still saw remains of the material with which the fletching was attached. Above there was no metal point. Only sometimes, small pins with which the lost arrowheads had been fastened. The stumpy part on which the arrowheads were set was mercury-red on some arrows." Thus did Wolfgang Menzel describe the found arrows in his 1847 excavation report. (6.2 b) This text was augmented by drawings of the finds. (Figures 11, 25) Two shaft pieces, about 190 mm long and 9 mm thick, from Grave 71–72 are still in existence today, preserved in the museum of the town of Spaichingen, district of Tuttlingen. (Figure 12)

4.1 WOODEN SHAFTS

The pieces of shafts consist of wayfaring tree viburnum and birch wood. Both are very suitable arrow materials, often found in European archaeological sites. The cited report uses the "Württemberg foot measure" for measurements. At a calculated 287 mm, the shafts had been some 574 mm long when intact. For such an arrow, considering the 135 mm bowstring distance and 25 to 30 mm of the point projecting, about 400 mm remain for drawing. Here the data in the secondary sources agree with the reconstructed bow qualities.

Figure 12: Viburnum and Birch (bottom) shafts grave NR. 70-71 (6,6, b)

In the 1846 drawing, the shaft thickness was 11 mm in front, after which came even tapering to 8 mm shortly before an offset area of 12 mm diameter.

In the full-scale replica, such arrows, weighing 40 to 50 grams with iron arrowheads, are not very flexible, because of the toughness of the shaft material and the meager overall length.

The flight qualities prove to be clearly better when the overall diameter is modified by about one millimeter forward, thus giving measurable "spine" values. The fragments from Grave 71–72 should also be noted, as they deviate from the finders' description, showing no thorough narrowing. (Figure 12) Obviously, both straight shafts and those that were thicker in front were used. Trimming them had to be done to suit the existing bow weight. Arrows of uniform thickness (as in the report) could not realistically have existed on account of varying bow weights.

4.2 ARROW FLETCHING

The detailed illustration of 1846, contrary to the report, which mentions only "remains of the material"—such as birch pitch—shows a shaft binding only about 90 mm long, unusually narrow and thick, beginning right after the arrow nock. In the middle, a quill line is indicated, its position when shooting with twofold fletching having none, with three- or fourfold fletching one of the vanes touching the bow from the side or front as it passed by. The latter represents an avoidable disturbance, which in fact exists on some of the Iron Age Germanic arrows from Nydam, too. (6.13 b)

Figure 13: Arrows with trapezoidal feathering and cup-shaped nocks ("Stuttgarter Bilderpsalter," fol. 74 r)

Further details are not documented for Oberflacht but can be deduced from alternative sources, so as to guarantee at least potential accuracy in reconstruction. Shaft bindings of softly spun wool fibers in S-cording occur on an Alemannic arrow found at Altdorf, Martinskirche, Uri Canton, Switzerland. (6.8) Used here to secure an arrowhead, it could have been used at the other end of the arrow for feather keels on a layer of glue.

In terms of shape, contemporary psalter illustrations are available, often showing arrows with trapezoidally cut flight stabilizers. (Figure 13)

Goose feathers were also used on shafts from Nydam and, because of their positive flight performance, were also used in the Middle Ages, as the detailed accounts of Roger Ascham show in his textbook of archery, *Toxophilus* (London 1545).

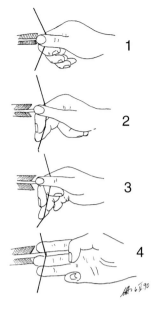

1

2

3

4

Figure 14: Traditional drawing techniques (A. Webb, *Archeology of Archery*, Tornworth 1991)

4.3 ARROW NOCKS

The nocks of the Oberflacht arrows were cut out of the tapering shafts in cup form. Similar shapes are also found on Germanic shafts from Nydam, Haithabu (Viking era), and in Carolingian iconography. (Figure 13) With such a widespread arrow end, there was sufficient material available on bowstring nocks. Furthermore, splitting the wood by the pressure of the string was avoided. For the so-called "secondary" or "tertiary means of drawing," that is, for grasping by the use of thumb and index finger supported for high drawing weights by middle or middle plus ring fingers (Figure 14, 203), offset nocks would likewise have been very helpful. One of these drawing methods, used for quick drawing plus immediate release of the string, would correspond well to the character of the Oberflacht bow's short draw and high speed. Compared with present-day usage based on "Mediterranean drawing" (Figure 14, 4), the thumb-supported techniques take some getting used to. But since the design of the Oberflacht bows differs so much from traditional longbows, one should consider unconventional shooting styles, which can prove very effecting with appropriate training, for the Merovingian-era situation!

4.4 ARMING THE ARROWS

Alemannic Arrowheads

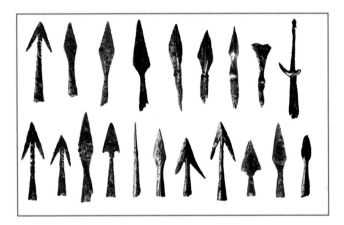

Figure 15: Alemannic projectile types of the late 6th and 7th centuries (J. Werner, Das alamann. Gräberfeld von Bülach, Basel 1953)

Only two iron arrowheads, along with arrow fragments, have been documented as coming from Grave 84 in the Oberflacht graveyard, but they have not survived. (6.6 c)

One is an example of a diamond-shaped leaf and the other a triangular point with barbs. Such shapes are typical of the Merovingian cultural area, that of the Franks, Alemans, and Bayuwars. In addition, bolts or pin-shaped points occur. Cross-cutters or trident points, such as were found at a graveyard in Bülach, Zürich Canton, Switzerland, rank among the exceptions.

The occasionally discovered three-winged types with a shaft thorn, that were imported from the Mediterranean area, are also interesting. (Figure 15) The shaping of the projectile was done, beyond stylistic aspects (oval, diamond, triangle), primarily on the basis of its purpose. Slim leaf points some 15 to 20 mm in diameter were used mainly for warfare. The conically tapered round or four-edged types, on the other hand, were used to strike through metal armor.

Deer hunting, the preferred kind of hunting in the early Middle Ages, required barbed heads 30 to 40 mm wide, often with twisted shafts. Probably the cross-cutters and trident points were also used for hunting. (6.14)

Smithing Techniques and Shafting

Metallurgical analyses showed a three-layered buildup, exemplary for an original Alemannic arrowhead, with a ferrite core with 182 HV 1 (Vickers hardness) enclosed by ferrite-perlite layers with 192 HV 1. (Figure 16) In this seemingly modern "sandwich construction," the harder zones gave stability of form while the softer middle section avoided brittle breaking because of its crack-stopping qualities. In the practical reconstruction (Figure 9, Color Plate 8), comparable material qualities were attained by manual smithing using modern steel S235JRG2 (DIN EN 10025), a simple iron steel without alloys. (6.12)

To unite the heads with the shafts, pinning was used. On the remaining birch shaft piece there is a pinhole at the beginning of the front part, which is pointed for 270 mm. (Figure 12, u) In the experimental replica, too, one such attaching element provides sufficient security.

The documentation from 1846, which shows two or three pins in text and picture (Figure 11, 25), surely exaggerates. If the case of "mercury red," coloring of some forward shaft areas is not the result of corrosion or even the remains of shaft painting, but traces of glue, then attachment with glue would have been practiced in Oberflacht, too.

Figure 16: Three-level arrowhead (Photo K. Becker-H. Riesch, FH Bingen)

4.5 ARROW QUIVERS

In the Oberflacht graves, arrows were usually three in number and buried without quivers. The living bowmen, though, must have had containers for the protection and transport of larger numbers of arrows.

The most complete Merovingian quiver found to date comes from the Altdorf grave inventory. The well-to-do Aleman buried there had a leather-covered linden quiver fitted with a lid, filled with eight hunting arrows of honeysuckle, hazel, and ash wood. Its body, long-oval in cross-section and widening toward the bottom, held the projectiles with the fletching downward; at the top they could be taken from a U-shaped opening at the front. (6.8) This trapezoid quiver design was brought into the Byzantine and Germanic areas by Huns and Avars, Asiatic mounted people, between the 5th and 8th centuries A.D.

For the Merovingian realm, the Altdorf discovery gives evidence of a slightly modified wooden body decorated with braided bands, and with a separate lid, features unknown to the Avars.

In practical use (Figure 17, see also Color Plate 8), the means of carrying the quiver at the right hip, allows an arrow to be taken just below the socket, so that it can be brought to the bow safely. Obviously coming to the Alemannic area from abroad, this method of carrying arrows with points upward perhaps also reached the Oberflacht archers.

Figure 17: Quiver design after a model from Altdorf (Photo and replica H. Riesch)

Figure 18: Hunting quiver of the High Middle Ages ("Krumauer Bilderkodex," vol. 97 v)

Just as the stirrup, brought westward by steppe nomads, was adopted successfully, the medieval sources appear to show that the Eastern type of quiver was also used permanently in Central Europe. (Figure 18)

Etymologically, it could only be suspected for a long time that the present-day German word "Köcher" (English "quiver," French "carquois") was a loan-word from Turko-Mongolian languages (Hunnish/Avarish "kur" or "kuhar") that came into Old High German in the early Middle Ages (Kluges Etym, *Lexikon*, Berlin 1975). The outstanding Altdorf discovery now supports this hypothesis on the basis of the adaptation of the object.

5. ALEMANNIC BOWYERS AND ARCHERS

The three long-range weapons from Oberflacht have a certain lack of homogeneity in terms of materials, functions, and stylistic details, which perhaps is attributable to the building of bows in the communities of the time not having been regarded as a specialized handicraft with strongly unified formation. Probably every archer or individual from his social group was himself responsible for production.

An optimal design like the one at hand always requires a high level of technical understanding, probably based on long practical experience in using hunting or fighting weapons. The Merovingian wooden bow from Altdorf also seems to belong to an older tradition, which will be outlined below.

In addition, the "Alemannic archery" knew fully different technical designs, as shown in the individual use of composite reflex bows, which will also be portrayed briefly.

Figure 19: Altdorf grave items as found (Picture: Swiss Landesmuseum, Zürich)

5.1 BOW TYPES OF THE MEROVINGIAN TIMES

Longbows from Altdorf and Oberflacht

In 1969 not only the quiver, but also fragments of a yew bow, were recovered from the Alemannic grave in St. Martin's church in Altdorf. It can be called a hunting weapon because of the wide barbed broadheads that were in the linden-wood quiver. (Figure 19)

At some 1,800 mm, it was probably as tall as a man, has an almost round profile without a specially strengthened grip area, and shows a specialty at one end, a point shaft 880 mm long, fixed with a thin iron nail. (6.8) This shooting weapon, buried circa 670 A.D., is thus comparable to such longbows as were found at the Nydam Moor (6.13 a) with round cross-sections and sometimes also with point shafts.

The Merovingian example may go back to an Alemannic tribal group, whose home was presumably in the lower and middle Elbe region before their emigration to the south, which began in the 2nd or 3rd century A.D., a (north) Germanic bow design carried into the early Middle Ages.

The great design difference of the Altdorf bow from the much more complex design of the Oberflacht bows is striking. Obviously, different bow types were used at the same time in the "Alemannia." No models for the Oberflacht objects are known to date, nor do bows of the High and later Middle Ages show a comparable form, though examples found in Europe are very few. The chronologically closest full-wood bow (made of yew) with offset but short grip area and five-sided (but slim) limbs, appeared only at the time of the Renaissance—also having been found in the South German area.

Reflex Bows of the 6th to 8th Century

The demanding handicraft of gluing a wooden core together with horn strips, bowstring attachments, and bone stiffening elements to make a reflex bow (English "composite bow") go back to models made by the Avars in Central Europe in the 6th to 8th centuries. A good example of the appearance of these weapons, with their angled sickle-like limbs and slightly offset grip sections, can be had from drawings in Frankish illustrated manuscripts. (Figure 20)

As a rule, finds in the ground contain only the flat plates of antler with which the grip zone and recurving limbs were strengthened.

Thus an Alemannic burial of the 7th century in Bad Cannstadt (6.4) contained a composite bow of the late Avarish type, with end pieces about 200 mm long and widening strongly in the area of the bowstring nocks. (Figure 21)

Because of the rarity of representative discoveries and the laborious means of building reflex bows, one may assume that their existence in what is now southwest Germany was based on a specialized handicraft or an import. In the 7th century this came either from Langobardic Italy, which itself was strongly influenced by Eastern archery, or from the Avars in the Carpathian Basin.

As a hand weapon of a mounted man, the use of such bows—as opposed to the easy-to-build full-wood bow—was limited to an Alemannic warrior elite.

For practical reconstruction, see the relevant literature. (6.7)

Figure 20: Carolingian portrayal of a reflex bow ("Utrecht Psalter," Ill. Zu Ps. 90)

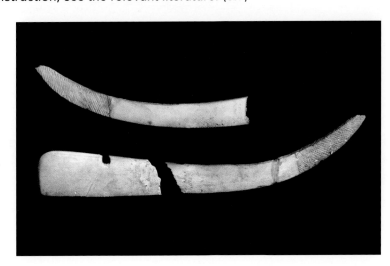

Figure 21: Bone bow ends from Bad Cannstadt (Photo: WLM Stuttgart, Inv. No. A 624)

5.2 BOW AND ARROW AS EVERYDAY TOOLS

Children, Youths, Rich or Poor People?

Among the Alemans, large numbers of remaining bows and arrows were discovered in the burials of children and young people, as well as in more simply furnished graves of adults. In Imperial Roman times, the latter were often buried with a battle-axe, and in Merovingian times with a single-bladed broadsword (Sax).

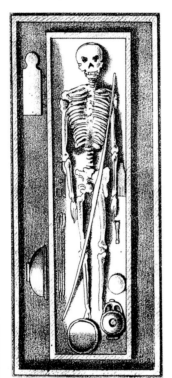

In the Oberflacht graveyard, about a third of the three dozen burials of men contained remains of bows and arrows. Thus the bow was quite often represented then. Its use must have been learned from early childhood and practiced constantly from then on.

The extensive decomposition of metal objects makes it difficult to organize contents as more or less wealthy from indications of social position. On the basis of the unfavorable preservation conditions in Oberflacht, no exact anthropological conclusions can be drawn.

But there exist from 1846, the only illustrations of bowmen's graves, two scale drawings of Graves No. 14 and 15. (Figure 22)

The individuals in them were about 1,650 mm tall, and the bows were about the same length. (6.6, h) If the yew staffs from Graves 7, 8, and 21 also matched the statures of their owners, then the archers—with an average height for men of the Merovingian era of some 1,720 mm—could not have been children. In this case the question arises of which group of users the bows belonged.

Figure 22: Burials No. 14 (left) and 15 from Oberflacht "in situ," 1846 (6.1, b)

Grave Furnishings for Hunters and Warriors

A bow design intended more for high firing speed than for far propulsion of projectiles, like the one at hand, shows its advantages chiefly in ranges of some 10 to 40 meters. This suggests hunting use in wooded areas. (Figure 23)

Actually, at the start of the Merovingian era hunting was still generally common, but in the course of the early Middle Ages it tended to be a privilege of certain groups of people belonging to privileged social classes. In addition, as is known from discovered settlements, it had only a subordinate importance for continually supplying agricultural village populations with animal foods.

The only need of the Oberflacht type of bow as a hunting weapon would thus probably be infrequent. In armed conflict, bows and arrows were usually used among West Germanic tribes by men of social levels for whom more expensive equipment, with two-bladed long swords (Spatha), lances, and shields, was not attainable.

Lightly armed Alemannic fighters of the 4th century went into battle with Roman troops just before the beginning of hand-to-hand fighting, thus at relatively short ranges against the rows of enemy soldiers (Ammianus Marcellinus, *Roman History*, Book 16-12 & 27-1). In a comparable event, "heavy" Oberflacht bows could also have been used effectively in the Merovingian era. So a wide range of uses was open to the existing type of longbow.

The two examples from Graves 7 and 8 might, of course, be assigned to hunting uses on the basis of their smaller dimensions and resulting weaker shot performance, while an example like that from Grave 21 (in complete condition) might represent a universal long-range weapon.

Figure 23: Bowmen with hunting arrow (Stuttgarter Bilderpsalter, fol. 69 r)

5.3 OPEN QUESTIONS AND FUTURE TASKS

The results of the depicted experimental archaeological tests could be amplified in the future, on the basis of the dates and descriptions cited here, with further information on the practical qualities of the Oberflacht bows, especially those from Graves 7 and 8.

The questioned use of elm wood could be tested, and appropriate performance data determined, to add to the existing material.

In practical use, the question could also be answered of whether an ideal shooting technique can be derived for the Alemannic bows and arrows, which might involve thumb-supported bow-drawing methods.

The results could consist of a compilation on the basis of numerous performance values of traditional archers, and thereby empirically confirmed, which would show both technical shooting characteristics and borderline areas of the existing design style. This purpose could be served by what is published in this *Bow Builder's Book*.

The author hopes for many replies from interested readers who can help to expand the present state of knowledge.

Thanks!

Hearty thanks to Frau Dr. Rotraut Wolf of WLM Stuttgart for the long years of co-operation. Many thanks to Herr Dr. Dieter Quast for his archaeological-factual advice and foreword, bow builders Ulli Stehli (Kierspe) and Alan C. Rogers (Stapleton, GB) for their friendly support. Thanks to Frau Dr. Heidi Amrein of the Swiss State Museum in Zürich for the pictorial material she provided, and naturally to Frau Angelika Hörnig for her support of this work.

Longbow from Grave No. 7

GRIP ZONE	Upper Bow Half	Lower Bow Half
Length of Grip	251 mm (between grip edges)	
Median Thickness of Grip	35.0 mm	
Thickness/Width in Center	34.7 mm / 23.0 mm	
Thickness/Width 70 mm from Center	35.9 mm / 23.4 mm (Ast)	34.9 mm / 23.9 mm
Thickness/Width at Edges	34.7 mm / 24.6 mm	35.1 mm / 25.2 mm (Ast)

LIMBS		
Distance to Grip Edge	Upper Half: Thickness/Width	Lower Half: Thickness/Width
10 mm	28.9 mm / 24.9 mm	31.9 mm / 25.7 mm
20 mm	26.5 mm / 25.0 mm	28.1 mm / 26.0 mm
50 mm	24.5 mm / 25.9 mm	24.6 mm / 28.0 mm
100 mm	22.2 mm / 28.5 mm	23.0 mm / 28.7 mm
150 mm	21.1 mm / 30.1 mm	22.5 mm / 31.0 mm
200 mm	21.5 mm / 31.2 mm	22.0 mm / 31.8 mm
250 mm	22.2 mm / 31.7 mm (Ast)	22.0 mm / 31.9 mm
300 mm	20.8 mm / 29.9 mm	21.8 mm / 31.0 mm
350 mm	20.3 mm / 28.7 mm	20.0 mm / 30.0 mm
400 mm	19.2 mm / 27.8 mm	19.0 mm / 28.9 mm
450 mm	18.8 mm / 26.2 mm	18.0 mm / 27.3 mm
500 mm	16.2 mm / 24.6 mm	17.0 mm / 24.9 mm
550 mm	15.0 mm / 22.5 mm	15.8 mm / 22.9 mm
600 mm	15.2 mm / 20.2 mm	15.2 mm / 20.0 mm
663 mm | 671 mm (Edge of Nock)	16.3 mm / 17.2 mm	16.5 mm / 16.1 mm
669 mm | 677 mm (Kerbenrand)	16.3 mm / 17.0 mm	16.3 mm / 15.8 mm
700 mm | 700 mm	16.4 mm / 15.7 mm	13.8 mm / 14.1 mm
716 mm | 724 mm (= End of Bow)	16.0 mm / 13.0 mm	13.4 mm / 12.8 mm (Damage)

BOWSTRING NOCKS AND ENDS	Upper Bow Half	Lower Bow Half
Light Width of Nocks	6.0 mm (at edge of bow limb)	6.0 mm (at edge of bow limb)
Maximum Depth of Nocks	3.7 mm	3.7 mm
Light Width of Double Nocks	6.2 mm (above-below)	—
Depth of Double Nocks	1.5 mm	—
Distance Double Nock to Bow End	13.5 mm (from edge of nock)	—

Longbow from Grave No. 8 (only general data because of damage)

	Upper Bow Half	Lower Bow Half
Length of Grip	237 mm (between grip edges)	
Median Thickness of Grip	34.0 mm	
Width in Center	26.0 mm	
Width at Edges	25.2 mm	28.5 mm
Effective Limb Length	679 mm	668 mm
Thickness/Width 1/3 Limb Length	18.9 mm / 30.2 mm	19.2 mm / 31.0 mm
Thickness/Width 2.3 Limb Length	16.5 mm / 29.6 mm	16.7 mm / 30.6 mm
Thickness/Width at Nocks (3/3)	14.6 mm / 17.7 mm	16.5 mm / 18.2 mm
Light Width of Nocks	6.5 mm (at edge of bow limb)	7 mm (at edge of bow limb)
Maximum Depth of Nocks	2.8 mm	3.5 mm
Distance Nock to Bow End	54.0 mm (from edge of nock)	56.0 mm (from edge of nock)
Thickness/Width at Bow End	3.2 mm (diameter)	—
Distance Hole to Bow End	18.0 mm	—
Thickness/Width at Bow End	16.6 mm / 14.3 mm	20.8 mm / 14.0 mm

Longbow from Grave No. 21

GRIP ZONE	Upper Bow Half	Lower Bow Half
Length of Grip	317 mm (between grip edges)	
Median Thickness of Grip	33.9 mm	
Thickness/Width in Center	34.9 mm / 24.8 mm	
Thickness/Width 80 mm from Center	33.4 mm / 25.1 mm	33.7 mm / 26.7 mm
Thickness/Width at Grip Edges	32.0 mm / 27.6 mm	33.9 mm / 27.8 mm

LIMBS		
Distance to Grip Edge	Upper Half: Thickness/Width	Lower Half: Thickness/ Width
10 mm	29.1 mm / 27.8 mm	32.0 mm / 28.0 mm
20 mm	28.0 mm / 28.0 mm	31.0 mm / 28.1 mm
50 mm	26.3 mm / 28.5 mm	29.2 mm / 28.1 mm
100 mm	25.5 mm / 30.4 mm	27.2 mm / 28.4 mm
150 mm	23.5 mm / 30.8 mm	26.1 mm / 29.2 mm
200 mm	23.0 mm / 30.7 mm	24.0 mm / 30.2 mm
250 mm	22.0 mm / 30.9 mm	23.7 mm / 30.5 mm
300 mm	21.0 mm / 30.1 mm	22.0 mm / 30.0 mm
350 mm	20.9 mm / 28.9 mm	21.3 mm / 28.3 mm
400 mm	21.5 mm / 28.8 mm	19.1 mm / 27.5 mm
450 mm	17.2 mm / 27.2 mm	19.0 mm / 26.9 mm
500 mm	18.4 mm / 26.3 mm	18.4 mm / 24.4 mm
550 mm	17.1 mm / 24.3 mm	18.1 mm / 23.0 mm
600 mm	15.4 mm / 21.8 mm	16.5 mm / 22.0 mm
650 mm	14.0 mm / 19.4 mm	14.8 mm / 20.8 mm
694 mm (edge of nock)	16.? mm / 18.8 mm (Damage)	14.7 mm / 19.2 mm
702 mm | 701 mm (edge of nock)	16.? mm / 18.9 mm (Damage)	15.0 mm / 18.8 mm
722 mm | 721 mm	18.9 mm / 18.7 mm	16.1 mm / 18.0 mm
740 mm | 740 mm	20.0 mm / 16.7 mm	18.9 mm / 16.2 mm
765 mm | 760 mm (= end of bow)	23.5 mm / 15.0 mm	23.1 mm / 14.7 mm

BOWSTRING NOCKS AND ENDS	Upper Bow Half	Lower Bow Half
Light Width of Nocks	8.0 mm (at edge of bow limb)	7.0 mm (at edge of bow limb)
Maximun Depth of Nocks	2.5 mm	3.0 mm
Hole bored in Limb	4.4 mm (diameter)	—
Distance Hole to Bow End	14.2 mm	—

6. CITED BIBLIOGRAPHY

6.1 Jahreshefte des Württembergischen Altertumsvereins, 1 (1846) 3
   a) on Tafel X, 1 profile drawing of bow from Grave 7, Oberflacht;
   b) on Tafel X, 18-19 drawings of wood chamber and tree coffin, Graves 14 & 15;
   c) on Tafel X, 25 arrow illustrations from (former) Grave 8.

6.2 Dürrich, Ferdinand & Menzel, Wolfgang: Die Heidengräber am Lupfen near Oberflacht, Stuttgart 1847
   a) on pp/ 8-10, 12 sporadic data on bows and arrows found;
   b) on p. 9 detailed description of arrows from Grave 6;
   c) on p. 18, collection of all bows and arrows found in graveyard.

6.3 Veeck, Walter: Die Alamannen in Württemberg, 1, 2, Berlin 1931
   a) on pp. 20-21 (Textband. 1) brief notes on bows and arrows from Oberflacht, after Dürrich & Menzel;
   b) on Tafel 6 (Tafelband 2) b/w photos (full views, grips, ends) of Oberflacht bows.

6.4 Paret, Oskar: Die frühschwäbischen Gräberfelder von Gross-Stuttgart und ihre Zeit, Stuttgart 1937
   Data on reflex bow from Alemannic graveyard at Bad Cannstadt, p. 24, p. 69.

6.5 Leier—Leuchter—Totenbaum: Holzhandwerk der Alamannen. Texts from special exhibition of 5/29-11/10/1991 at Württembergisches Landmuseum Stuttgart, Stuttgart 1991
   Basic data on the Oberflacht bows on p. 24, further literature on pp. 39-40.

6.6 Schiek, Siegwalt: Das Gräberfeld der Merowingerzeit bei Oberflacht, 1, Stuttgart 1992
   a) on pp. 26-28 & 97-98, descriptions and detail drawings of 3 yew bows; wood analysis on p. 127;
   b) on p. 45 & p. 127, Tests 204, 206 & Tafel 41, B, 3-4 arrow pieces of birch and snowball wood;
   c) on p. 56 data on diamond and barbed points, last in Museum of Early and Prehistory, Berlin;
   d) on p. 101, No. 31 & Tafel 103, 4 a bow (?) fragment, unknown wood (WLM Inv.-No. F 83, 96);
   e) on p. 26 & Tafel 10, C, 3 & p. 125, Test 93 bow fragment of elm (WLM Inv.-No. ?);
   f) on p. 101, No. 30 & Tafel 101,11 limb piece of yew bow (WLM Inv.-No. 83,101);
   g) on p. 56 data on yew bow from Grave 84, last in Museum of Early & Prehistory, Berlin;
   h) on p. 31, 32 description of burial chamber or tree coffin of burials No. 14, 15.

6.7 Szöllösy, Gabor: Neuere Beiträge zum Fragenkreis der völkerwanderungs-zeitlichen Bogentypen. In: Evkönyve 1987-89, A Nyiregyhazi Josa Andras Muzeum, Nyireghaza 192, pp. 349-374. Reconstructed models for performance levels of Avarish and Hungarian reflex bows (with German summation).

6.8 Marti, Reto: Das Grab eines wohlhabenden Alamannen in Altdorf. UR-St. Martin. In: Jahrbuch der schweizerischen Gesellschaft für Ur- und Frühgeschichte, 78 (1995)
   Description and pictures of the yew bow, arrows and quiver on pp. 95-99.

6.9 Riesch, Holger: Archery in Renaissance Germany. In: Journal of the Society of Archer Antiquaries, 38 (1995)
   B/W photos and dimensions of a late 15th century bow from Schloss-Hohenaschau in Germanic National Museum, Nürnberg (Inv.-No. W 741) on pp. 66-67.

6.10 Schmand, Rudolf: Untersuchungen zum statischen und dynamischen Verhalten von historischen Langbögen mit der Methode der finiten Elemente, Fachhochschule Bingen, Fachbereich Maschinenbau, Dipl.-Arbeit, 1966 (unpublished manuscript)
   Static & dynamic calculations for the Oberflacht and Altdorf bows on pp. 43-45, 52, and 31-34.

6.11 Wolf, Rotraud: Schreiner, Drechsler, Böttcher, Instrumentenbauer—Holzhandwerk im Frühen Mittelalter. In: Die Alamannen, Archäologisches Landesmuseum Baden-Eürttemberg, Stuttgart 1997 (also exhibition catalog)
   Color photos of Oberflacht bows & replica of author's Grave 21 bow, pp. 385-386.

6.12 Becker, Klaus & Riesch, Holger: Untersuchungen zum Metallurgie alamannischer Pfeilspitzen in Original und Reproduktion. In: Archäologisches Korrespondenzblatt. RGZM Mainz, 28 (1998) 2, pp. 305-310
   Metallurgical arrowhead analyses.

6.13 Paulsen, Harm: Bögen und Pfeile. In: Der Opferplatz von Nydam, 1, Neumünster 1998
   a) on pp. 387-399 Description of Nydam bows; b) on pp. 404-421, documentation of Nydam bows.

6.14 Riesch, Holger: Untersuchungen zu Effizienz und Verwendung alamannischer Pfeilspitzen. In: Archäologisches Korrespondenzblatt. RGZM Mainz, 29 (1999) 4, pp. 567-582. Experimental tests of function of Merowingian era projectile types.

THE BOWS OF THE VIKINGS

Viking bows are known from the Viking city of Haithabu on the Schlei near present-day Schleswig and the Irish Ballinderry. They date from the 9th to 11th centuries A.D. A presumed child's bow fragment was also found in the settlement at L'Anse aux Meadows, Newfoundland.

The bow fragments from Haithabu, which were thoroughly studied and replicated by Harm Paulsen, Schleswig-Holsteinisches Landesmuseum für Vor- und Frühgeschichte, Schlos Gottorf, Schleswig, are the most important source of information on Viking bows (Harm Paulsen: Pfeil und Bogen in Haithabu, in: Berichte über die Ausgrabungen in Haithabu. Bericht 33. Wachholtz Verlag Neumünster 1999). The information cited here comes for the most part from this publication. The weapon was depicted only rarely in its own time, as in the early medieval manuscript from the Pierpont Morgan Library in New York (picture at right).

Figure 1
Archers with longbows of the Viking type in the manuscript from the Pierpont Morgan Library, New York. 11th century.

THE DISCOVERIES

In all, two completely preserved bows, one from **Haithabu** and one from **Ballinderry,** can be referred to for the type definition. It is a variant of the so-called longbow used in Northern and Western Europe throughout the Middle Ages.

The difference from the usual longbow is mainly that both ends of the bow are bent backward.

Yew wood was almost always used as the material. Only exceptionally, as an example from Haithabu shows, was a bow made of the qualitatively less suitable elm wood. The unusual bow ends were meaningless for the functioning of the bow, since the curved parts were beyond the string nocks. Their meaning was to be found in a decorative or ethnic sense. Since these bent ends occur only in Viking bows, then can be interpreted as an identifying mark, lending a Viking "identity," so to speak, to the bow.

In two of the Haithabu bows, an iron nail with a round, projecting head was driven into the belly ten centimeters below the upper string nock, which could have served to define the bowstring length and to prevent the sliding of the loop when the bow was unstrung. The driven-in depth of a few millimeters did not affect the bow's stability.

The further technical features, such as the one-sided string nock, the rather D-shaped cross-section, and the stick-like appearance of the bow without a recognizable grip are typical of the normal medieval longbow.

The string was apparently attached only at the upper end with the help of a nock. Since the lower end of the bow has no means of fixing the string, the bowstring must have been attached there by a permanent binding.

Length

The two completely preserved Viking bows can be described as the most powerful battle bows, measuring 191 cm (Haithabu) and 185 cm (Ballinderry) and having mighty limbs. The Haithabu bow measures 4.0 x 3.3 cm, the Ballinderry bow 3.8 x 2.86 cm in the middle. The effective length, that is, the usable length between the attachment points of the bowstring or the projecting bow ends, is only 178 cm in the Haithabu bow, and about 169 cm in the Ballinderry bow.

The other bow fragments from Haithabu belonged to clearly thinner and weaker bows, which were probably used only for hunting. Perhaps young people's bows are also among them.

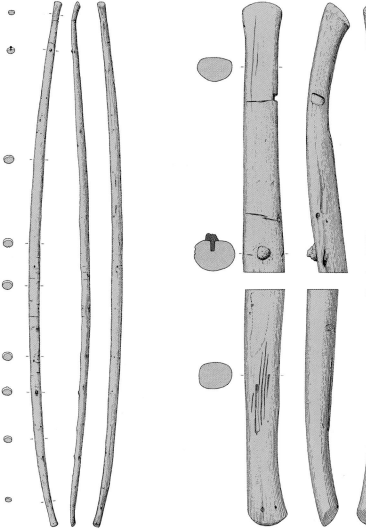

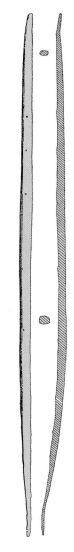

Viking longbows of yew
HAITHABU, 9th-11th century A.D.
Left: front, side and inside views.
After Paulsen 1999, Viking Museum

Center: Upper and lower bow ends

BALLINDERRY: 10th century after J.
G. D. Clark 1963 (GB)
Haithabu, Haddeby near Schleswig (D)

THE CROSS-SECTION

Viking bows have the typical "D-shaped" longbow cross-section. As in other medieval longbows, this varies from "almost round" through "classic D-shaped" to nearly rectangular profiles. Despite the small number of discovered Viking bows, it is clear that their cross-sections are somewhat flatter and wider than those of the other longbows.

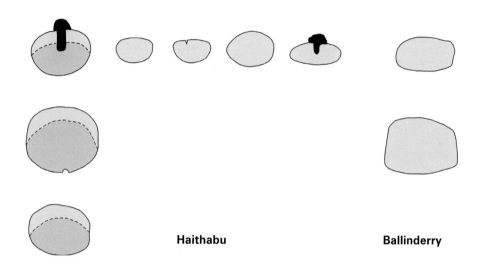

Haithabu
Ballinderry

Figure 2
Cross-sections of Viking longbows from Haithabu (D) and Ballinderry (GB). Scale 1:2. After H. Paulsen 1999 and J. G. D. Clark 1963.

The belly of the bow usually consists of the outside of the yew trunk just under the scraped-off bark and thus shows its natural bending, which is more or less striking depending on the trunk diameter. Usually this arching is clearly flatter than the inside of the bow.

On the belly is a layer of elastic yew sapwood, which forms an effective protection against breaking.

STARTING MATERIAL

The yew trees used to make the Haithabu bows were all of very small diameter, between about 4 and 6 cm. Perhaps this is an indication that no larger or older yews were available any more in that region at that time.

The strength of the sapwood layer can appear very different in yews. It seems that in the Viking times, just as earlier in the Neolithic and Bronze Ages, almost all the available yew trees had only a few millimeters of sapwood.

The complete Bow 1 from Haithabu has a sapwood layer some 4-5 mm thick. In present-day yew trunks, on the other hand, a sapwood layer several centimeters thick can be found, which requires reducing the sapwood on the belly of the bow for bow building.

The thickness of annual rings in the Haithabu bow is between 12 and 15 rings per centimeter. The wood used has thus grown relatively quickly for yew. Prehistoric bows were usually made of yews with thicknesses of 30 to 40 rings per centimeter, such as can only grow in thick, shadowy wooded areas. There is a connection between annual ring thickness and yew quality: more slowly grown trees usually have a harder wood than quickly grown ones.

Traces of grip wrappings of leather or cloth have not been found to date, so that it is to be presumed that the Viking bows, like all prehistoric and medieval longbows, were used without them.

What material was used for the bowstring is not yet known. One can thus assume that, as described in the applicable literature several centuries later, (R. Ascham, *Toxophilus,* 1545), use was made of flax or linen fibers for their high degree of resistance to tearing among natural fibers.

PERFORMANCE
Shooting Tests by H. Paulsen

Harm Paulsen of Schleswig built a total of three replicas of the complete Viking bow from Haithabu for testing purposes. For them, he used yew stems of 6-10 cm diameter, aged for 2 to 3 years. Although the three replicas correspond roughly to the dimensions of the original bow, they have different draw weights (38, 42, and 46 kg or 84, 93, and 101 pounds, based on 70 cm draw length), which derives from the different firmness of the used yew staves. These are very strong bows for present-day conditions.

"After lengthy training," H. Paulsen was able to shoot the three replicas. The shooting test stretched over five years. In this period the draw weights of all the bows decreased by some two kilograms; the strongest bow broke after about a thousand shots.

It is very interesting that the strongest bow did not show anything like the power of the two weaker bows. Perhaps this bow would have needed heavier arrows to be able to transmit the energy in it to an arrow effectively.

With arrows weighing 25 to 30 grams, H. Paulsen attained maximum shot values between 190 and 195 meters; arrows of 30-40 grams flew 170-180 meters, and with heavy 60-gram arrows, he could still reach 150-160 meters. In various series of tests, a very high performance ability of the replicas was shown in shooting at various targets, from dead animals to wooden shields, chain-mail shirts, and wooden plates. Except for arched metal plates (such as shield-bosses), these bows, with suitably chosen arrows, were able to penetrate all tested materials without problems.

BUILDING A VIKING BOW

Essentially, one builds a Viking bow just like any other longbow. The most suitable native wood is undoubtedly the yew, probably followed by the considerably less suitable elm. Very good self bows can also be made of hickory.

Yew should be aged at least two years. If one is lucky enough to get a yew stave with a sapwood layer no more than 1 centimeter thick, this eliminates the otherwise necessary, difficult reduction of the sapwood.

After removing the outer and inner bark and doing some polishing, the belly side is already prepared in this case. If the sapwood layer is too thick, it must be cut down to the needed thickness with a sharp draw knife, carefully following the unevenness of the wood.

In any case, the sapwood should be thinner than the planned thickness of the bow at the ends, so as to avoid having the ends made only of sapwood.

The diameter of the bow's belly follows the curvature of the outside of the trunk: it is little in larger trunks, and more in thin staves. The inside of the bow can be arched more or less strongly, as you choose.

Flatter insides are essentially *more strongly pressure-strainable* than more arched ones, tend less to bend permanently (stringfollow), and attain a high degree of performance. On the other hand, rounded cross-sections have a somewhat lower inherent weight, which likewise has a positive effect on the attainable arrow speed. Both flatter and more curved cross-sections can be seen in Viking and other medieval bows.

In considering how long the bow should be, it must be remembered that the effective bow length is less than the overall length because of the projecting, angled ends. The *effective length* should more or less correspond to your own *body size.* If it is somewhat smaller, the bow will be faster, but it can also break, perhaps during tillering, with a little bad luck. The effective length should be somewhat greater if you have very long arms.

It is very important to deepen the string nock(s) only *after bending* the projecting ends*. Otherwise the end, from the nock out, will break while being bent.

The bending places should not be too thick (at most about 1.5 cm), and should contain no branch holes or annual rings.

Before bending, the ends must be cooked in a big pot with lots of water. After boiling for about 20 minutes, the wood is soft enough for carrying out the bending process.

It is best to make a wooden form in which the end of the bow can be fastened and fixed in a bent position after being bent. If need be, it can also be clamped between the ribs of a radiator.

Figure 3
Bending the ends of a Viking bow with the help of a wooden form.

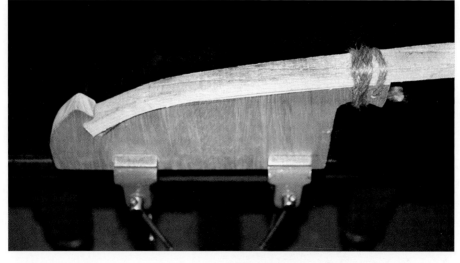

After bending, the wood must cool off in its new shape for several minutes; otherwise the bend will straighten out again. Once the wood has cooled, the bend remains permanent, although it unbends a little after being taken out of the form.

One day after the cooking and bending, the bow can be tillered. Both limbs are equally long and are tillered *symmetrically.*

Since these longbows have no thickened grip sections, they bend over their entire length, thus also in the grip area. It cannot be said that this causes problems in shooting (hand shock or the like), as many authors claim.

With high pulling weights, there is naturally a bit of "backlash" through the sudden muscular relaxing when you release the arrow; but this is the case with all strong bows and cannot be eliminated.

A prerequisite for good shooting qualities is, first of all, a careful tillering of the bow limbs, plus the straightness of the bow as you look at it from the front.

The upper string nock of the Viking bow has, like all medieval bows, a one-sided nock on the right side of the bow (seen from the front). When unstringing by the step-through method (see page 30), this has the advantage that the bowstring loop can be pushed out of the nock with the thumb of the right hand.

Upper bow end with one-sided string nock and restraining nail.

Left-handers should put the nock on the left side of the bow, provided they hold the bow by the step-through method when unstringing it, with the upper end to the left.

Whoever wants it truly original attaches the string at the lower end by a firmly attached wrapping. The attachment of the strung bowstring should be in the middle of the bent end.

Less authentic, but simpler, is the making of another string nock, which can be placed on the other side of the bow, opposite the upper nock, to avoid one-sided straining of the bow.

In all yew bows with one-sided string nocks, you should think about a wrapping right under the nock (see photo at left). Yew is very easily splittable, and cracks often occur in a place strained so much by the one-sided pull of the string.

A replica of an Alemannic bow broke on me while shooting one day, with a part of the bow end splitting off. The cracked surfaces were so smooth that the bow could be repaired by regluing the split-off piece.

HAITHABU TYPE (built 4/99)	Overall Length: 191 cm Effective length: 179 cm		Permanent bending" 2% Wood type: yew		Draw weight: 77 lb/70 cm	

cm	place	width	thickness	cm	place	width	thickness
96,0	bow end			95,0	bow end		
89,5	upper nock	--	--	-89,5	lower nock		
80,0		2,01	1,65	-80,0		2,03	1,49
70,0	branch	2,34	2,11	-70,0		2,22	1,85
60,0		2,58	1,92	-60,0		2,48	2,00
50,0		2,67	2,11	-50,0		2,65	2,18
40,0		2,81	2,25	-40,0		2,82	2,30
30,0		2,94	2,33	-30,0		3,00	2,34
20,0		3,09	2,46	-20,0		3,09	2,41
10,0	branch	3,15	2,95	-10,0		3,19	2,67
0,0	middle	3,20	2,93	0,0			

Figure 4. Dimensions of a reproduction of the Haithabutype bow

A replica of a Viking bow, completely corresponding to the Haithabu bow in dimensions but clearly less thick (see Figure 4), had a pulling weight of 77 pounds at 70 cm of draw.

This bow also developed a crack at the lower, one-sided string nock, whereupon making a second nock for relaxing and adding a binding became necessary.

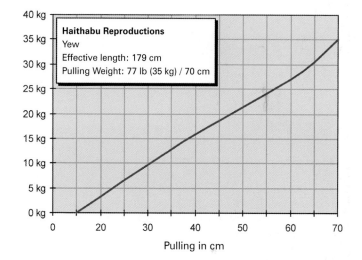

Haithabu Reproductions
Yew
Effective length: 179 cm
Pulling Weight: 77 lb (35 kg) / 70 cm

Pulling in cm

Figure 5
Charted curve (power-path diagram) of the Viking bow replica

The replica shot a 20-gram arrow in speed tests at an initial velocity of 198 kph.

Bending behavior of the replicated Viking bow.

THE AUTHOR

ULRICH STEHLI

Born in Zürich in 1948, wood and metal fascinated him equally, and he decided to be trained as an artistic locksmith. Since the beginning of the seventies he has been active in the non-ferrous metal industry in the Sauerland, Germany.

He began shooting bows in early childhood and made his first laminated bow in 1983. In the early nineties he began to build traditional longbows.

Outside of his profession, Ulrich Stehli is also busy with the technical reconstruction of historic arrow- and lance-heads, as well as smithing Damascus steel.

10

THE ENGLISH LONGBOW

1. HISTORY FROM THE HUNTING WEAPON TO THE WAR BOW

Technically defined, the bow is a device by means of which slow human energy is converted to fast mechanical energy. Unlike all other early weapons, the bow stands out for its ability to store energy. This technical characteristic and the relatively simple means of production from organic materials explain the wide spread of the bow among the cultures of the earth. Its invention, or better, its discovery, wherever it was first made, became one of mankind's great achievements.

Early Times

Let us look at the simple bow and its development in the western part of Europe. Archaeological finds prove its use after the end of the last Ice Age, at the transition from the late Paleolithic era to the Mesolithic era. Through the warming climate, woods and shrubbery spread over the tundra-like cold steppes of central and northern Europe. The people, who lived as hunters and gatherers, had to adjust to new conditions in a relatively short time by changing their hunting methods.

As an example of this, we know of a dwelling place of the so-called Ahrensburg culture, in the Stellmoor north of Hamburg. This cultural group, which spread from western Poland across northern Germany to Holland, was dated in the time period from 9000 to 8300 B.C. Like their forerunners, the "Ahrensburger" were mainly reindeer hunters. Thanks to a wealth of found material, their use of pine wood (*Pinus silvestris)* for bows and arrows by these early hunters is documented.

The next time block (8300–5000 B.C.), called Preboreal and Boreal, can be called a high point of the hunting culture. The Maglemose Culture spread over all of northern Europe. Bows and arrows were still the most important weapons. Several bows have survived from the end period of this epoch. The best-known are two examples found in the turf bog of Holmegaard, Denmark. Both are made of thin elm (*Ulmus glabra)* trunks. Seen technically, these "early" types nevertheless show the product of a millennium-old development in bow building.

The preferred use of elm by these peoples is explained by the relatively late post-Ice Age growth of the yew in the Northern Hemisphere.

On the basis of wood structure and physical-mechanical qualities, the yew (*Taxus baccata L.)* has decisive advantages over the other types of bow wood. The soft, yellowish sapwood (laburnum) is much more elastic in comparison with the hard, dark heartwood (duramen) that grows in the inner trunk. Unlike it, the hard, sturdy heartwood develops a very effective release of power under dynamic pressure. These ideal qualities were recognized and used by man to build bows very early.

To meet their needs at that time, they used a stave about as thick as their arms, which they worked according to ancient experience so that the sapwood formed the back and the heartwood the underside of the bow. Several Neolithic bows from the "yew-rich" south German and Swiss areas have survived. They are all made of yew.

As for the way these European Stone Age bows were made, they can be divided in terms of their occurrence, aside from exceptions, into two main types:

• The examples coming from the southern regions generally have a high, rounded cross-section somewhat like longbows.

• In the northern regions, flat, rounded cross-sections were common.

This can be explained by the climatic differences. Bows with flat cross-sections are less sensitive to low temperatures. The yew bows from the Lötschen Pass (Switzerland), for example, which date back to the end of the Neolithic era and the transition to the Bronze Age, are all flat bows. If one considers the Alpine area where they were found, the thesis stated above would be confirmed in this case.

Replicas of early bow types made of elm and yew document draw weights from about 35 to 70 pounds. This was sufficient for hunting purposes. Modern tests in experimental archaeology confirm this.

In the course of the Iron Age, when the migrations of tribes began, the first changes in the war bow can be found. The "Nydam bows," named after the place where they were found, a bog area on the German-Danish border, can be classified as early longbows by the way they were made. Together with numerous needle-shaped arrow ends, they were doubtless used for warlike purposes. Even though they do not show overly high draw weights, they were suitable for the means of fighting at that time and extremely effective, as tests with replicas have shown! This is the prehistory of bows in general.

Angles, Saxons, Vikings

Following the further development, we turn our gaze to the west, to the coasts of Britain. According to historical records, members of North German tribes settled England from A.D. 450 on. It would be illogical to assume that the Angles, Saxons, and Jutes who moved to England in their longboats had left their bows and arrows at home.

In the formerly Roman-occupied parts of the island, as well as Wales and Scotland, the bow was in use, though we have no sources that prove a tactical use of the war bow at that time.

In the following centuries, this was to change! From the year 633, a report on "Ottfried, the Son of Edwin, King of Northumbria" has survived, telling of his death from an arrow in a battle with the Welsh.

After the numerous waves of migration by the Angles, Saxons, and Jutes, who gradually conquered the land and founded various small kingdoms, King Egbert of Wessex (802-839) gained the upper hand. But not over Wales and Scotland.

In the same century, Norwegian and Danish Vikings fell upon England, but could be driven out at first. As for the war bows of these "Northmen," archaeological discoveries of arrowheads in great numbers confirm their active use. In one study, the Swede Erik Wagreus shows a specialization in arrowheads for the later Viking era. On the basis of examples from more than 1,000 investigated graves, he shows a differentiation into typical hunting and war heads, sometimes with different shafts.

Through the discovery of a splendidly preserved yew bow from the harbor basin of Haithabu, the former Viking trade city in Schleswig, we know of the appearance and construction of the "Nordic" bows in use at that time. In his reconstruction he documents the respectable pulling power of 100 pounds.

For hunting purposes, such enormous draw weights were not needed. Considering the various criteria, as shown by developments and events of this time, a perfection of the bow as a weapon of war is recognizable.

The country was not able to withstand the second great invasion of "Northmen." The Danish kings, including "Canute the Great" (1016-1035), ruled all England for 26 years. Though bowmen were not yet decisive in battle because of their tactical action at the time, finds of arrowheads in great numbers still confirm their involvement!

Excerpt from the Bayeux Tapestry

When the English army under King Harold was beaten by the Norman conquerors under William I, Duke of Normandy, at the Battle of Hastings on October 14, 1066, there were numerous bowmen on each side. This is confirmed authentically and in detail by the famous Bayeux Tapestry.

The ensuing forced restructuring of the English society by the Norman conquerors, and the resulting and gradual loss of the nobility's power, as well as the persecution of the free farmers, secretly turned the bow into a more and more popular weapon, especially in outlying and wooded areas, where it was easy to make. As to the questions of when, where, and by whom the bow was first used strategically in England, English historians and authors are not of one mind. Reports of the use and action of strong, long bows exist, though, aplenty.

Longbows and Crossbows

Before we turn to these disagreements, which play a key role in the development of longbow strategy, the fact that the longbow would be preferred against the commonly used crossbow deserves a closer look.

Despite the ban on the crossbow and the "condemnation of mercenaries" proclaimed by the Pope in 1139, bowmen with crossbows served as mercenaries in the armies of Edward I and Edward II. They came from Gascony and Aquitania.

According to history, we know that at the same time bowmen were on hand in sufficient numbers!

As for the financial situation, several price comparisons from the time around 1300 show us that, according to quality and workmanship, approximately three longbows could be bought for the price of one crossbow.

The same applies to the price of crossbow-bolts and bow-arrows. The price of a longbow ranged from twelve pence to one shilling sixpence, depending on quality. Twenty-four arrows (one sheaf) cost about threepence. There were differences between bows of branchwood and those made of "good tree trunks."

Now to the strategic aspects. A longbowman in action on the battlefield is able to shoot six aimed arrows per minute. On the other hand, the crossbow, because of its laborious winding technique, could fire only two bolts in the same time. Contemporary reports stress, among other things, the vulnerability of the "composite" crossbow to moisture.

A further disadvantage was that of ballistics in general. In experimental tests, representative data were produced that gave the crossbow of the time a zero point of about 80 meters. Since shooting was done in battle, at least at the beginning, at long distances, a crossbowman, because of the fact cited above, had to aim far above his target! There was also a hindrance of free sight by the broad shaft and massive bow. The relatively short, fast-flying bolts could be followed only with difficulty while in flight, which made aim correcting of salvo shots hard at great distances.

In comparison, shooting with a longbow gave better possibilities for aiming and observing targets being hit! To the information above, it should be added that in large battles, only massive salvo fire could lead to a decisive victory. Everything else was called skirmishing in military language.

Considering the various factors—social, financial, and strategic—it is not surprising that under Edward I and II the longbow weapon was promoted for its powers.

Salary and Cost of Living from the Times before and around 1300

A report from the mid-13th century gives us valuable information on the preparation of arrowheads. It tells of one "John Malemort" who worked as an "arrowsmith" at St. Braviels Castle on the River Wye, near Chepstow, in the royal Forest of Dean, from 1228 to 1266.

At the beginning of his career in 1228, he received a daily pay of four pence. In 1265, as a "master arrowsmith," he earned seven and one-half pence for making 100 arrowheads (quarrels) per day and threepence for the shafting and feathering of arrows.

For the year 1257, the production of 50,000 arrowheads was cited; they were sent to all parts of the land from this factory.

Around 1300, a stonemason earned between nine pence and twenty-four pence per week. An "armbruster" 14 pence, the "harness maker" 18 pence. The cook boy of a garrison was paid 15 pence for six months. A plumber earned threepence, his helper 1.5 pence per day.

The salary for a bowman was 60 shillings per year (5 s. per month), Between 1300 and 1305, two arrows cost a quarter of a penny (a farthing), a lance sixpence apiece, helmets (bascinets) 2 s. 2.5 d. Twenty ells of sailcloth (45 inches per ell) to make bow covers cost 6 s. 8 d., wooden containers for storing arrows cost eight pence apiece.

At the same time, one paid 3/4 d. for a pound of wheat, 2 s. for 28 pounds of oatmeal, and 16 d. for the same quantity of salt. Around 1300 a gallon of wine cost 2.5 pence, a side of bacon 9.5 pence. For a slaughtered ox 3 s. 8 d., had to be paid, for a pig 2 s. 8 d.

If one looks at these prices, which varied greatly at that time, influenced by economic factors, one can get a picture of the economic pressures that were caused by large standing armies.

The Scottish Wars

In the disagreements with their northern neighbors, who vehemently opposed every English invasion, the use of bowmen deserves special attention. Yet the mistake of viewing the bowmen's role in isolation must not be made, for they were an integrated part of a whole.

In the battle of Dunbar in 1296, for example, bowmen were present, but the victory can be ascribed in the highest degree to the cavalry.

It was March 1298; King Edward was back from France and gathered a large army of 2,500 riders and 10,000 to 12,000 men on foot, including a great number of bowmen. Wallace had fewer horsemen available, about 500, and a smaller number of bowmen. The battle took place near Falkirk. The Scots posted their bowmen between four great masses of foot soldiers armed with long spears. On the flanks they protected themselves with palisades against flank attacks from English cavalry. The English mounted men, attacking in several waves, were able to decimate the Scottish bowmen strongly, who were hindered by the masses of their own men. The English bowmen, set up in rows, fired so heavily on the Scottish spearmen that, with the last attack waves of the cavalry and the use of infantry, the Scottish front could be broken. That decided the battle!

In a reversed situation, the English, under King Edward I, began to feel the results of strategic errors in the battle of Bannockburn on June 24, 1314. The Scots, led by Robert the Bruce, who had fought on the English side under Edward I and was familiar with their tactics, dealt the English a miserable defeat. The English lines were not yet formed; the foot soldiers with the bowmen were behind nine squadrons of cavalry at the time of the Scottish attack.

The bowmen were hastily ordered to the right flank before the main line to take the attacking Scottish spearmen under fire. They could secure their position well, but Bruce threw a cavalry reserve in behind his forces and fell upon his enemy's flank. The bowmen posted there could not withstand this extremely heavy cavalry attack, they were partly wiped out, partly scattered in the English lines. Thus they were forced to shoot over their own troops at an enemy whom they could not see. At the same time, the Scottish bowmen had reformed their lines and now took the English cavalry under systematic fire. The catastrophe was perfect!

The Battle of Bannockburn, after Geoffrey Regan, Enfield, 1991

The lessons that can be learned from this: only absolute discipline and a protected arrangement of bowmen, who have to be positioned so that they have sufficient freedom of movement and were thus able to attack the enemy on sight, could bring victory.

In 1332, a small English expeditionary army headed to Scotland by sea. It was a small force, consisting of 500 knights, armed men, and 1,500 bowmen. The young King Edward III was not with them. After their landing, they marched toward Perth and encountered a large enemy force of some 10,000 men, commanded by the Earl of Mar, who were waiting for them at Dupplin Muir. The forces formed their battle lines on the following day, both forces dismounted, the horses with the reserves. The English, with the knights and armed men in the center, the bowmen on the sides, were positioned in the form of two unequally long wings. The Scots attacked frontally against the center. The English knights could hold off the first attack.

Meanwhile the bowmen, with full freedom of movement, took the Scottish attackers under crossfire. The effect was terrible. Driven together in the center, hindered by each other on both sides, unable to fight, the dead piled up. At that, the rear ranks of the Scots began to flee and were pursued by the hastily mounted English knights. The result was a massacre. On the English side, only thirty-three knights and armed men fell, but not a single bowman!

When the young King Edward III led an army against the Scots himself the next year, Baliol, Umphraville, Beaumont, and Atholl, who had planned the battle of Dupplin Muir, were among his commanders. Edward besieged Berwick with his troops and was attacked by a strong Scottish army. The battle positions were taken in a hilly landscape called Halidon Hill, and were as before at Dupplin Muir. But the bowmen were in the form of long truncated triangles, their points turned toward the attackers, to the sides of the dismounted cavalrymen, who formed the center along with the other armed men. Here, too, the English forces were fewer and more mobile than those of the enemy. This fact caused the Scots to attack. They stormed over the hill in four great waves. Few of them made any contact with the English men-at-arms; they were simply shot down by the bowmen. The "Bridlington Chronicle" reports on this encounter: Many Scots were "slaughtered," but on the English side only one knight, one nobleman, and a few foot soldiers fell.

As we see from this historical information, the tactic that was to be used in France a short time later was nothing new, but resulted from long development. We can say that the Scottish wars show us a system of developing the bowmen, not simply to have them, but because the battle depends on them.

The great novelty, as which the bow now entered military history, was not a revolutionary new weapon, but the use of a great number of bowmen who, with strategically well-chosen positions, outstanding discipline, and cooperation were in a position to let loose an overwhelming hail of arrows on men and horses!

The Great Victories

The three military victories of English armies that follow here took place during the Hundred Years' War against France were based on this strategy that was developed in long years of warfare with the Scots.

The first meeting was to take place at Crecy. In this battle the English had 13,000 armed men, including a large number of 36,000 to 40,000 bowmen, opposing the French.

The battle began during the afternoon of August 26, 1346. While the French troops were still taking their positions, a torrential rainstorm fell on both armies. At the front of the French lines were several thousand Genoese crossbowmen, who opened fire on the British lines, shooting and loading as they moved forward in stages. Eyewitnesses reported that their weapons were soaked and not fully usable on account of the heavy rain. The English bowmen took the crossbowmen under heavy fire. The arrows, falling on the crossbowmen like hail, frightened these soldiers so much that many threw their weapons away and tried to flee. At this moment, the leader of the main French forces, the Comte d'Alencon, gave the signal for the main attack.

The Battle of Crecy, after Croissart's Chronicles, 1877

The Genoese crossbowmen got in their way by being present in the front lines; many of them were ridden down. Now "fate," as the history writers say, began to break in on the "flower of French cavalry." The well-disciplined bowmen shot ceaselessly at the attacking horsemen without leaving their positions. They were able to shoot down sixteen waves of attack, and the French knights under King Philip were helpless. The field was littered with dead and wounded men. The losses were shattering. On the French side, more than 1500 knights and a great number of foot-soldiers fell. Edward III had lost only "a few" of his men and moved triumphantly to Calais.

Ten years later, on September 19, 1356, a French army of 16,000 men, under King Jean II was shattered under similar circumstances at Poitiers by a smaller force, numbering only 6,000 men, under the command of the 26-year-old Edward III.

On July 12, 1369, King Edward III proclaimed a law saying that every strong man of the city (London) should use bows and arrows in his spare time and on holidays, so as to learn the art of shooting. In addition, he forbade, under pain of punishment by prison sentences, games such as stone, wood, and iron pitching, handball, football, cockfighting or other vain, worthless pastimes.

In the battle of Agincourt on October 25, 1415, 9,000 Englishmen, 6,000 of them bowmen, under their young King Henry V, faced almost four times as many French troops. Here, too, the defeat of the French army was catastrophic.

The ensuing years, though, show certain signs of dissolution among the English war parties. The enemies also seem to have learned a lesson. After varying fortunes of war, the French side was able to decide the Hundred Years' War in their favor and break the English positions of power on the French coast.

In the English civil wars that lasted from 1455 to 1485, called the "Wars of the Roses" because of the emblems of the royal houses of York and Lancaster, bowmen, crossbowmen, and musketeers fought side by side in various battles. English historians thus are defensive about the charge that English warfare was antiquated and only based on the longbow!

In 1470, Edward IV enacted a law with the following contents: every Englishman or Irishman who lived in England should own a bow of his size, made of yew, hazel, ash, laburnum, or another usable wood. Training sites were to be set up outside every city for the purpose of practice in spare time or on holidays. Worthless games like bowling, football, and tennis were banned under penalty of punishment. Every person of strong stature and healthy body should use his bow, because the defense of the land lay only in the hands of the bowmen.

Because of the enormous need for bows, King Edward IV enacted the Statute of Westminster in 1472, by which dealers were instructed to import four "bow staves" for every ton of imported trade goods and deliver them to government offices. Considerable fines would be levied otherwise. Ten years later, ten bow staves had to be turned in for every imported barrel of wine.

This English trade policy of forced importation led to an early capitalistic monopoly in the central European forest and wood business. Because of the conditions, the trade organizations strove to make appropriate contacts with continental European landowners to secure their supply of yew wood.

The needed quantities of wood came from the western parts of Russia and the Carpathians, moving down the Vistula on rafts to the main trade port of Danzig and to England. From the German language area, the yew wood was transported to London via Cologne and Antwerp. Looking back, we find that the first bow-wood export to England is documented in the city records of Dortrecht on October 10, 1287.

Around 1483, the price of a bow was set at three shillings fourpence for the best quality, but because of political unrest in Lombardy, an increase of prices from two pounds to six- to eight pounds for a hundred bow staves had to be accepted.

From monopoly contracts of a sixteenth-century South German trade association it can be calculated that over a period of sixty years, 500,000 to 600,000 bow staves were exported. And this organization was not the only one active at that time.

When one notices the very sparse occurrence of the yew in central Europe today, the reason for it can be found overwhelmingly in its excessive export during the 15th and 16th centuries.

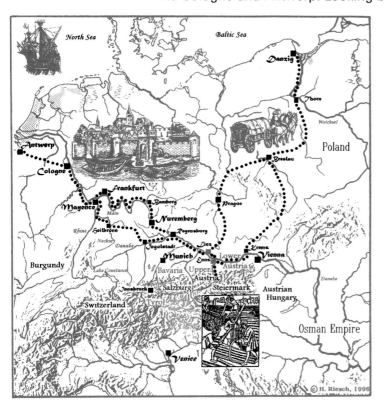

Figure 1
Transport routes of yew bow staves from the German language area in the 16th century, after H. Riesch, 1996

140

But let us turn back to the events in England.

Although 2,000 French mercenaries with muskets served on the Tudor side in the last battle of the Wars of the Roses, at Bosworth in 1485, in which the last Plantagenet king, Richard III, met his death, they were not decisive in the victory.

In the times that followed, though, a slow return to the longbow weapon began. Infantry armed with pikes (long spears) and halberds, musketeers, and light cavalry, along with the "new" artillery that grew ever stronger, dominated warfare more and more.

The longbow experienced a last renaissance during the reign of Henry VIII, the "last great bowman." Henry was eighteen years old when his reign began in 1509. Of mighty stature, he even outdid the men of his guard as a bowman. In 1510 he asked the Doge of Venice, via Piero Pesaro, for permission to buy 40,000 bow staves. This contravened the laws of Venice, but the Doge approved the sale at a price of 16 pounds per 100 staves.

Figure 2
Battle of Dixmuede

Henry VIII initiated warfare against France. His first engagement, though, was the sending of 1500 bowmen to support his father-in-law, Ferdinand of Aragon, against the Moors. In 1513 Henry attacked France with his troops. A short time afterward the Scots attacked England. On September 9, 1513, there was a battle at Flodden Field. Along with musketeers and artillery, a great number of bowmen fought in the English ranks. The Scottish forces suffered a destructive defeat. Their king, James IV, fell, fighting with the bravest of his country, by an arrow shot to the head. On the battlefield there lay 12,000 Scottish and 4,000 English dead. That was the last battle of which it was said that it could have gone the other way without the bowmen.

An impression of the quantities of military goods that were stored in the arsenals then is given to us by an ordnance report from the Tower of London on September 21, 1523. Listed as "ready for use" were:
- 11,000 finished bows and 6,000 bow staves
- 16,000 sheaves of (384,000) arrows, 4,000 sheaves of (98,000) arrows with nine inches of fletching, and 600 gross of (86,400) bowstrings
- 5,000 sets of horses' reins, spare parts for 70 wagons, 80,000 horseshoes, and 500,000 hoof nails.

Figure 3
Excerpt from an
altar picture, 1493

When Henry VIII took his bowmen, plus great numbers of musketeers, field, and siege guns on a campaign against France, the royal bowmen accepted the value of the new weapons. Henry believed in the tried and true, but promoted the use of new weapons as well.

After his reign, the criticism of modern-thinking military experts was heard ever more loudly against the use of the longbow. On the one hand, the "horrendous import prices" of the bow staves was noted, on the other, the high expense of maintaining the bowmen, who needed "a great quantity of fodder" to stay in good condition and fight effectively.

In 1590, "Sir John Smythe" wrote a long and convincing argument for the maintenance of the longbow, in which he accused his opponents and some of the queen's advisors of corruption and incompetence. At that time, many arguments were advanced for and against the longbow, but time was against it.

On October 6, 1595, a formal request was made by the County of Hertfordshire to replace the last 100 longbows in the country, which were finally unusable, with muskets. Three weeks later, on October 26, Queen Elizabeth I gave the order via the Privy Council that all longbows of the militia should be replaced by firearms.

The fact is that the firearms used at Waterloo, barely 200 years later, were less effective than longbows, in both rate of fire and precision. But there were no more longbows!

Timeline

Norman Kings

William I, the Conqueror	1066-1087
William II, Rufus	1087-1100
Henry I	1100-1135
Stephen of Blois	1135-1154

House of Anjou (Plantagenet)

Henry II	1154-1189
Richard I, Lionheart	1189-1199
John, Lackland	1199-1216
Henry III	1216-1272
Edward I	1272-1307
Edward II	1307-1327
Edward III	1327-1377
Richard II	1377-1399

House of Lancaster

Henry IV	1399-1413
Henry V	1413-1422
Henry VI	1422-1461

House of York

Edward IV	1461-1483
Edward V	1483
Richard III	1483-1485

House of Tudor

Henry VII	1485-1509
Henry VIII	1509-1547
Edward VI	1547-1553
Mary I	1553-1558
Elizabeth I	1558-1603

2. THE "ART" OF BOW BUILDING

On the following pages, I would like to draw the interested reader into the events of my involvement in the building of traditional longbows of yew wood.

First, though, a few basic determinations.

In general it can be said that one must not necessarily be an artisan to be able to build a bow! As with every qualified and serious activity, a portion of discipline, endurance, patience, and a certain amount of ability belong to the basic equipment. Bow building is not fun, but bow building can make fun!

It is a proud and uplifting feeling when you let the first arrow fly from a bow that you have built. This ancient fascination can only be experienced fully by someone who is interested and strives to see his ability. In our highly technical, hectic times, almost everything can be bought, but only almost!

THE MATERIAL

Yew wood is the best bow wood in our hemisphere because of its physical characteristics. As noted in the previous chapter, our forefathers recognized this and used it thousands of years ago. This awareness, though, rested on a purely empirical basis. To give not only the specialist, but also the interested layman a scientifically based insight into this highly interesting material, there follows an exact explanation of the aforementioned characteristics. In the next sections I shall draw, among others, on the 4th International Yew Congress of 1997, held at the ETH in Zürich, where Prof. Dr. Dr. h. c. Ladislav J. Kucera, Professor of Wood Science at the ETH of Zürich, reported.

Of special interest for the subject of bows and bow building are the structural composition and physical-mechanical qualities. For better understanding, here are some basic details of wood structure.

Wood

Wood has a plant structure consisting of millions of extremely small cells with a diameter of a few hundredths of a millimeter. Chemically, wood consists mainly of cellulose and lignin.

Growth in Length

A young living cell consists of protoplasm, a material similar to albumen, and is enclosed by a thin wall. Such a cell can reproduce by splitting, in which the mother cell forms an internal wall and thus two daughter cells come into being. This cell division takes place steadily at the outer edge of the trunk, the branches, and roots. In addition, the cells at the outside stretch, so that the long growth of the tree takes place.

When the cells become older, the cell walls thicken and die off. The protoplasm disappears and is replaced by air, water, or frequently colorful products of metabolism.

Growth in Thickness, Annual Rings

Along with their growth in length, the trees also constantly grow in width. This so-called secondary thick growth takes place in that the cambium cells between the wood and inner bark constantly give off wood cells to the inside and inner bark cells to the outside. These cells maintain their ability to divide during the entire life of the tree.

The tree grows by constantly producing a new layer of cells on the already formed wood, while on the other side just as many (though much thinner) layers are formed new on the inner bark. This growth in thickness extends steadily through the whole period of vegetation, but the thickness of the new layer formed in one year (growth) can vary considerably according to the type of wood, age of the tree, precipitation, location, etc. When the growth stops for a time, as in our regions in winter, that can be determined by the growth rings on the cross-section of the wood. The inner bark constantly dies on its outer side. The bark at first has a protective function, but it cannot follow the continuing growth in thickness of the trunk, it becomes broken and finally splits off in part.

To live, the tree needs a number of nutrients. The roots take in mineral substances with the ground water and send the stream of water (transpiration stream) up the outermost splint layers to the leaves (or needles). There the greater part of the water evaporates, and the resulting suction pulls more water up. Some of the water is needed in the leaves or needles, where with the help of light and chlorophyll it turns the carbon dioxide of the air (by photosynthesis) into carbohydrates. The assimilation products are moved in solution down the trunk, which builds up its structure of them, via the living part of the inner bark. Thus a stream of transpiration moves steadily up the trunk through the wood, and a stream of assimilation goes downward through the inner bark.

a b   Annual ring border
c   Resin channels
d   Pith rays
e   Tracheids

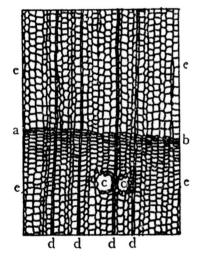

Figure 1
Arrangement of tracheids in coniferous wood (enlarged)

Cell Building in Coniferous Wood

The more lightly colored part of the annual ring, which is formed in spring, and thus called early wood, consists of very thin-walled cells. In the darker part, the summer or late wood, the cell walls are thicker. In addition, the late wood cells are arranged in a radial form, let less light through, and thus appear darker. These cells have an oval-round cross-section in the early wood and a flat rounded shape in the late wood. On their long axis, these cells, in microscopic enlargement, appear very long in comparison with their cross-section. They are called tracheids in coniferous wood. They serve to increase rigidity (supporting tissue) as well as to conduct water (conductive tissue).

The stream of sap is made possible by openings (microtubules) in the cell walls, through which the sap can diffuse. A closer look at the smoothly planed surface, seen at best with a loupe, shows a great number of fine lines, the pith rays, perpendicular to the annual rings.

Under the microscope one can recognize them as thin bands made up of more or less brick-shaped cells, which transport sap horizontally as well as storing reserve substances. Such non-pointed, usually thin-walled cells are called parenchym cells. The water flow between the parenchym cells, in them and to the tracheids takes place through thin, semi-permeable places in the cell walls, simply called "Tüpfel."

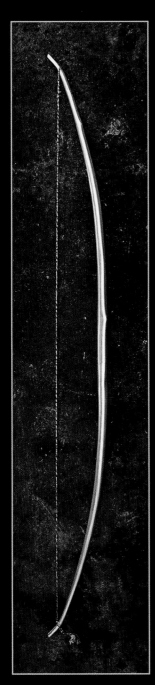

Upper bow end with one-sided string notch and holding nail, strung at left, unstrung at right

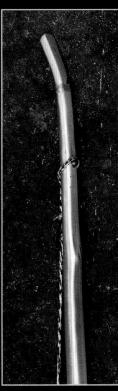

Replica of a Viking longbow, made of yew.
Length 191 cm (effective 179 cm).
Pulling weight 77 lbs at 70 cm distance.
(Photos and replication: J. Junkmanns)

Lower bow end with string notches

Bending behavior of the replica.

Figure 46
Classic English long-
bows
Grip wrapping of
leather, arrow plate of
bone over it (Photos:
U. Stehli)

THE YEW
Figure 3
Left side: back growth, diameter ca. 20 cm, 110 years old.
Right side: fine annual rings, at 1 inch (25.4 mm), 62 annual rings.

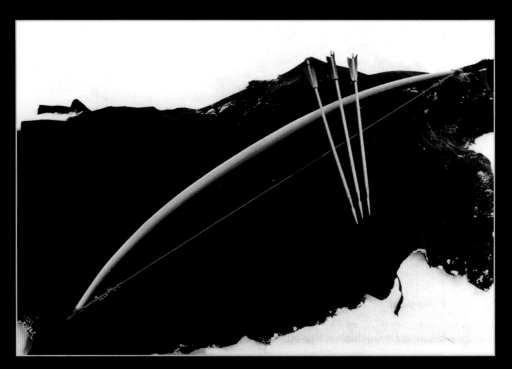

Figure 42: War bow, "Mary Rose" type: 100 lbs. at 28 inches

Grip parts ready for gluing
Right: various grip versions

Bows by Achim Stegmeyer

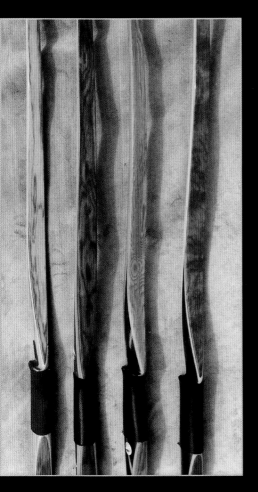

Limb woods on finished bows and before working.

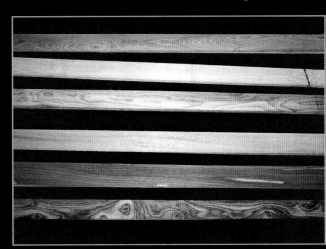

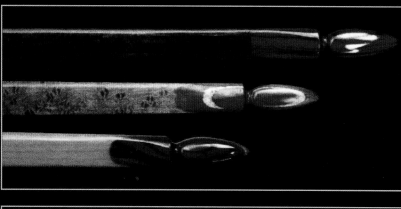

Bows by Achim Stegmeyer

THE YEW (*Taxus baccata L.*)

Macroscopic Description

"It forms thin and irregularly curved annual rings. A series of irregular annual ring buildings are splint-back stem cross-sections, such as are found, for example, in the hornbeams.

"The sapwood is thin and yellowish, and usually includes 10 to 20 annual rings. The obligatory heartwood has a unified brown to reddish color. It can border on sapwood in the area of branches. The natural removal of branches takes place very slowly in the yew. Only in inner competition does it form a natural 'dead-branch zone.'

"The series of them are dead branches grown into the wood and additionally disturbing the annual rings." These factors, along with general growth deformation, constitute the main reason for problems in the selection of good yew stems for bow wood. "Often one finds traces of sleeping buds and water shoots in the wood; they were favored by the thin rings and are found even in outer annual rings of old trees. In both the trunk and the branches of the yew one often finds pressure wood. The heartwood of the yew is regarded as very sturdy! Falling and destruction caused by fungi are rare and require much exposure. The same applies to wood-destroying insects"

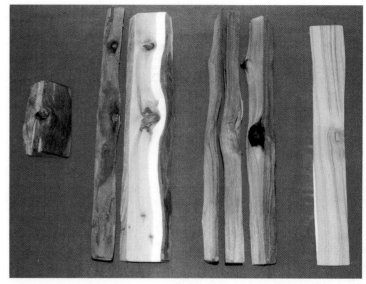

Figure 2 Dead branches and old wounds in the yew. From left: 1.) dead branch; 2.) dead branches cut off; 3 & 4.) cut-off branches with wound overwalling (see also Color Plate 10)

Wood Structure

The wood of the yew has a very simple construction. The annual rings have an even color, the annual ring border is marked, to be sure, but the transition from early to late wood is gradual, and the late-wood area is relatively small as a rule. The yew wood consists of just three cell types: the early and late wood tracheids and the ray parenchym cells. In comparison with most conifers, the ray tracheids and the vertical as well as horizontal resin channels are missing.

The screw thickenings are an important anatomical feature of the yew. These are generally spread through the row of *Taxalidae* (yew-like trees). They are also found in types of the genera *Picca* and *Pseudotsuga*. (Greguss 1955)

Between the screw thickenings of the yew and those of the *Douglasiae*, though, there is a major quantitative difference. The screw thickenings of the yew, which are found in both the early- and late-wood tracheids, are very massive. In comparison, those of the *Douglasiae* occur only in the early-wood tracheids and are formed very delicately.

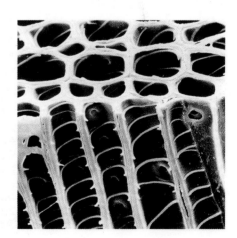

Figure 4 Yew wood, cross and radial cuts, shown by an electron microscope, enlarged 865 times, H. Hegnauer, with screw thickenings in the tracheids.

Physical-Mechanical Statistics	Fir	Douglas Fir	Yew
Darr thickness g/cm	0.42	0.50	0.62
Volume contraction percentage	11.8	12.0	8.8
Lengthwise break resistance to fibers N/mm			
Under pressure	45	55	57
Under pulling	85	94	108
Under bending	71	85	85
Lengthwise bending E-module to fibers N/mm	11000	12100	15700
Breakage activity Nm/cm	4.5	4.9	14.7
Brinell hardness lengthwise to fibers N/mm	31	45	70

Figure 5. Average values of selected physical-mechanical figures for fir, Douglas fir, and Yew, after Zell (1987) and Wagenführ (1996), slightly rounded off.

Physical-Mechanical Characteristics

These characteristics of wood are among the best researched.

In the table, Figure 5, one finds the most important physical-mechanical statistics of the fir, Douglas fir, and yew.

The yew is the heaviest conifer. The volume contraction percentage is positively amazing, for it shows a good stability of form for things made of yew. The statistical fractional values of yew are impressive, but exceed those of the Douglas fir only slightly. Yew wood, though, stands out for its bending elasticity and especially its resistance to breaking (striking bending firmness, tested as per DIN 52189).

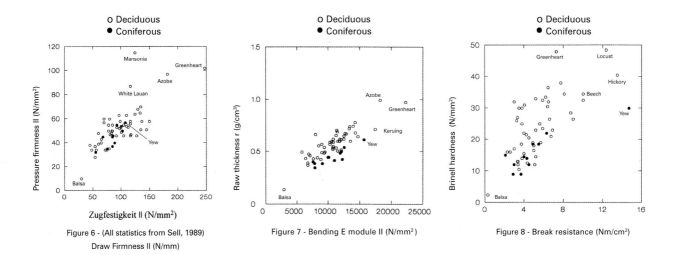

Figure 6 - (All statistics from Sell, 1989)
Draw Firmness II (N/mm)

Figure 7 - Bending E module II (N/mm²)

Figure 8 - Break resistance (Nm/cm²)

The bending elasticity module is a measure of the required reforming energy, the break-striking work, also called strike-bending toughness, is the only dynamic firmness of the wood. According to that, yew lets itself be reformed only with great difficulty, and it can withstand extremely dynamic (striking) pressures.

The importance of yew for making bows can be derived from these last figures. To round off the figures, several physical-mechanical values of yew were compared with those of the native and the most important foreign coniferous and deciduous wood types.

In the process, Figure 6 shows the draw and pressing firmness and provides an average positioning of yew. From Figure 7, the relatively high raw thicknesses and the very high bending E module of this wood can be taken. Finally, Figure 8 shows the excellent hardness and the unequaled bend-striking firmness of yew wood.

This shows the basis of the advantages of yew wood in its use for making bows.

AN ENGLISH WAR BOW MADE OF YEW

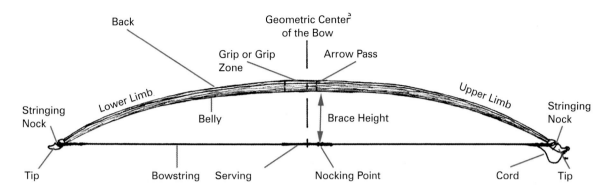

Figure 9. Parts of the English longbow and their names, in strung condition.

As a beginner in bow building, you should not make the mistake of stubbornly sticking to yew wood. It is hard to obtain in bow quality, and when it is, it must be stored for several years, to do what it promises!

I recommend that you begin with hazel, ash, elm, or hickory wood to gain experience. Only someone who already has experience in bow building should venture to use a piece of yew. The following notes are based on yew wood!

TOOLS

Ideals are described; improvisation is possible.

We need:
• Measuring stick, ruler, pencil, felt-tip pen, note paper
• Thin cord, such as a black nylon cord
• Workbench with mounted vise and padded jaws
• "Workshop block" with padded surface
• Drawknife, not too long
• Hand plane
• Rasp, medium fine, half-round files, medium and fine, round files, 5, 6, 8, 12 mm
• Draw blades, straight, arched, and profiled
• Flot (old bow-builder's tool, multiple blades)
• Sandpaper, various grades, 100/150/180/240/320/400.
• Fine steel wool
• Spiral drills, conical, 12/13/15, for the horn tips
• 3 clamps, 200 mm long
• Bowstring with leather caps for tightening and loosening during tillering
• Flat cutting knife, 4 mm wide

Figure 10. Bow making tools and materials.

Before we begin the work, the following should be noted for the sake of your health:

All of the yew is poisonous except the fruit calyx (arillus) of red berries that grows on female plants.

Thus it is important to wear a dust mask during the fine smoothing, and to vacuum up sawdust. Through this little bit of hygiene we avoid letting the toxins in the wood get into our blood through the mucus.

Figure 11. Splitting the piece of the trunk

Figure 12. Stacking the staves

CHOOSING THE WOOD

From a straight-grown yew trunk, a good two meters long and about 25 cm thick, free from branches and with no distortions, cracks, bumps, or dead branches, it is possible to make up to four good longbows.

Such fine examples are, of course, very rare. Of a hundred trunks, one often finds only a few that are usable for bow building at all. Often the criteria of choice apply to only a quarter or half of a trunk.

But one should not get depressed!

If it is possible to get a good bow stave, we split the chosen trunk piece carefully into segments 8 to 10 cm wide, using steel wedges.

From the "stave" so obtained, the pith will be removed with a hatchet and its splintery side angles cleaned up with a drawknife.

The cleanly sawed ends will be sealed with paint or simple carpenter's lime, so as to prevent the wood from drying too fast, which causes cracking.

If long stems are not available, there is the possibility of making longbows of shorter pieces. These will be spliced in the middle with a "double fishtail," as the specialist calls it. As for the choice of wood and the raw working, they get the same treatment as long pieces.

I'll go into the splicing technique later.

In the subsequent drying and storing period of at least two years, better three or four, there is the possibility of "experimenting" with more readily available kinds of wood.

I store the fresh wood for a year, carefully stacked in an airy outdoor space protected from sun and rain. In the second year I bring the pieces inside, but not into a heated room. That is done only a short time before the work starts.

Three "long years" have passed. Our first hickory longbow, built in a bow-building course, is long since finished. Through experimenting with hazel and ash wood we have gained valuable experience. Among other things, we have mastered the technique of the "Flemish splice" important in making "standard" bowstrings.

Inspired by reading one of the inclusive historical books, we are firmly determined to venture to replicate an English war longbow of our aged yew wood.

Compared with the "comfortable" traditional longbows used today, which are usually made with hickory backing and have a stiffening zone with a velvet or leather grip in the middle, this gripless type of bow makes a very archaic impression!

The medieval English war bows, though, were built that way. It may seem repellent to us today, but other concepts of war prevailed in those days.

No yeoman archer at the time of Edward I or afterward would have thought of wrapping a leather belt or velvet band around his bow just to be able to hold it better—what for?

On the basis of the heavy draw weight, sometimes more than 100 pounds, these bows were long (74 to 78 inches) and had to be tillered so that they bent in semi-circular form over their whole length. That means the grip part and the limb ends were included in the bending. Only thus was it possible to transmit the pressure needed to send the arrows, weighing up to 75 grams and 29 to 32 inches long, on their "deadly business."

Since our bow, unlike its medieval ancestors, is to serve peaceful purposes, a draw weight of 60 pounds with a length (between nocks) of 72 inches is enough.

THE RAW BOW

For our bow, we choose a stave, remaining straight after storage, a good 1.9 meters in length. Fixed in the vise, it will have its bark carefully removed with a drawknife. Upon closer inspection we determine that the debarked raw bow has an irregular, wavy surface, with a slight twist at its upper end (upper part of the stem).

The stave, lying on the workbench with its sapwood up, is now lined up and arranged with small wooden wedges so that the main limb zones are as horizontal as possible. Above and below the raw bow we fasten two wooden blocks, each fitted with a nail, to the workbench with clamps. Between these two nails the test string will be stretched.

Through precise sighting and lateral adjustment of the stave, it is possible to position it so that we mark points on the sapwood surface along the string and link them together to form a center line.

After drawing it, we transfer, following the next drawing (Figure 16), the recommended raw measurements and contours of a bow of this type to the back of the sapwood.

Figure 15. Draw outlines with enough left over

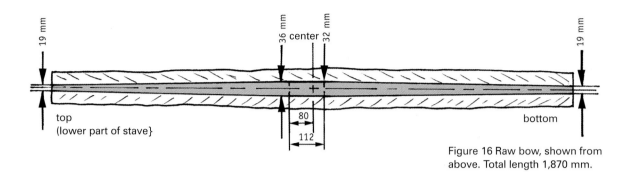

19 mm

36 mm center 32 mm

19 mm

top
(lower part of stave}

80

112

bottom

Figure 16 Raw bow, shown from
above. Total length 1,870 mm.

Figure 19. Reducing sapwood
delicately with a draw blade.

With hatchet, drawknife, and hand plane, and with a band saw if we have one, we remove the excess wood on the sides.

Since the sapwood is usually thicker than we want, it has to be reduced to a thickness of about 7 mm. For this purpose a pencil line is drawn freehand on the side, following an early-wood annual ring.

Now a hard job begins, depending on the fine-year quality of the sapwood. With extreme care, beginning from the middle of the bow, we cut and scrape with a draw knife (crudely) and draw blade (finely) one annual ring after another from the wood surface, until we reach the line we drew on the side. In no case should layers in the main bending zone be cut through!

The light-dark contrast of the early and late wood makes this subtle work easier. To avoid any "breaking places," next comes a careful pre-smoothing of the debarked back with 100 grit sandpaper.

The side surfaces of the raw bow are now worked clean with a hand plane.

Figure 22. Raw bow seen from the side; overall length 1,870 mm.

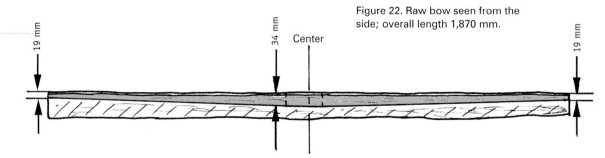

19 mm

34 mm Center

19 mm

Now we can lay out the raw side dimensions (thicknesses) of the bow.

In the following working of the inside, caution is recommended, depending on the growth of the wood and the available tools. Using the drawknife, again from the center out, we make small, controlled cuts to remove the excess wood in stages until we reach the drawn line.

150

As on the back of the bow, waves on its belly cannot simply be eliminated just to form a nice straight surface. Being careful of the annual rings, we follow the contour of the backing. Around an unavoidable, fast-grown branch we must leave a little more material—better more than less at this stage.

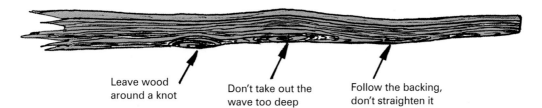

Leave wood
around a knot

Don't take out the
wave too deep

Follow the backing,
don't straighten it

Figure 23. Working the
front

A loose, thin knot sitting in the middle of a limb is carefully bored out and the hole is filled with a glued piece of hardwood. Here too, wood is to be left to protect this spot.

The stave has now attained an almost square form. The following work, rounding the belly, begins when we draw a center line on it and two lines on the left and right sides. They afford better control over this work process. Working again from the middle out, we carefully cut off wood, piece by piece.

Here caution must be used with the drawknife. As firm, tough, and elastic as the yew wood is, it tends to splinter. A cut that goes too deep has ruined many a "hopeful" limb!

It is better to recognize the danger that is always present when the wood has grown unevenly, and to use a rasp or a file. To attain an even, half-round contour, the use of variously profiled draw blades is recommended.

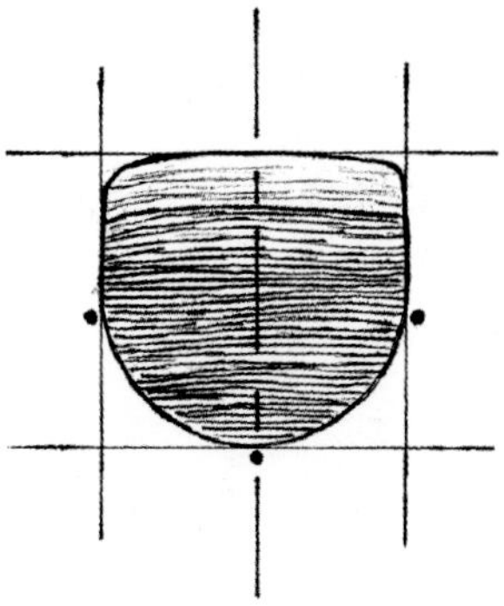

Figure 24. Rounding the
bow

DRAW BLADES

These tools are meant only for taking off very fine bits of material.

For repeated working of long areas, in our case the rounding of the bow belly and the subsequent tillering, there is the danger of making waves (the "Cellulitis effect"). To avoid this, the use of a "flot" is recommended. This tool, which was used by the English bow builders of the Middle Ages, is in principle a "multiple draw blade."

Because of the blades being one after another on the same level, this special instrument glides along over the wood surface when used, and thus prevents the formation of waves by the longitudinal scraping.

Figure 26. Fine work
with the flot

Figure 27. Flot

151

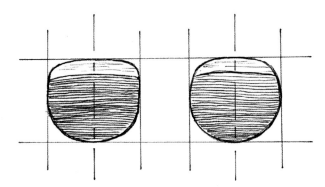

Figure 28. Cross-section profile of English war bow (Mary Rose)

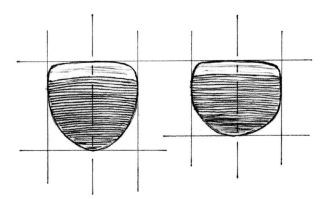

Figure 29. Cross-section profile
1. high (fast)
2. flat (soft)

Different longbow profiles have come to use out of the past. In this regard, note the following:

The optimal ratio of measurements for the cross-section is 1.1 width to 1 thickness.

In my opinion, this is a standard, from which, depending on the type and growth of the wood, and the projected qualities of the bow to be built, limited deviations may be made.

In general, the higher the limb cross-section, the livelier and quicker the shot is!

To be sure, the wood experiences a greater strain, which, in turn, affects the sturdiness.

A somewhat flatter cross-section gives a softer shot, but the bow is more likely to "follow the string." At the beginning, I would rather play it safe in this respect.

Now, the tapering, rounded rough bow is sanded with 100-grit sandpaper and given a precise examination. Drawing a center line again on the back is vital. The yew wood is full of surprises!

Figure 30 Stave rounded, tiller grooves put in

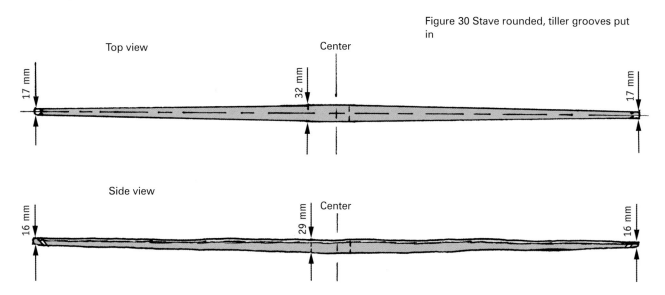

There is the possibility that, because of the considerable reduction in material on the belly and sides, the stave will warp despite being stored. For this reason, we have left a certain amount of spare wood in the width. If this negative situation should occur, there would still be the possibility of making slight one-sided corrections to retain the recommended width of a 60-pound bow. To attain such a draw weight with a projected length of 72 inches (1,829 mm), the stave should have the following dimensions:

152

TILLERING

First, provisional string nocks (tiller nocks) are made on the ends. It is important here not to let these nocks run over the back of the bow, but only on the sides.

At this stage, the stave already shows some flexibility. Of course, we should not make the mistake of stringing it yet. That would be too soon! First "it" must learn to bend itself. This is called "tillering" in bowyer's language.

For this purpose it is advisable to build a simple device, a tillering board. On a paper sheet a meter wide and 2.1 meters long, we draw with a felt-tip pen the scale shown in the following sketch.

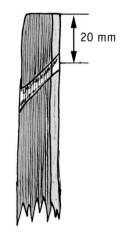

20 mm

Figure 31. Making the tillering grooves

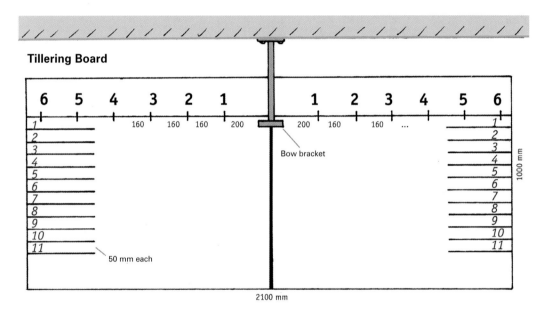

Figure 32. Tillering Board

Tacked onto a light piece of wood, the whole thing can be attached to a wall at eye level. A bracket attached near the top serves to hold the bow.

A small guiding pulley is fastened at the bottom, so that it stays exactly vertical under the middle of the tiller scale. Now we put an overly long loose string on and locate it on the layout. An unbreakable nylon cord with a hook is hung on the middle of the string. The loose other end is led around the pulley, which allows us to observe the bending behavior of the bow at a distance and to judge it. By a first cautious drawing, we bend the stave about 7 centimeters and find that it is up to 3.4 stiff at the ends.

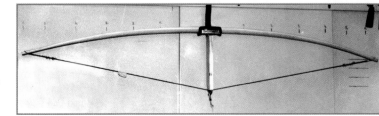

Figure 33. War bow, Mary Rose type, before tillering—much too stiff.

153

Down from the tillering board!

With the draw blade and the flot, from 2 to 4 on both limbs, bit by bit, is scraped from the belly of the bow. But always carefully, not too much, you can always take off but not put on!

And again, check it on the tillering board.

Now we pull carefully until past 2. Result: still too stiff. After several repetitions of this process, both limbs begin to bend somewhat evenly.

On closer examination, the upper limb shows too strong a bend from 2 to 3.

Down from the tillering board!

The lower limb, because of the offset grip zone, is shorter and thus stiffer. Again, carefully reduce the whole inside of the lower limb. If we have the feeling that the limbs bend evenly at about 15 cm after several pulls, we put a shorter string on. To do this simply and with no risk, we use our "leather-capped" special string throughout tillering.

The bow is now strung flat, with only a brace height of 7 cm at most. Now, for the first time, we check the string distance. A paper strip with a scale on it makes this process, to be repeated often from here on, easier.

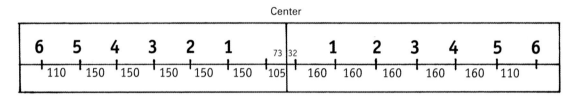

Figure 34. Scale and measuring points for the string distance.

We place the unstrung bow in the center of the scale and transfer the measuring points to the belly side. Then it is strung again and set up centrally so that the string is on this line.

In comparing the measurements, the distance between the string and the bow at the various measuring points on the upper limb must be about 2 to 3 mm more than on the lower one.

After that, we carry out a first side check, by sighting over the string on the belly side to check its exact central extent. If one limb should show a sideward deviation at this stage, a "cast" in bowyer's language, it is now early enough to react to it and correct it in the further course of the tillering.

In our case, that is what has happened!

In the area of points 3 and 4, the upper limb shows a slight deviation to the left. First we check the bending behavior once again on the tiller wall. Pulling carefully, several times to 3 and 4, we find the following:

At the same position between 3 and 4 where the cast begins, a stiff place appears.

Down from the tillering board, unstring it!

With the draw blade we first remove some wood from the arch of the belly, so as to weaken the stiff zone. Then we reduce the arch by taking some material from the right side over the determined points and beyond.

Why Is That So?

There, where a limb deviates, the wood is too weak. So this unevenness must be countered by taking material off the opposite side. Should it not be possible to equalize a cast completely by this method, we also deepen the string nock on the side to which the limb leans.

There are various reasons for deviations of this kind:
- An imprecisely applied center line,
- Irregular growth of the wood,
- In most cases, though, the unevenness is in the workmanship.

A right-hander easily tends to take too much wood from the side bulge off the left side of the upper limb and the right side of the lower one while working on the bow. If there is no check of the "string middle" from the start, it can easily happen that, because of the aforementioned fact, the lower limb of the finished bow shows a deviation to the right and the upper one to the left. When strung, the bow forms an elegant but "unqualified" S-curve when you sight along the belly.

As for the bending of the limbs in the direction of drawing the bow, the following should be kept in mind:

If one limb should enter a position in which it bends too strongly, we must immediately relieve this "kink" by reducing the material on the belly side, before and after!! Stiff zones are weakened by removing material from the spot outward and thus included in the bending!

In these processes it is important to know that every material reduction affects the bending behavior slowly! Thus during the entire tillering process, time has to be allowed for it to "set" through repeated numerous drawings on the tiller string.

If one moves too quickly, there is the danger that the processes will go too far, meaning that one "rocks" the bow down through misjudged actions on its draw weight.

The final result then is usually a child's bow!

Thinking clearly about every action, we go on, pulling the flat-strung bow more and more on the tiller wall. We carefully observe its bending behavior and correct mistakes, always keeping in mind that every weakening of one limb also affects the behavior of the other. Meanwhile, checking the string distance and the central control of the string goes on steadily. Symbolically, one could compare the tillering process with hiking a ridge. That means that every step must be considered well.

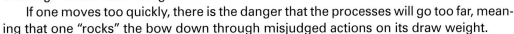

The farther we go, the finer measures we must take.

In one check we find that the bow, drawn by hand to about 45 cm, already shows some flexibility. Now we raise the string distance by pulling the provisional string to some 10 cm. In comparing the measuring points, a difference of 4-5 mm from the upper to the lower limb appears. If we observe the bending behavior on the tiller wall, these values are confirmed.

In a strung condition, the upper limb shows a clearly stronger bending than the lower one. But if we begin to put the bow under tension with the tillering string, then both limbs work together! The string runs over the bow exactly in the middle. If it is unstrung now, it shows a slight bend toward the string over its entire length. This is normal in the use of a straight raw bow; in the specialist language, the bow has set itself back.

In a reflex bow, meaning one that is bent toward the sapwood, this bending would, of course, be less. Strung again, after pulling several times to 2/3 of the drawing length, we have a "good feeling." In view of its whole distance, it still seems to us to be somewhat too strong. But we must bear in mind that through the smoothing still to come, a weakening of the wood will occur over its entire length.

It is also important to give the bow 3 to 4 more pounds of draw weight, since it will lose power after breaking-in. Keeping this in mind, we smooth the belly of the whole bow vigorously with 100-grit sandpaper and slightly round the edges of the back.

If the condition still does not change, then we repeat the smoothing process.

Of course we do this only after checking on the tiller and then comparing the measurements of the string distance. After sanding again, the situation has relaxed!

On the basis of its length of 72 inches, the bow can now be drawn relatively softly to 60 cm. Drawing it for a short time to 70 cm, we still sense what is in it.

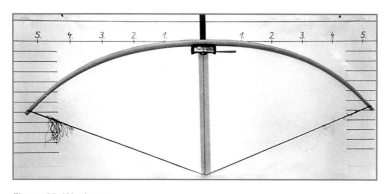

Figure 35. War bow, Mary Rose type, bends at 26 inches

TEST SHOOTING

Now the time for the first test shots has come. Because we carefully carried out the described work, nothing should really go wrong. But as already noted, yew wood is full of surprises.

On the basis of the extremely high pulling and pressing stress to which the wood is exposed, reactions can occur afterward. If the bending of the limbs should change again in this last stage, this must be eliminated by retillering in the previous manner.

The first test shots have gone successfully, and a check afterward confirms that nothing has changed in our bow.

Now the "work of art" can be sanded with 150-, 180-, and 240-grit sandpaper. Through further turning of the string, we bring the distance to 140 mm. After more test shooting, the obligatory checks are made again. In comparing the string distances, we have now reached the measuring points of the upper limb, always some 5 to 6 mm higher than those of the lower limb. Drawn on the tiller, the bow forms an even semicircle, slightly flattened in the middle.

Afterward we still want to retain the aforementioned distance of 140 mm for a time, until the bow is well broken-in. After that we'll raise it to about 150 mm.

How Does the Bow Influence the Arrow's Flight?

In the moment of shooting, an arrow, influenced by its mass inertia, is bent by the accelerating forces affecting it. It sort of winds itself around the bow and still makes some snakelike movements after it is released. This is called "archer's paradox."

For lateral flight behavior, then, it is true that the better the arrow fits the bow in regard to its bending behavior, the faster it has stabilized itself and reached its straight trajectory. If the arrow does not fit the bow, then its stabilization is faulty, and a deviation to one or the other side will occur.

For right-handed shooters this means that if the stave is too stiff, it will deviate to the left; if it goes to the right, it is too weak! For the left-handed shooter, the opposite is true.

What the right behavior of the arrow amounts to in its vertical trajectory is chiefly dependent on the correct tillering of the bow.

The difference in mass of 5 to 6 mm in the string distance of our bow, attained through careful work, has the following cause: because of the offset grip zone, the upper limb is longer and thus has a greater mass than the lower one. If the string distances were the same above and below, it would mean that both limbs had about the same power.

But since the upper limb has a greater mass because of its greater length, it would influence the arrow negatively in giving off energy because of this fact. Let's put it this way: through this difference in mass, an added power is documented in the lower limb. Through this, the arrow is lifted slightly when shot and glides "cleanly" over our bow hand.

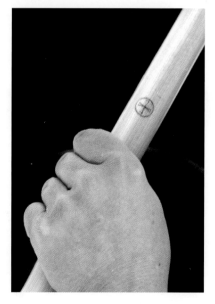

In the now attained condition it would be possible to determine the draw weight of the bow. For starters, though, we should not concentrate with all our powers on the maintenance of an exact value. More experience would be needed for that. Let's be satisfied with the fact that the bow works well, suits us, and shoots without problems!

Peck Mark and Arrow Pass

To maintain a reference point for an exact grip position on this bow, it is advisable to make a sign (peck mark), as was customary in olden times. For this purpose, a marking applied on the left side, 25 mm over the middle of the bow, will be sufficient, and will be covered by the bow hand when you hold the bow.

Directly over it goes the so-called "arrow pass," the place over which the arrow leaves the bow when shot.

Figure 36. Grip zone with peck mark

In order to give the bow some additional shooting comfort in the end, we taper the limb ends down conically at a length of about 13 cm, so that they have a diameter of 15 mm. If we should not succeed, despite all our efforts in the process of tillering, in eliminating a sideward deviation in one limb, there is now one last possible way of correcting it. By slight one-sided application of the aforementioned tapering, the position of the bowstring to the opposite side will be corrected.

HORN TIPS

Finally, we make two tips to protect the end of the limbs. With conical holes, and glued to the fitted bow ends, they give the string loops a secure hold. Most suitable for them are the compact points of cow horns.

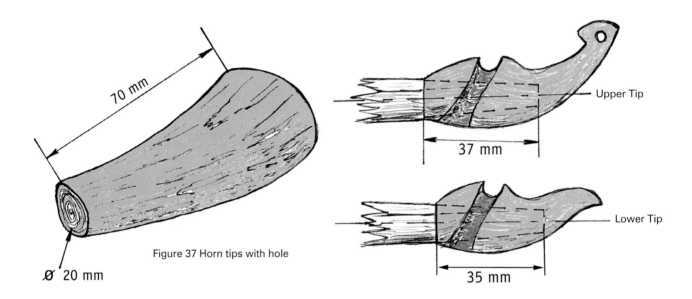

70 mm

Ø 20 mm

Figure 37 Horn tips with hole

Upper Tip

37 mm

Lower Tip

35 mm

By means of a conically ground spiral drill of 15 mm diameter, we bore holes 37 mm deep on the thinner side of the horn tips. Provisionally glued onto prepared wood with Pattex, the horn pieces can be worked with various half-round and round files. The upper horn tip gets a 4 mm hole to hold a thin cord called the string keeper.

This is spliced into the bowstring at one end and tied fast to the tip with the other, so that when the bow is unstrung it prevents the string from sliding down. (Figure 38)

After the crude shaping with files, the two horn pieces are smoothed with sandpaper of the finest grain.

By warming with a hot-air blower, the contact glue loosens, so that we can attach the finished horn tips, after cleaning the holes thoroughly (nitro-thinning) to the pointed limbs with two-component epoxy.

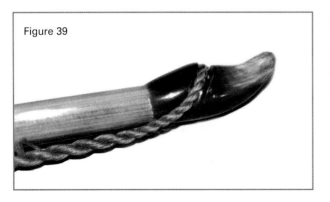

Figure 39

Now comes the final finishing of the entire bow with 320 and 400 grit sandpaper and fine steel wool.

To protect the wood from hand sweat, moisture, and dirt, it is advisable to impregnate the bow. I use stock oil for this. This oily, slightly silicon-holding means of preservation, used to protect gun stocks, has the advantage of not penetrating into the depths. By the fast evaporation of the liquid, the silicon settles in the uppermost layers. Applied several times, it protects the wood in a natural way against environmental influences.

Our bow, equipped with an 18-ply Dacron bowstring, is now ready to shoot!

The end measurements given in the following charts are taken from a bow of this type that I built. They should, of course, not be taken dogmatically, but only as a guide!

Figure 38. Mary Rose bow with upper tip and string keeper.

War Longbow, Mary Rose type
Yew (1988): 28 annual rings/inch
Bow length: 72" (1,828 mm)
Draw weight: 63 lb./28"

End Widths

6	5	4	3	2	1	M.	1	2	3	4	5	6
15	19	24,6	27,6	29,6	31,2	32	31,5	30	26	22,5	18,3	14,6

End Thicknesses

6	5	4	3	2	1	M.	1	2	3	4	5	6
14,6	15,3	20	21,7	22,5	26,6	28,5	26	24,7	22	20	16,2	15,2

In comparison to them, here are the dimensions of a replicated "Mary Rose type war bow" that, built according to original measurements, produced a good 100 pounds of draw weight when drawn to 28 inches.

War Longbow, Mary Rose type
Yew (1988): 28 annual rings/inch
Bow length: 76.4" (1,940 mm)
Pulling weight: 103 lb./28"

End Widths

6	5	4	3	2	1	M.	1	2	3	4	5	6
13,3	21,3	26,1	30,5	34	36,8	39,5	37,1	33,7	30	26	20,6	13,7

End Thicknesses

6	5	4	3	2	1	M.	1	2	3	4	5	6
13,5	17,4	22,4	26,2	27,7	30,3	32	29,5	26,7	25	21,8	17,5	13

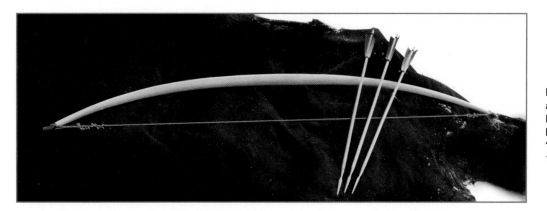

Figures 15, 19, 26, 36 and 42 document the building of this bow. Figure 42. War bow, "Mary Rose" type, ca. 100 pounds/28 inches

An English Longbow with Sapwood Back

Since, as already noted, it is very difficult to obtain long yew staves for the building of self longbows, the description of two alternatives follows.

Splicing

First of all, there is the splicing technique.

Best suited for this are so-called sister pieces. These are two billets, lying next to each other in a trunk piece about 1.1 meter long, that suit the purposes of bow building. From such partial pieces we can build a traditional longbow with a sapwood backing.

The two chosen, well-seasoned yew billets first have their bark removed. Laid on the workbench with their backs upward, they are evaluated as to the run of the sapwood.

If this has grown straight in both pieces, then we trim the billets angularly with a hand plane to a measurement of 30 mm wide and 35 mm thick. Should it prove, after the bark has been removed, that the surfaces are irregular and fall off to the sides, then there is a possibility of correcting it with this technique.

By turning them slightly, they are laid out before being worked so that the sapwood surfaces lie horizontally on the main bending zones. That means there is a slightly angled course of the annual rings to the axis of the bow, which is easier to accept in the grip than in the bending zones of the limbs.

Considering the course of the annual rings and the criteria stated above, we decide which ends of the two billets are going to be spliced together.

To make the fishtail connection, both billets must be squared off and trimmed exactly for a length of 20 cm, to the measurements of 32 mm wide and 35 mm thick. A possible reduction of the sapwood will be undertaken after the splicing. After laying out the obligatory center lines comes the marking of the first fishtail piece.

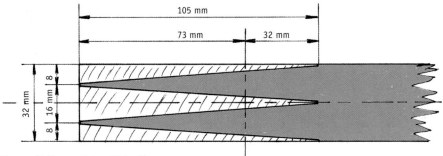

Figure 43 Bow splicing (fishtail)

The cross-hatched wood is now cut out with a band saw so that the remaining points are 1.5 mm wide and the saw cuts are likewise 1.5 mm wide.

Now we put the piece that isn't cut yet into the vise, put the other one on it, line it up, and support the free end with a block.

By sighting over the center line, we straighten the cut piece and copy the lines of the fishtail onto the lower piece with a pencil flattened on one side. In sawing out the second piece, be sure to make the cuts as neat as possible. That means that the two pieces must fit together at the joint without "using force," avoiding the danger of splitting.

For the gluing which follows, I use Klebit 303 be Kleberit. This high-quality glue works with hardwood and has flexibility characteristics after drying.

Straight billets are glued with 20 mm reflex, to maintain a reserve for the "set-back."

After applying glue to both pieces, we put one piece into the vise, push the other piece in, and support it temporarily. Then we fix the gluing point with a clamp.

Straightening

For this purpose, the aligning string, held with two clamps, is stretched tightly over the center lines of the two glued-together staffs. Checking longitudinally, we test the "flight" so as to correct any occurring deviation by adjusting the supported stave. By applying two more clamps, which are carefully tightened alternately, we achieve a tight, lasting and unloosenable joint. After 24 hours, the work on the rough stave can continue.

Regarding the raw measurements and a possible reduction of the sapwood, we follow the previous directions. As far as the dynamic pressure on the raw stave is concerned, this should be left to rest for several days to give the glue time to make a final union. This is important, for this process, in terms of time, is influenced by moisture in the wood and air. That means that the drier the wood is and the less moisture there is in the air, the longer the final drying takes.

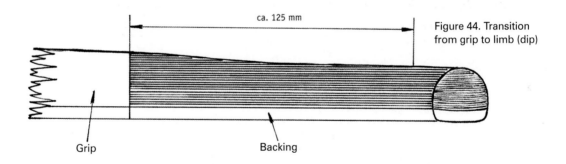

ca. 125 mm

Figure 44. Transition from grip to limb (dip)

Grip

Backing

Dip: Transition from Grip to Limb

Unlike a medieval war bow, the modern type to be built now has several major differences.

This type of longbow shows a definite stiffening in the middle and a thickened handgrip. The grip zone here is under tension and absolutely inactive. This provides a quiet shot with minimal hand shock. The stiffening of the middle of the bow, already mentioned, is attained through a defined slimming (dip) in the thickness of the bow at the transition from the grip to the limbs.

The further conical extension to the ends creates the attained measure of thickness. Through this almost abrupt tapering, the bow limbs are also included equally in the bending, even at their thickest areas near the grip.

As for the bending behavior of this bow, it must be kept in mind during tillering that the limbs have a slight thickening at the ends, at a distance of about 15 cm. Yet in view of the equal strain on the material, it is important that some 8-10 cm above and below the grip, the bending begins gently, continuing steadily to the outside and, as noted above, running out about 15 cm from the ends.

Arrow Plate

In view of these differences, tillered according to the experience gained with the first bow, equipped with horn tips and ready to shoot, we equip it at the place where the arrow passes by with a small plate (arrow plate) made of bone. This serves to protect the wood against the abrasion of the arrow sliding over it.

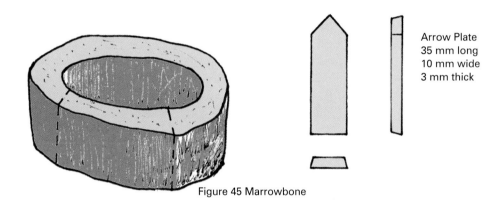

Arrow Plate
35 mm long
10 mm wide
3 mm thick

Figure 45 Marrowbone

To make this inset part, marrowbone, as thick as possible (such as a beef leg bone), is suitable. After being washed four or five times in the dishwasher, the clean bone is cut with a saw, smoothed flat and handled as shown in the drawing.

After marking the outlines on the bone, we stick it vertically onto the wood by means of a small flat knife and take off the intermediate material about 2 mm deep. This inlaying work should be done very carefully, for it is done on a finished bow!

Using two-component epoxy, it is set into the prepared cutout, and the projecting material, after hardening, is removed with sandpaper.

Grip Wrapping

As an added thickening of the handgrip, we glue a curved piece of wood (block), 90 mm long, 30 mm wide, and 7 mm thick, onto the belly of the grip zone, and neatly round or smooth its angles and transitions after attaching it. To complete the comfort, we equip this bow with a grip wrapping. According to individual taste, velvet ribbon, leather, or rawhide strips are suitable glued on with Pattex and wrapped in spiral form over the grip zone to give a good grip.

To finish the job, here are the end measurements of a bow made in this way.

Figure 46 Grip wrapping made of leather, and arrow plate

Traditional Longbow, spliced, with sapwood backing
Yew (1984): ca. 40 annual rings/inch
Bow length: 69.5" (1,765 mm)
Draw weight: 67 pounds/27"

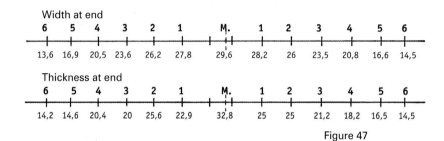

Width at end

6	5	4	3	2	1	M.	1	2	3	4	5	6
13,6	16,9	20,5	23,6	26,2	27,8	29,6	28,2	26	23,5	20,8	16,6	14,5

Thickness at end

6	5	4	3	2	1	M.	1	2	3	4	5	6
14,2	14,6	20,4	20	25,6	22,9	32,8	25	25	21,2	18,2	16,5	14,5

Figure 47

Traditional longbow, spliced, with sapwood backing
Yew (1989): ca. 45 annual rings/inch
Bow length: 74" (1,880 mm)
Draw weight: 57 pounds/28 "
62 pounds/30 "
Thickness at end

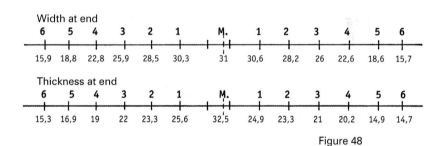

Width at end

6	5	4	3	2	1	M.	1	2	3	4	5	6
15,9	18,8	22,8	25,9	28,5	30,3	31	30,6	28,2	26	22,6	18,6	15,7

Thickness at end

6	5	4	3	2	1	M.	1	2	3	4	5	6
15,3	16,9	19	22	23,3	25,6	32,5	24,9	23,3	21	20,2	14,9	14,7

Figure 48

Variant with Hickory Back

To finish my directions, I come to the aforementioned second alternative, the building of a traditional longbow with hickory backing. This variant is made most often at the present time.

Here there is the advantage of a free choice of wood. That means that, for this type of work, we are able to evaluate good heartwood pieces without concern for the sapwood, which is often not suitable for making a bow. By using the fishtail technique, and fitted with a backing of hickory wood, the opportunity exists here of building a high-quality longbow. An added important aspect is the better utilization of valuable yew wood.

We begin by making a heartwood raw bow, to the same dimensions as the first bow, but reduced in thickness by the thickness of the sapwood.

In choosing wood, it is important to remember that for "pairing" we only use pieces that are as straight as possible, with similar longitudinal grain.

Using the technique described in detail above, we make a slightly reflex raw bow of the best yew wood. In place of the sapwood of the back, we use the aforementioned hickory. This wood, because of its tremendous elasticity and toughness, is the best alternative.

A lamination 7 mm thick, fitted to the width of our raw bow, is smoothed fine and prepared for gluing.

More precise directions are needed for the gluing process:

One should not try to do this with two dozen clamps, "free hand provisionally," for it would damage the material and spoil the work.

Shape

To guarantee problem-free work, a form is needed. This involves a certain amount of work, of course, but guarantees the best results.

For gluing raw bows, I use a press form two meters long, made of rectangular steel tubing.

On the upper side of this apparatus lies a "wooden coulisse" (of hardwood!), which shows a slight radius in its longitudinal direction. Thus the raw bow takes on a reflex of 35 mm as a reserve against the "set-back."

For the lateral holding of the glued pieces of wood, ten adjustable-height flat irons, their upper ends equipped with adjustable screws, are used.

Figure 49. Middle: Press form for gluing longbows with hickory backing. In the foreground: sister billets. On the wall: bow, ready for tillering.

Set exactly, they prevent the displacement of the wood, which the viscous qualities of the glue make unstable. Such set screws are attached at the top, preventing the glued pieces as well as the pressure blocks from sliding longitudinally.

The application of pressure is done with two blocks (of hardwood!), as noted above, which are padded on their undersides with 20 mm thick rubber.

Six T-irons, welded to the steel tubing on each side, provide the vertical control over these pressure pieces. To transmit an even pressure to the glued material via the pressure blocks, three brackets, with set screws on their tops, are pressed onto each side of the form from above. Through holes bored in the bottom of these brackets, there is the possibility of attaching them under the form with bolts. Held fast in the change, these set screws provide a necessary pressure for a firm gluing.

However this work is done, it is important to make sure that no lateral displacement takes place because of the pressure. An error of this type would bring catastrophic results in the building of a bow. The result would be a displacement (cast) that would be difficult to overcome.

For gluing, as for splicing, Klbit 303 by Kleberit is recommended.

Absolute cleanliness is important! That means that the prepared, smoothed contact surfaces of the woods must be dust-free and degreased with acetone before the glue is applied. They can be touched only with clean gloves.

To prevent the bow from sticking fast to the form, the latter is covered with oiled paper. The glue is applied liberally on both sides with a short-bristled flat brush. During the pressing, the excess glue will ooze out of the joint. At this time the glue bonds completely and develops its optimal qualities.

As for the further building of the bow, we proceed as before. The following measurements of two bows of this type, like the previous examples, can serve as a guide.

Traditional longbow, spliced, with hickory backing
Yew (1984) ca. 35 annual rings/inch
Hickory: 7 mm
Bow length: 74" (1,880 mm)
Draw weight: 62 lb./28"

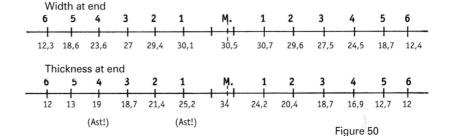

Width at end

6	5	4	3	2	1	M.	1	2	3	4	5	6
12,3	18,6	23,6	27	29,4	30,1	30,5	30,7	29,6	27,5	24,5	18,7	12,4

Thickness at end

6	5	4	3	2	1	M.	1	2	3	4	5	6
12	13	19	18,7	21,4	25,2	34	24,2	20,4	18,7	16,9	12,7	12
		(Ast!)		(Ast!)								

Figure 50

Traditional Longbow, spliced, with hickory backing
Yew (1988): ca. 40 annual rings/inch
Hickory: 4.5 mm
Bow length: 68" (1,727 mm)
Draw weight: 36 lb./27"

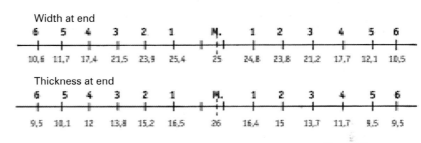

Width at end

6	5	4	3	2	1	M.	1	2	3	4	5	6
10,6	11,7	17,4	21,5	23,9	25,4	25	24,8	23,8	21,2	17,7	12,1	10,5

Thickness at end

6	5	4	3	2	1	M.	1	2	3	4	5	6
9,5	10,1	12	13,8	15,2	16,5	26	16,4	15	13,7	11,7	9,5	9,5

Figure 51

Stringing and Care of Yew Bows

To string finished bows, a two-ply stringer should always be used. Only by this method is absolutely even stress on the two limbs guaranteed during this process.

One should never let a stranger draw a yew bow! A wooden bow is not an expander; it cannot stand that. Every "dry" drawing means a wasted shot! By remembering this advice and generally taking care of a yew bow, it will give good service for years. As for its shooting power, it is slightly below that of a glass-backed longbow with the same draw weight.

Easier to draw and to shoot, it also forgives more. And if it should grow tired over the years, then we simply build a new one!

I hope that by portraying my experiences gained over long years, many a reader will be led to build a bow, for that, among others, was the reason why I organized it and wrote it down.

Ulrich Stehli

Bibliography

Bellwald, Werner: *Aus Archäologie der Schweiz: Drei spätneolithisch/frühbronzezeitliche Pfeilbogen aus dem Gletschereis am Lötschenpass*

Bradbury, Jim: *The Medieval Archer*

Cole, Hector: *The Manufacture of Arrowheads in the Medieval Period*

Duff, James: *Bows and Arrows*

Hardy, Robert: *Longbow, A Social and Military History*

Kucera, Ladislav J.: *Das Holz der Eibe, Schweizerische Zeitschrift für Forstwesen*

Paterson, W. F.: *A Guide to the Crossbow*

Pope, Saxton: *Jagen mit Bogen und Pfeil*

Radatz, Klaus: *Pfeilspitzen aus dem Moorfund von Nydam*

Rahlenbeck, Friedel: *Pfeil und Bogen im steinzeitlichen Skandinavien, Sehnengebrumm 2/1983*

Riesch, Holger: *Journal of the Society of Archer-Antiquaries*, Volume 39, 1996.

Scheeder, Thomas: *Die Eibe, Hoffnung für ein fast verschwundenes Waldvolk*

Wagreus, Erik: *Pilspetsar under vikingatid, Tor 15, 1972/73, p. 191-208*

11

AN ELM LONGBOW
FROM THE MIDDLE AGES

Translated from the Danish by Wulf Hein (in collaboration with Kerstin Wieland and Ole Nielsen)

He will always be there—the man in green with the long bow.

This little description is dedicated to him and to all those who believe in adventure and romance.

Although the High Middle Ages are no more than 650 years behind us, our knowledge of bows and arrows from this time is exceedingly meager. If we include the whole Danish Middle Ages from circa 1050 to 1536, we can determine that the greatest knowledge is in the written sources. Unfortunately, there is nothing about the technical aspects of bows and arrows, but only about their use in many famous battles. There is also data in the displays and records of the armories of those days, as well as in laws and orders as to how a bowman was to be equipped according to the king's command.

Archeologically, there are almost exclusively discoveries of arrowheads that tell of the uses of the weapons, but these are hard to differentiate from crossbow bolts, which confuses the picture in every aspect.

There is no doubt that various bow types were used in the Middle Ages, but the discoveries are extremely rare, especially in Denmark.

Over several centuries, England developed the bow to perfection. In the 13th century, the feared English longbow was a reality, and it only ceased to be used by the military after the year 1600.

But although millions of bows were probably made, only one single bow from the 13th century has been found.

But fortunately for us, the *Mary Rose* sank at Portsmouth in 1545. The craft was a fully equipped warship that met its fate at French hands and thus became a gift for the underwater archaeologists of our times.

Among the thousands of objects that were salvaged in the 1970s and 1980s were numerous bows and arrows.

The "Mary Rose" bows are classic longbows made for war. The various arrows are likewise war arrows. Even though these bows and arrows come from the times when the weapon was already out of fashion, one can assume that they looked the same in the mid-13th century.

The following directions are based on the *Mary Rose* discoveries.

The definition of a longbow is rather difficult, but in the Middle Ages they differentiated between a "longbow" or "hand bow" and a "short bow" or "crossbow." The latter is the name of a bow that rests on a shield (and is called a "Schloss" or "Verschlussbogen" in Old Danish).

Horn tip with string nock

"Bodkin point," a hardened steel point for piercing armor and chain mail

Crossbow bolt point

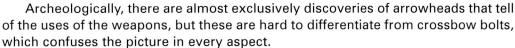

One should not confuse the longbow of the Middle Ages with the traditional English longbow.

They have much in common, but differ in essential ways.

The medieval longbow bends in the handle when it is drawn. The traditional bow does not do that. It has a stiff handle section.

Wing feather of a goose, right wing

The medieval bow was made of yew, but it is not wrong to assume that elm was also used.

The wood in these instructions is elm. (For substitute woods, see also page 17.)

The medieval arrow shafts were made of pine, ash, aspen, birch, etc. The bowstring of the time was made of hemp or flax (linen).

LONGBOWS MADE OF ELM

"A simple beauty without splendor"

The following directions lead, step by step, through the process of building a longbow of elm, as it could have looked in the High Middle Ages.

Felling and Storing Wood

In principle, a tree can be felled regardless of the season, but it seems to me that the winter is the best season for it. Then it is easy to go into the woods, easy to evaluate the individual trunks, and finally, the least sap flows in the tree, which means a shorter storage time.

The trunks for this bow should have a diameter of 8 to 15 cm. Such trees are 12 to 25 years old.

Pay attention to the age of the tree.

Woods that are straight for a distance of two meters, without large branches, dead branches or other flaws, are what we need.

We want to build a nice bow, and for that we seek good wood. Small branches and twigs don't matter so much.

When you find the tree, be critical.

Take your time, walk around it a few times, get to know it before it is felled.

It is a living thing, and there is much medicine in good bow wood. Irresponsible people without respect for nature will never be able to build good bows.

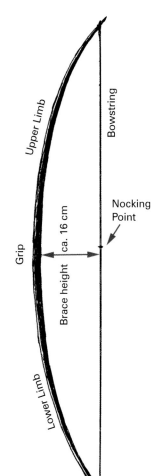

Upper Limb

Bowstring

Grip

ca. 16 cm

Brace height

Nocking Point

Lower Limb

Medieval Longbow

Use a regular "foxtail" saw or bow saw to fell the tree, and cut only as many trees as you are allowed to, or as many as the environment can stand to lose.

A few days, at most, after the tree is felled, the bark should be removed.

Trunks with a diameter of up to about 13 cm can be stored whole; thicker trunks, though, must be split or sawn. Before you do that, think about where to separate the trunk—the best pieces are found when you turn the wood over a few times.

The ends of the wood should be sealed with paint, glue, or the like, and the wood should be stored in an airy place, in the shade, and shielded from rain.

Mark the wood with the date and year, plus the place where it was felled, and then wait at least 7 to 8 months.

The longer the wood is stored within two years, the better it will become.

Unfortunately, there is no other way, but the time can be used for reading books about bows, making bowstrings, or, not least, making arrows.

Foxtail Saw

Bow Saw

PREPARING THE BOW STAVE

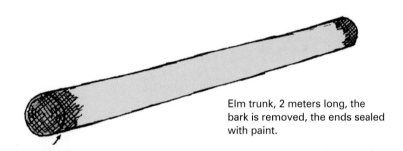

Elm trunk, 2 meters long, the bark is removed, the ends sealed with paint.

Elm Leaf

After storage, take a look at the results. Probably some of the pieces have warped, contracted or cracked—so they are firewood or, at best, a couple of small bows for children. It is good that several trunks were felled.

Naturally, the bow will be laid out on the best side of the trunk.

But before that, it is necessary to quickly review the drawings on pages 18 and 19 (placing the bow in the trunk).

Mark with a pencil immediately where the back should be.

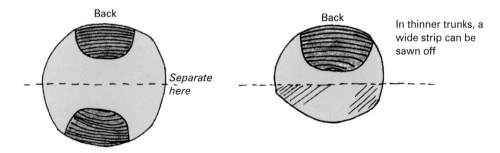

Back

Separate here

Back

In thinner trunks, a wide strip can be sawn off

If the trunk has a diameter of about 13 cm or more, it should be sawn or split. Maybe two bows can be made of it—but don't be too greedy. Better one good bow than two bad ones!

Marking the Stave

As a ruler, you can use a planed piece of pine. Make sure that it is straight before you buy it at the lumber yard.

The bow must not lie crooked on the trunk, but should lie straight, so that the fibers run smoothly in the bow stave without being cut through. Naturally, this does not include the necessary cutting at the ends.

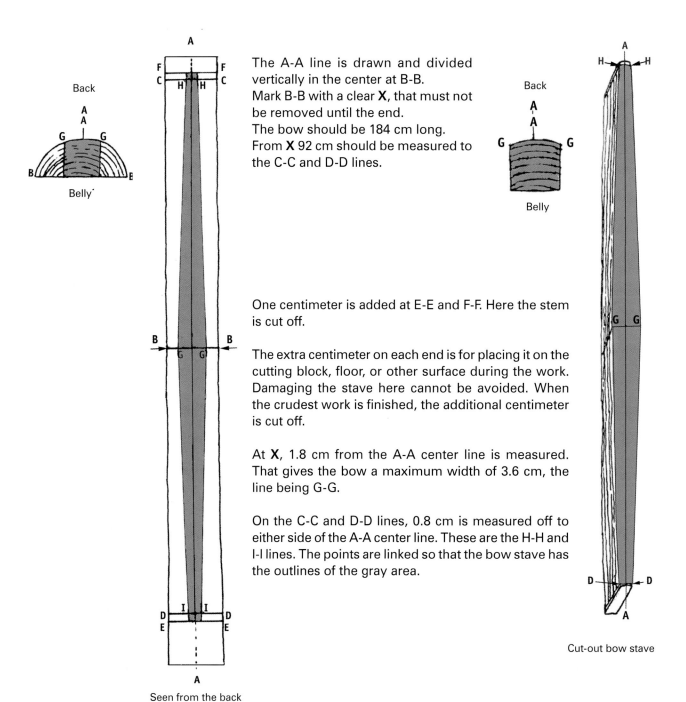

The A-A line is drawn and divided vertically in the center at B-B.
Mark B-B with a clear **X**, that must not be removed until the end.
The bow should be 184 cm long.
From **X** 92 cm should be measured to the C-C and D-D lines.

One centimeter is added at E-E and F-F. Here the stem is cut off.

The extra centimeter on each end is for placing it on the cutting block, floor, or other surface during the work. Damaging the stave here cannot be avoided. When the crudest work is finished, the additional centimeter is cut off.

At **X**, 1.8 cm from the A-A center line is measured. That gives the bow a maximum width of 3.6 cm, the line being G-G.

On the C-C and D-D lines, 0.8 cm is measured off to either side of the A-A center line. These are the H-H and I-I lines. The points are linked so that the bow stave has the outlines of the gray area.

Back

Belly

Back

Belly

Cut-out bow stave

Seen from the back

Please note: The drawing is not to scale!

If you have access to a band saw, you should use it. If not, spit on your hands and grab an axe. Begin the cutting work from below (from the tips of the limbs) and work toward the middle. Then the stave will be turned, etc.—cut off only enough so that the line is still visible. Check often, very often!

It is tremendously important that the sides be parallel and at right angles to the surfaces of the back and belly. Check it, check it, and check it again. For what is once taken off cannot be put back on again.

After a lot of time and trouble, including "spitting on your hands," the stave looks like the right drawing.

But before we can go on to work on the belly, it is worthwhile to take care of knots, bends, and other problem areas in the wood.

Knots, Bends, and Problematic Wood

Before the tree is felled, you have convinced yourself that there are no large branches or big overgrown knots (bulges in the bark) present.

There are big differences in the knots.

Black knots are the dead remains of branches. The dead wood must be scratched away and the rest examined to see whether it is worthwhile to go on working.

"Fresh knots" consist of good, thick wood, and generally cause no problems. Knots from small branches or twigs are of no importance.

Where the knots are located is important. Are they on the back, the sides or the belly?

Are they in the handle area or somewhere out on the limbs?

The best places are around the handle, where the bow is thickest, and preferably on the back. Everything else ranges from "not so good" to "throw it away." The most important rule is: "Never work against the annual rings, but with them."

If you work against them, the axe, plane, or knife goes under the rings and lifts them up.

Then it is always necessary to turn the stave in one direction and the other alternately when you work on knots.

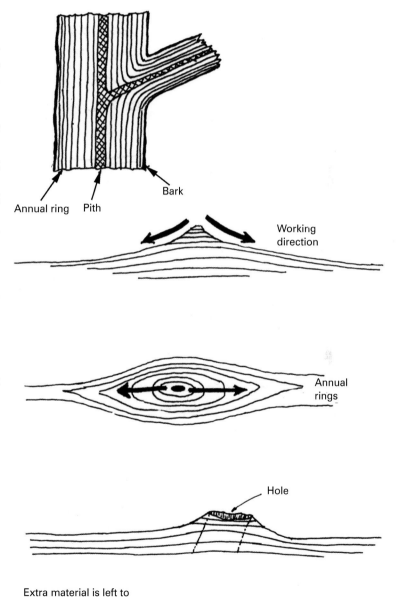

Annual ring Pith Bark

Working direction

Annual rings

Hole

Extra material is left to strengthen the weak spot.

The wood in and around fresh knots is hard and tough. Work slowly and let caution prevail. Dead branches are scratched out to see if it pays to continue.

If it is worthwhile, the hole is bored out and a wooden plug is glued in. Use white glue. The plug should be made out of elm, and the annual rings should run the same way as in the trunk.

Seen from the side

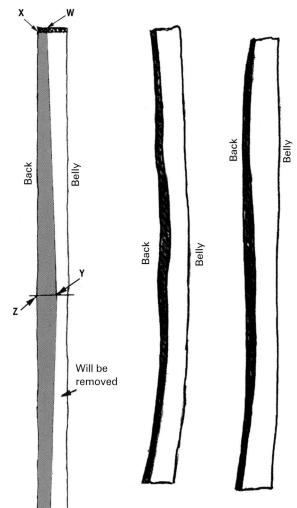

Working out the Bow Stave

Be sure that the **X** mark is now drawn all the way around the stave. It should remain marked throughout the work.

Difficult wood, bends, and the like are often not spotted until the axe suddenly sticks fast in the wood. Do not try to break the wood out, but pull the axe out, turn the stave around, and work from the other side.

That can get on your nerves, but it is one of the many demands that are made on the bow builder. It does not pay to make the wood obey you by force. The bow that lies hidden in the trunk is to be made in cooperation with the wood. The art is in being able to recognize the possibilities.

So have patience, get rest, and take your time. Never work on the bow when you are in a bad mood, or stressed, or have had a few too many beers. That doesn't work. Building a bow is a process—but it is more of a condition.

Now the sides are cut right, and now the belly should be shaped.

On the sides the center line **X** is drawn (it should be marked on both sides).

From point **Z** on the back, measure 4.5 cm down to point **Y**.

At both ends, before the added centimeter, measure 1.6 cm from point **X** on the back down to point **W**. The points are linked, and now the whole thing should look like the gray-colored area.

Everything else is to be removed. Now be careful to check both sides. It is not rare that a stave bends, conforming to the back, as in the two drawings at the right. It is very important that all measurements are made from the back.

You cannot draw the W-Y-W lines with a ruler, but must draw them so that they run parallel to the back.

The bow stave has now been worked down to a "square" stave with a slightly arched back. From here on, the rest should be formed, and now it is important to keep in mind: "Now there is no more waste!" The closer the process comes to the finished bow, the more carefully you must work.

The "work pieces," the extra centimeter at the end of each limb, can now be removed carefully with a fine saw.

The pencil marks that you drew on are all intact, neither cut nor sawn away. The lines on the back can all be removed with an eraser. The **X** line is again drawn all around the staff.

CROSS-SECTION

The next step is working out the cross-section of the bow, which is best done with a cleaning plane with a flat bottom.

To guide the work, do it in two stages.

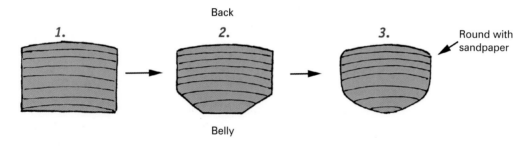

Notice, drawings are not to scale!

The bow stave is finished, 1-3 show the processes. The cross-sections always show the middle of the limbs.

While you give the limbs the right cross-sections, work gently and evenly on both limbs. Thus it is easier to guide and check the process.

As for sandpaper, start with 80-100 grit, followed by 180. When going from the sides to the back, be sure only to "break" the angle by rounding it a little. Make sure that it is not too much.

And think about how the knots are to be handled.

When the whole bow stave has been through the process, remove all pencil marks. Clean up with 180 sandpaper.

Mark **X** again around the entire bow with a steady hand.

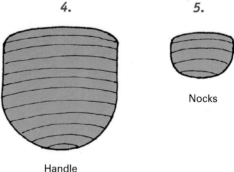

TILLERING

When you can tiller the stave "on the ground," it is time to make the string nocks. Tillering "on the ground" means that when you hold the bow stave in one hand by the end of one limb and put the other end on the ground, you can make it flex by pressing the middle of the bow with the other hand. Push a few times, turn the stave around, and feel the elasticity of the wood.

That is the signal for the next process, called "tillering the bow," which can be explained best as "balancing out" or "trimming" the bow. But first the string nocks have to be made.

String Nocks

Draw the nocks around the bow, as in the drawings.

It is advised that you cut the **X-X** line with a jigsaw, then do the rest with a good carving knife. It should not be too long; the blade should be about 7 centimeters long.

Put a lot of work into the string nocks. Be very careful and round off all the edges. A file doesn't do the job. Sandpaper is much better.

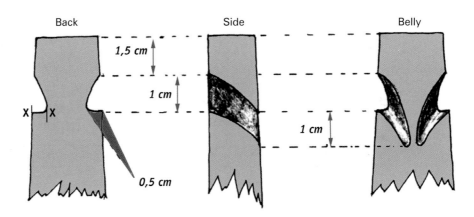

The forming of the ends beyond the string nocks is a matter of taste.

Where the string is supposed to run, all sharp edges must be rounded off with sandpaper. Otherwise the linen-thread fibers will wear through on the sharp edges, and the string will have a very short life.

Now be absolutely sure which is the back and which is the belly.

Do not cut into the back under any conditions. Only the edges between the back and sides may be rounded nicely with sandpaper.

Now we get to tillering, which is the process in which patience, self-criticism, and precision are rewarded and the able worker proves him/herself.

Tillering should mean that the limb will bend nicely and evenly through its entire length; at the same time, both limbs should bend equally strongly and be equally round.

A golden rule, simple bow physics: "Only wood that bends builds up energy."

Wood that doesn't bend is "taking it easy" and causes the bending wood too much stress, finally making it break.

Tillering Stick

An important tool for tillering is one that you can make yourself: a so-called tillering stick, which you can make out of a piece of thin wood.

Be sure that the slot to hold the bow up on the stick fits the dimensions of the handle.

The bow should stay firmly in place during the tillering.

The string is strung on the bow. Use the knots (shown on page 28), since they will need to be untied again and again. The string should remain tight.

The bow is placed on the tillering stick so that the center of the bow is at the center of the stick. Make sure that the angle between the bow and tiller stick is 90 degrees.

Pull the string down to the first attachment and see what happens. Surely not much will, so pull it down to the second one.

Keep going like that until the bow begins to bend. The string has now reached its limit, so take the bow out, shorten the string and begin all over again.

When the bow begins to bend, step back a little and observe the result. You still won't see much, so pull to the next attachment and then to the next until you see where the limbs are bending.

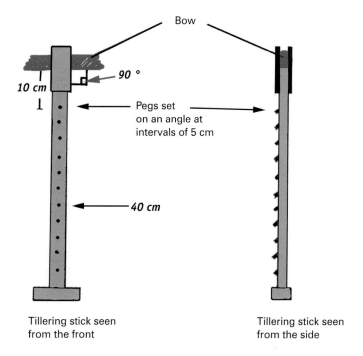

Bow

90 °

10 cm

Pegs set on an angle at intervals of 5 cm

40 cm

Tillering stick seen from the front

Tillering stick seen from the side

Medieval Longbow

A "medieval" longbow bends over its entire length, including in the handle.

When the bow is fully drawn, the limbs form a part of a semicircle.

"Classic English" Longbow

The "Classic" does not bend in the handle. That is stiff. Thus it follows that the limbs must be tillered differently, so that the lower limb remains a little stiffer.

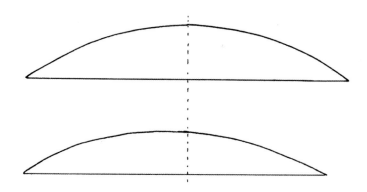

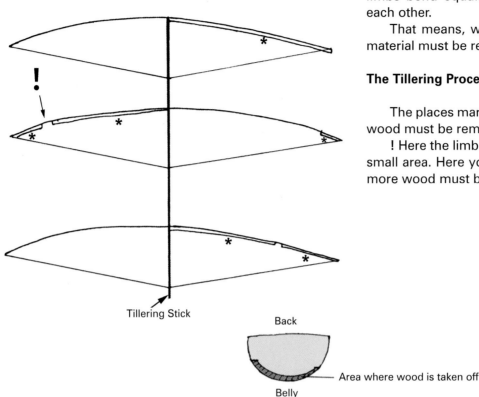

The job is now to make sure that the two limbs bend equally in themselves and with each other.

That means, where the limbs don't bend, material must be removed.

The Tillering Process

The places marked with * are too stiff. Here wood must be removed.

! Here the limb bends quite strongly in one small area. Here you must be very careful. No more wood must be taken off at this place.

Tillering Stick

Back

Area where wood is taken off

Belly

If it is necessary, you can work with a plane, but it is really a job for the draw knife. This is a piece of flat steel with sharp 90-degree angles, which can be used like a scraper. It takes off very fine shavings, which is also necessary, since the work must be done very carefully.

Mark with a pencil where wood should be taken off, take the bow out of the tillering stick, and work with the draw knife.

Observe the bow in the stick and check it. If it has not helped, take off a little more.

This process takes time. Turn the bow, look at it mirror-inverted and think about it. . When the bow is drawn to 40 centimeters, take it out of the tillering stick.

The string can be shortened by moving the bowyer's knot (timberhitch, see page 28) at the lower tip. Don't cut the string. Make a new timberhitch so that the string is 7 cm shorter than the distance between the nocks.

Now take off the string from the upper tip. Fix the bowyers knot tightly and string the bow. (Stringing methods, see page 28.)

The distance from the string to the belly surface of the handle (fistmele) should be 16 cm. Observe your work carefully and critically. If something has to be changed a little bit, that can be done with the bowstring strung. If, on the other hand, it is more inclusive, the bow has to go back to the tillering stick.

How Many Pounds?

When the string is strung, check again and again to make sure the string sits correctly in both nocks. Test the bow by drawing it a little, and feel the strength.

Pull it halfway out, but don't hold it there long. Hold the string firmly and move it slowly back to the bow.

If the bow is too strong, some more wood must be taken off, and equally on both limbs. Make sure that it is still in tiller.

Take off only so much that it is still a little too strong. A wooden bow can lose between 5 and 10% of its draw weight when being shot.

Finishing the Tillering

The work goes on until you shoot the bow or draw it for one or two days. Then it goes back into the tillering stick, in case some changes are still needed. When you can draw the bow all the way, its strength can be measured with a scale.

Finally, the bow should be cleaned with fine (320) sandpaper. For a protective coating, you can chose between shellac, linseed oil, wax, or lacquer.

BORIS PANTEL

Born in 1961, Boris is a development engineer and works professionally with adhesives.

I actually came to archery via technology. A good bow is a component strained to its physical limits. In spite of that, man understood how to attain this perfection thousands of years ago without having modern means of production and analysis at his disposal.

In the end, my goal is not only to make the work of our ancestors usable, but also to understand the details of it.

12

ADHESIVES IN BOW BUILDING

This article is meant for all archers who think about laminating their own bows, want to splice their staves, or need to carry out essential repairs. After I was asked for the Xth time at a tournament whether this or that can be glued and what the best glue to use is, I decided to write down, in a comprehensive manner, all the information that was available to me and that might be of use in our hobby. I also find that it is time to put an end to the secrecy that is still found now and then among bow builders.

After a short historical outline of the origins of adhesives, I must then pester you with a bit of theory. For many contemporaries that is annoying, of course, but important for the better understanding of adhesive conditions and the quality that I can expect from an adhesive. It includes an overview of the adhesives that are relevant to us, whether they are of natural or artificial origin.

Then a few tips and tricks of working with glue, and what dangers arise from them. And finally, a glossary in which the most important concepts are explained again, so that we are all speaking the same language.

HISTORY OF ADHESIVES

Long before man knew of screwing, riveting, soldering and welding, gluing was already done. Gluing is one of the simplest and oldest attaching techniques that mankind knows. The people of the Paleolithic era (80,000–10,000 B.C.) were regarded as the earliest users of adhesives, but according to the newest research at the Doerner Institute for Pigment Research in Munich, it is possible that the Neanderthalers be regarded as such (Staatsministerium für Wissenschaft, Forschung und Kunst Bayern).

In 1963, "resins" from the Neanderthal era were discovered in the central German lignite mines. These discoveries are more than 80,000 years old, and it can be seen that they were formed by hand (fingerprints) and used as an adhesive for stone (silex) blades in wooden handles. In 1999, for the first time, precise analyses were carried out at the Doerner Institute and showed that this adhesive clearly consisted of *birch pitch* (the presence of betulin proves it). This discovery is sensational in the eyes of archaeologists.

For birch pitch is not a product that the first humans picked up somewhere by accident, but one that they must have produced deliberately in a laborious technical process with special implements, such as suitably formed containers. The analyses made at the Institute allowed the conclusion that this adhesive was made out of birch bark without the presence of air and at temperatures between 340 and 370 degrees C.

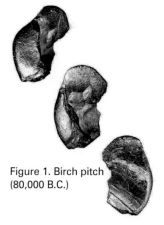

Figure 1. Birch pitch (80,000 B.C.)

The first historical evidence comes from the antique cultures of Mesopotamia, between the Euphrates and Tigris rivers, from the sunken city-states of Sumer, Akkad, Assur, and Babylon (ca. 7000 B.C.). The Sumerians cooked a kind of *gluten glue* out of animal hides, and seem to have used *asphalt* as a means of binding for mosaics as well as in building their houses and temples (Emil Hoffmann, Lexikon der Steinzeit).

It is also to be assumed that at this early point in time, sinew backings for hunting and war bows were already in use, though archaeological discoveries do not exist. Further evidence of prehistoric glue production is found among the Egyptians. From the 18th Dynasty (ca. 3500 B.C.), the use of *skin and bone adhesives* is known. From somewhat later times (1500 B.C.) there also comes the first definite evidence for the use of composite bows by the Egyptians (W. McLeod).

Glue boiling was later taken over by the Greeks and Romans. The Romans expanded the known types of glue by adding fish glue. The fish glues mentioned by the Romans turned up in our latitudes only in the 6th century A.D. At that time they were obtained by cooking fish by-products. Glues for certain uses were made especially from the air bladders of fish.

In the ensuing times of the Early Middle Ages, development in central Europe seems to have stagnated. While the composite technique of making bows was used in China, Japan, and Mongolia, and ever-newer and higher performance was asked of glue, until the 15th century almost no interesting evidence of gluing technology is known to us. Only with Johannes Gutenberg and his invention of moveable letters in printing did the development begin anew. The bookbinder's trade absolutely required a greater amount of special glue for book production.

When the technique of veneering enjoyed a renaissance in the 16th and 17th centuries, a great need for suitable adhesives was born. As a result, the first adhesive factory was founded in Holland in 1690, and the first patent for the production of a carpenter's glue was issued in England in 1754.

Before the final development of artificial resin glues began, the use of *natural latex* as a glue was already common around 1830. With the invention of the vulcanizing of rubber by Charles Nelson Goodyear, his technology experienced another great advance.

The actual origin of *modern adhesives* took place in the late 19th and early 20th centuries. In 1846 cellulose was nitrated for the first time. In 1864, W. Parks was able to produce the semi-synthetic plastic called celluloid. In the thirties, carboxymethyl and methylcellulose were invented for the glue and adhesive market; they are used today as paperhangers' and painters' glue. In short succession, urethane, melamin and phenol resins (bakelite), synthetic rubber such as polychlorophane, buna (polybutadine), and the group of silicon rubbers were developed. Before the war, they were followed by the epoxies and polyurethane, which are produced from the components diisocyanate and various alcohols.

After World War II, the development of adhesives has gone on just as tempestuously. In the fifties, the methylacrylates that harden in the absence of air were discovered, as well as the large group of cyanacrylates, which are based on methyl, ethyl, and butyl ester of cyanacryl acids and harden quickly from moisture in air, being known by the somewhat spongy term "second adhesives." In the sixties, the anaerobic adhesives, closely linked with the name of Loctite, came on the market.

All over the world, a thousand adhesive producers offer a palette of an estimated 250,000 different adhesives and thickeners, and earn a total of about 13 billion Euros a year with them.

THE CONCEPT OF ADHESION

Adhesives are non-metallic materials; they unite bodies by surficial sticking *(adhesion)* between a substance and the adhesive, and the inner firmness of the adhesive itself *(cohesion)*. Adhesives show characteristics that one should always be aware of, so as not to experience any surprises.

They have many **advantages** such as:
- Even distribution of tension and power transmission,
- Binding very different materials,
- Easy attainment of smooth large-surface adhesions,
- Exceeding the tolerances of components with adhesives,
- Good damping qualities,
- Thickening and isolating,
- They can be chosen for specific uses.

Adhesives also have **disadvantages**:
- Limited firmness of adhesives, generally less than the glued components,
- Gluing is always flat binding; where there is no flat surface available, even the best high-tech adhesives cannot work,
- Specific processes are required, which means that gluing allows absolutely no errors,
- Limited thermal resistance,
- Loss of firmness through long-time influences must be considered.

Now let us leave the adhesives alone for a time and look at the first important link in the chain of gluing connections, the glued surface.

QUALITIES OF THE GLUED SURFACE

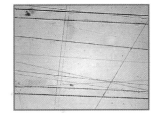

Surfaces are never clean, no matter how clean they seem to us. One finds guaranteed dirt (dust, grease, means of separation), adsorption layers (microscopically thin layers of water, especially on glass-fiber laminates and metals), and oxides (on metals). These layers have a negative effect on the adhesive ability of the surface and the long-time holding of adhesives.

Figure 2. Polished stainless steel (200x)

Along with the condition of the surface layers, the roughness of the surface itself has a major influence. Thus in gluing, one must differentiate between geometric, true, and effective surfaces.

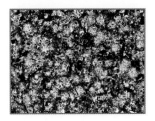

The geometrical surface results from the dimensions of the components, but is fully insufficient for observing adhesion in the molecular realm.

The true surface can differ from the geometrical at a ratio of 2-8, depending on how rough I make my surface.

The effective surface, which cannot be conceived at all in its size, differs from these again, for possible inclusions of air and dirt prevent the use of the true surface.

Figure 3. Radiated stainless steel (200x)

ADHESION AND SURFACE ENERGY

Under the concept of adhesion, one understands the sticking of similar or also different materials to each other. The adhesion has the following causes.

Physical Attraction:
• Dispersion forces, caused by alternating effects of electrons in molecules near the surface of the object and the adhesive,
• Dipole powers, brought forth by electrostatic alternating effects between positively and negatively charged areas of molecules,
• Van de Waal's forces: electrostatic alternating effects through induced dipole moments.

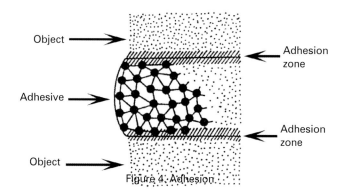

Object →
Adhesion zone ←
Adhesive →
Adhesion zone ←
Object →

Figure 4. Adhesion

Chemical Unions:

• Covalent binding (atomic binding)
• Ionic binding
• Coordinated binding (complex binding, between object and adhesive)

An adhesion that is based only on physical attraction is basically weaker than those that are based on chemical exchange effects.

So that a successful adhesion takes place, it is necessary that the adhesive covers the object as thoroughly as possible. This coating on the surface of an object by the liquid adhesive is the second important link in the chain of processes in an optimal adhesive bond. It depends mainly on the surface energy of the liquid adhesive on the one hand and the surface energy of the object on the other.

Here is the principle: Only when the surface energy of the object is *greater* than that of the adhesive does a bonding occur that is sufficient for the adhesion.

Here, for comparison, are the surface energies of several adhesive and other surfaces:

Material	Surface Energy
PFE (Teflon)	18.5 mN/m (material with lowest known surface energy)
Silicon oil	22 mN/m
Polymethymetacrylate	40 mN/m
Polyamid 6.6	46 mN/m
Epoxide resin	47 mN/m
Water	72.8 mN/m
Aluminum	1200 mN/m
Steel	2550 mN/m

Figure 4. Edge angle measurement

Interesting here is that the epoxide resin with its surface energy (also called surface tension) can only penetrate the water present on the surface of any chosen object very weakly. That means the water must be removed in other ways. The ability of a surface to be coated can be measured by the so-called edge angle measurement. The edge angle is the expression of the varying surface energies between the surface of the object (solid) and the adhesive (liquid).

The greater this difference, the smaller the angle, the better the coating.

182

In many adhesions, the surface energies of the objects and that of the adhesive are not so far from each other as would be desirable; all the more important is the appropriate preparation and cleaning of the surface here.

DIFFERENTIATION OF ADHESIVES

We differentiate first between *organic* and *inorganic* adhesives.

The *inorganics* include, for example, chalk mortar, cement, water glass (natrium silicate), and ceramic casting materials. They remain outside our study, for they have no importance for bow building.

The *organic* adhesives divide into the groups of **physically binding** and **chemically hardening** systems.

The natural adhesives (gluten, casein, fish lime) belong to the physically binding systems, and there to the subgroup of watery adhesive dispersions, to which we shall return later.

All other hardening organic adhesives are basically artificial. There are the macromolecules (polymers), which have come from smaller molecules through chemical reactions. On account of the variety of their chemical structure, they possess very varying technological qualities. From a chemical standpoint, they can be divided crudely as follows:

PHYSICALLY BINDING SYSTEMS
- Adhesives without solvents (melting)
- Ferr-L-Tite, Beman, Pattex, hot glue sticks
- Sticking adhesives (glue bands)
- TESA-Band
- Adhesive solutions
- Easton Fletching Cement, UHU universal adhesive, Arrow Mate
- Watery adhesive dispersions
- Acryllate, White lime (PONAL), natural glues

CHEMICALLY HARDENING SYSTEMS
- Polycondensation adhesives
- Silicon resins, phenol resins, polyamides
- Polymerization adhesives
- Cyanacrylate, methacrylate, anerobic glues
- Polyaddition adhesives
- Epoxide resins, polyurethane

Along with this division, there are also other criteria by which adhesives can be classified. For example, thermoplastic or duroplastic adhesives, single or multi-component adhesives, cold or hot hardening, plus adhesives that have combined hardening mechanisms, such as reactive hot melts (in principle, they are polymerisates), which are applied like melting adhesives and use the moisture in the air to form a coating, but they are of less importance to our uses.

TECHNOLOGICAL PROPERTIES

Here I would like briefly to present the most important groups of adhesives for us in terms of their technological properties, and limit myself to the following groups:
• Melting adhesives
• Solution adhesives
• Natural adhesives: gluten glues, fish glues
• Polymerization adhesives: cyanacrylate, anerobic adhesives
• Polyaddition adhesives: Epoxide resins, polyurethane

Melting Adhesives
Single-component thermoplastic adhesive, that heats (to a molten state) and is then applied.
Advantages: fast binding, problem-free storage, free from solvents, little loss in applying, easy to dispose of, good holding and toughness when struck, always soluble.
Disadvantages: limited temperature resistance, no large surfaces glueable.
Use: arrowheads, repairs.

Birch Pitch (wood tar)
Single-component, based on long-chain hydrocarbons, melting adhesive. In destructive distillation (ca. 300-400 C), the lignin of the material turns into pyrolysed products like wood tar and wood gas (yellowish smoke).
Advantages: One of the oldest known glues (80,000 years), easy to apply, lasts practically forever.
Disadvantages: Not available in the trade in small quantities, so it must be homemade. Little firmness, is unfortunately always "pitch black."
Use: Fletching, attaching heads and blades (especially silex, obsidian, or bone), Stone Age replicas.

Solution Adhesives
Single-component thermoplastic adhesive. The thermoplast is completely dissolved in organic solvents; after application the adhesive evaporates and the glue hardens.
Advantages: Easy to use, easy to spread on surfaces, even problematic surfaces are glueable with this aggressive adhesive.
Disadvantages: Solid portion only 15-25%, evaporating solvent is usually dangerous to health, limited life.
Use: Lacquer for bows and arrows, glue for nocking points, arrow inlays, fletching.

White Glue
Synthetically produced watery adhesive dispersion. The thermoplast PVAC = polyvinyl acetate) is completely dissolved in organic solvent (water), the water evaporates after application and the glue hardens.
Advantages: Easy to apply, no problems with surfaces. White glue is always ready to use, can be stored a long time, and is easy to work. In liquid condition still covered in white, but becomes transparent when hardened.

Disadvantages: Solid portion only 20-35%, normal white glue does not resist water and heat. Watertight modifications are available in the trade, as are some two-component white glues, which have other hardening mechanisms and higher firmness.

Structural gluing with white glue is problematic because of its limited resistance to environmental influences and requires a thorough study of the available data. Normal white glue (such as Ponal) is thus unsuitable.

Note! Not to be put into contact with iron, copper, or aluminum materials. The white glue reacts with a strong color change (to black).

Use: Arrow shafts, handle leather, arrow inlays of wood, stabilizing of leather wrappings.

Gluten Glues

Single-component dispersion adhesives based on long-chained animal collagens (albumen, particularly bindings). As a rule, commercial glues contain only 10-15% moisture, raw glues (plates or flakes) must thus be softened first in lukewarm water before use and then heated. Various additives can favorably influence the water-solubility after hardening.

Advantages: Natural product, generally not poisonous except for some additives, and, of importance to purists, stylistically right and appropriate for your Holmgaard replica.

Disadvantages: Moderate firmness, sometimes takes weeks to dry, sensitive to dampness.

Use: sinew and rawhide backings on longbows and Asiatic cavalry bows, stiffening and fixing string wrappings, gluing of self-nocks.

Above: skin glue as "granulate"; below: bone glue in plate form

Fish Glue

As with the gluten glues, single-component, long-chained collagens, but from fish. The top product of this group is the bladder glue, which is no longer made from the waste products of whole fish, but only from the air bladder of a certain kind (sturgeon).

Advantages: Sometimes much higher firmness than with animal gluten glues, the gluing combinations are comparable with those of modern epoxy resins.

Disadvantages: Except for the firmness of them, as with the gluten glues, fish glue is considerably more expensive than glues made from mammals.

Use: Same as the gluten glues. Notice: taboo for Stone Age bows, as it did not exist then.

Cyanacrylate

Single-component thermoplastic adhesive. In polymerization, *identical* short-chained monomers combine into long-chain polymers. The reaction requires a catalyst that affects the whole; in this case, it is the water, provided by the natural dampness of the air.

Advantages: Very simple to use, sometimes hardens extremely fast (10-30 seconds), also visually clean gluing are possible, high firmness (to 30 N/mn^2). Glue is, as a rule, transparent to clear, meanwhile a great number of modifications, from water-thin to gel-like, are available.

Disadvantages: The polymer is relatively brittle, with little toughness when struck, the hardness reaction is dependent on the dampness of the air, meaning that under 40% humidity nothing happens, poor crack covering, sometimes gives off gases from remaining monomers on the hardening glue, with white precipitate.

Use: arrow inlays, fixing wrapped nocking points, securing string wrapping, emergency repairs.

Anerobic Adhesives

Single-component, duroplastic adhesive. Polymerization reaction as with the cyanacrylics, with the difference that the starting reaction can be released by lack of air and contact with metal (more precisely: alkaline metal surfaces).

Advantages: easy to use, hardening only in the applied area, free of solvents, high firmness, high resistance to temperature.

Disadvantages: little covering of cracks, the polymer is relatively brittle, no metallic surfaces (as with brass, copper, bronze, nickel, and steel) are available, must be used with activators. This applies especially to plain or eloxal aluminum and stainless steel.

Use: screw clamps.

Polyurethane

The group with the most variety in hardening mechanisms. There are one- and two-component systems, thermo- or duroplastic, hardening in moisture, in heat or cold, and watery dispersions. Unlike the polymerisates, two different monomers always react with each other and form the polymer chain.

Advantages: firmness, toughness, elasticity, good use time. All freely usable within certain limits.

Disadvantages: The exact mixing ratio of two-component systems must be followed. Use times limited to 30-45 minutes as a rule. Many modifications cannot stand ultraviolet light.

Use: One- and two-component lacquers for bows and arrows, a few glues are suitable for structural gluing on the bow itself.

Epoxy Resins

Always two-component duroplastic adhesives. As with the polyurethanes, two different monomers react with each other. No remainder of one of the two components should remain. To achieve maximum firmness, it is thus extremely important that the mixing ratio be followed exactly.

Advantages: highest firmnesss (45 N/mn^2), toughness, and elasticity in wide ranges, good adherence to many surfaces, long use times (2-4 hrs) possible, little drying away, free of solvents, cold or hot hardening systems usable.

Disadvantages: Exact mixing ratio necessary, epoxies are sometimes very expensive.

Use: structural gluing on the bow, splicing arrow shafts, gluing tips and arrow inlays, high-value two-component lacquers for bows and arrows.

TRICKS AND TIPS

1. Surface Preparation—Smoothing and Degreasing

As already mentioned, surfaces are never clean. So we must do things to achieve the desired adherence of the adhesive to the surface of the object, so that perfect adhesion between them occurs.

Surfaces generally should be smoothed, not too rough, but not too fine. Sandpaper grades between 100 and 150 generally give the right results.

With metals, it is to be noted that they must be degreased even before smoothing if they show crude dirtiness.

After the surface is smoothed, the dust is removed, best with oil-free blown air. If you don't have that, take a clean, lint-free cloth and wipe the dust off. Then wipe several times with a degreasing solvent.

By **degreasing** solvents I mean:
• Acetone,
• Isopropanol 99% pure,
• MEK (methylether ketone),
• Trichlorethylene and perchlorethylene.
I do **not** mean:
Alcohol, washing benzene, diesel oil, shaving water, or the like.

Sometimes surfaces cannot be smoothed (points, nocks, etc.); then they should be degreased all the more. Note that our solvent degreases but does not dissolve (nocks, arrow inlays, etc.), so test it first.

Figure 6: eloxal surface clean

On eloxal surfaces, smoothing is not normally done, for aesthetic reasons, but they should be thoroughly degreased. In and of itself, the eloxal layer forms an optimal surface for gluing; for reasons of easy application, the layers should usually be degreased or waxed from the work out, so that appropriate advance treatment is still necessary.

Some tropical woods are an exception, as their oil content is so high that any surface degreasing is useless. Here you must play a trick. The wood is smoothed and dust removed, then the surface to be glued is dipped completely in the solvent for several minutes. Thus practically all the oils are dissolved out of the uppermost 1/10 of a millimeter. Let it air briefly and work it right away. By the time the oils have risen to the surface again, the glue has already hardened.

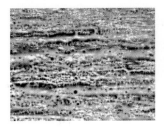

Figure 7: eloxal surface oily

This process can be used with most types of palisander, ebony, cocobolo, bongossi, greenheart, and olive wood.

After the surfaces have been smoothed and degreased, they are not to be touched by bare hands. Every fingerprint and every subsequent befouling have a drastic effect on the adhesion. Besides, even when the glued parts are protected, not too much time should pass between the smoothing and the gluing (maximum 2-3 days).

187

2. Preparing the Object and the Field

Let's be honest; normally chaos rules in the workshop, except when gluing. Dust, dirt, and meter-high stacks of tools and utensils on the workbench dependably prevent the success of our endeavors.

First, the pieces to be glued are put in a safe place, then things are straightened up thoroughly. Now we can begin to set up the equipment that we need for gluing. These include the pieces, the bow form or other rigs, clamps for holding or a pressure line for pressing, an exact scale, one-way gloves, containers for mixing the glue, tools for mixing, solvents, cloths for wiping, a trash can, and the glue.

If you have something big in mind, such as a complicated recurve, the preparation can go so far that the whole process, from putting the laminate in the form to tightening the clamps must first be given a dry run without glue. For as soon as the two components of the glue are mixed, time flies; there is no more going back.

Naturally, this detailed preparation is not always necessary; even I repair a broken tip on my feet. But to create highly firm, lasting gluings in lamination of bows, cleanliness and exact work are essential, and that applies in extended form to all gluings.

3. Mixing the Glue

Before you open the container, you should already have disposable gloves on. They not only protect your hands from aggressive solvents and hardeners, but they also protect the gluing surfaces from your fingers.

In the one-component system, the procedure is simple: put glue on both the glued sides, let it dry if necessary, press them together, clamp them, let the glue harden, and you're finished.

In two-component systems, the resin and hardener have to be mixed in a precise ratio. Precise means precise to the gram here, and that applies to an amount of glue that may be 50 or 100 grams. A small letter scale is necessary for that reason.

As a rule, the mixing ratio is expressed in weight percentages for some glues, but also in volume percentages. Make sure you know in advance what it says in the instructions.

You should also take note of the following four points:

• Mix a little more glue than you think you need. The rest serves as a control, to show whether the hardening reaction is working properly.

• The use time runs from the first contact of the hardener with the resin, and it depends on the quantity of material and the surrounding temperature. Usually, the use time at room temperature (20 degrees C) is stated. So think about that when you work in the garage in the heat of the summer. On the contrary, a low temperature prolongs the use time, and also the hardening reaction. One can say that at temperatures under 15 C you should no longer work with room-temperature guidelines.

• The greater the amount of glue, the shorter the use time becomes (exotherms, self-hastening reactions). With quantities that are too much, 500 grams and more, the adhesive can literally begin to cook. One can make the mixture in one pot, of course, but the mixture must then be divided among several containers.

• Mix the components thoroughly, even though at first they only mix badly; mixing for 2 to 4 minutes is normal.

In closing, one more trick. If the time grows short and the glue is already beginning to solidify (you notice that from a clear increase of viscosity), but you are still not finished, the glue mixture can cautiously be warmed in a water bath. Soon the viscosity decreases again, but the reaction time increases significantly. You can't take more than ten minutes, but perhaps that will be enough.

When the two-component adhesive is mixed, both pieces are coated and pressed together. Then they remain fixed in the form or apparatus until the glue hardens. A special pressure must then be put on them if the pieces do not lie up against each other.

4. Hardening, and What Comes Next

A new day, a new joy. The workshop is locked up and the tension becomes immeasurable. Is the gluing working, has the glue hardened?

Now you make use of the remaining glue that was left over the day before. With it you can test whether the hardening reaction appears to have gone correctly. The stuff should be hard as stone now. But be careful! Usually, epoxy resins attain some 60% to 80% of their hardness at room temperature after 24 hours. Normal procedure with the parts is thus not an issue, but checking the just-formed bow for full drawing is.

In heat-hardening, everything is clear after the stated hardening time, for example, just about 100% after three hours at 90 degrees C. This applies to polyurethanes and epoxy resins equally.

For those that harden at room temperature (epoxies, polyurethanes), you can now do what the specialist calls tempering. In the case of adhesives, this means subsequent warming to some 50-75 degrees C to attain a late bonding of the adhesive.

The molecular chains don't become longer this way, but the links between the individual chains become more numerous. Firmness and toughness increase. Tempered resins generally have greater firmness than those that harden only at room temperature, and also the advantage of not having to put the form or apparatus in the oven.

So that's the essence of the work. Now quickly clean up the workshop and put the glue away. But wait, stop, stop!

189

There are More Points to Consider

• Adhesives, as a rule, have a limited lifetime, and this is to be kept in mind, especially in very firm adhesions. The expiration date is given in the instructions and usually even on the wrapper; it is normally one year after manufacture. That does not mean that the adhesive is unusable after this period, but only that the manufacturer no longer guarantees it for the stated firmness and other parameters after that time. Despite that, "aged wine" glues that are ten years old and more should no longer be used for structural gluing.
• The environment has much influence on the firmness. Adhesives are to be stored as dry and cool as possible—not frozen in the deep-freeze drawer, but a cool place in the cellar is ideal. Moist warmth is an absolute pestilence and ruins every adhesive in a very short time.
• Most hardeners of epoxies and polyurethanes are hygroscopic. That means that they attract moisture like cooking salt and are then no longer useful. Thus you should also make sure that the binding of the still-present quantities of resin and hardener is not too great. It's better to fill a small container, so that as little air as possible is enclosed.
At this point we must talk again about the dangers in working with adhesives. No finger-shaking, but a few rules that are sensible and easy to follow. They don't harm the gluing, and they do protect your health.

WORKING WITH ADHESIVES
Rule 1 "Thou shalt not eat glue with a spoon." That means don't swallow any glue or rub it in your eyes. Avoid any skin contact as much as possible, for except the natural adhesives, **all** glues are poisonous and dangerous to your health. Therefore:
Rule 2 Wear gloves whenever possible to protect yourself and use the glue. The reason is that all epoxies and polyurethanes are addictive, meaning that you can acquire an allergy in time. Especially aggressive organic solvents, hardeners with free polyamines and the diisocyanate compounds of the epoxies and polyurethanes are critical in this respect.
Rule 3 "Thou shalt not stick thy trunk into the pot." Don't open containers and wrappings under your nose, and provide good ventilation as much as you can.
Rule 4 Unhardened adhesives are special garbage in principle; they don't belong in the trash can. Hardened adhesives, on the other hand, are no problem, and you can discard them normally.
Rule 5 Food and glue cannot stand each other. All organic solvents and many components of hardeners or resins dissolve grease and get into foodstuffs. So don't leave a sandwich lying around when you glue your bow or fletch your arrows.

SELECTED ADHESIVES FOR STRUCTURAL GLUING

Scotch-Weld 9323 B/A   Made by: 3M

Scotch-Weld 9323 is a tough, elastic two-component construction adhesive that hardens at room temperature. It was developed for gluing metals like aluminum and steel and a great many artificial and combined materials such as GFK and CFK laminates. Characteristics include, little tendency to flow; highest shearing, scaling, and striking firmness in the temperature range from -55 C to +120 C; and good stability against oils, propellants, and moist warmth. When mixed, 9323 B/A has an opaque (not transparent) pink coloring. In the use of transparent laminates, care must be given to an exact division of adhesion, since the adhesive will otherwise show color changes.

Scotch-Weld 9323 B/A	Basis	Hardener
Color	white-coated	red-orange
Chemical basis	mod. epoxy resin	mod. polyamine
Consistency	thixotrope paste	gel-like
Viscosity at 20 degrees C	1,500,000 mPas	150,000 mPas
Specific gravity	1.15 g/cm³	1.05 g/cm³
Portion of solid bodies	100%	100%
Mixing ratio, weight	100 parts	27 parts

Attainable firmness according to DIN53283		42 N/mm³
Use time	25-gram mixture	2.5 hours
	130-gram mixture	2.0 hours
	160-gram mixture	1.0 hour
Hardening time: 48 hrs at 25 degrees C or 2 hrs at 65 degrees C		
Firmness increase at room temperature:	after	
	6 hours	10%
	8	30%
	12	40%
	24	70%
	48	80%
	15 days	100%

Araldite AW 106 (basis) / HV 953 U (hardener) also Araldite 2011   Made by Vantico

Araldite AW 106/HV 953 U is a tough, elastic two-component construction adhesive that hardens at room temperature. It was developed for gluing metals like aluminum and steel and a variety of artificial and combined materials like GFK and CFK laminates. Characteristics include, little tendency to flow; high shearing, scaling, and striking firmness in the temperature range from -50 C to +80 C; and good chemical stability. In a mixed condition, the adhesive has a whitish transparent color, which makes it especially suitable for gluing transparent laminates.

Araldite AW 106/HV 953 U	Basis (AW 106)	Hardener (HV 953 U)
Color	cream-white, transparent	yellowish transparent
Chemical basis	mod. epoxy resin	mod. polyamine
Viscosity at 20 degrees C	40,000 mPas	30,000 mPas
Specific gravity	1.20 g/cm	1.0 g/cm³
Portion of solid bodies	100%	100%
Mixing ratio, weight	100 parts	80 parts

Attainable firmness according to DIN53283		25-30 N/mm²
Use time:	25-gram mixture	3.0 hours
	130-gram mixture	2.0 hours
	160-gram mixture	1.0 hour
Hardening time: 15 hours at 20 degrees C or 50 minutes at 70 degrees C		
Firmness increase at room temperature:	after	
	6 hours	50%
	10	70%
	15	80%
	48	100%

UHU-Plus Endfest 300   Made by: Henkel

UHU Endfest 300 is a tough, elastic two-component construction adhesive that hardens at room temperature. It was developed for gluing metals like aluminum and steel and a variety of artificial and combined materials. Characteristics include, little tendency to flow; high sharing, scaling, and striking firmness at temperature ranges from -40 C to + 80 C; and good chemical stability. In a mixed condition, the adhesive has a whitish transparent color, which makes it especially suitable for gluing transparent laminates.
The advantage of UHU-Endfest 300 is its transparency and utility on small glueings (ca. 20g). But if its usual sales price is reckoned by the kilo, you find that this product is 2 to 3 times more expensive then the presently best hi-tech adhesive.
For structural adhesion, UHU-Plus Endfest should also be tempered at ca. 120-130 C for 20 minutes.

UHU-Plus Endfest 300	Basis	Hardener
Color	whitish opaque	yellowish transparent
Chemical basis	mod. epoxy resin	mod. polyamine
Consistency	tough liquid paste	honey-like flowing
Viscosity at 20 degrees C	50,000 mPas	25,000 mPas
Specific gravity	1.20 g/cm	1.0 g/cm³
Portion of solid bodies	100%	100%
Mixing ratio, weight	100 parts	100 parts

Attainable firmness according to DIN53283		12-30 N/mm²
Use time:	5-gram mixture	120 minutes
	20-gram mixture	100 minutes
	100-gram mixture	90 minutes

Temperature	Hardening Time	Stability
20 degrees C	12 hours	1,200 N.sq. mm
40	3	1,800
70	45 minutes	2,000
100	10	2,500
180	5	3,000

Stability increase at room temperature:	after	
	6 hours	50%
	12	70%
	24	80%
	48	100%

Birch Pitch (wood tar)

It occurs in the absence of oxygen and application of heat in a range between 340 and 420 degrees C. Both the so-called pit-kiln and double-pot procedures are of historical significance. They differ very little technologically. Since birch pitch, as far as I know, cannot be had in the trade, the devout archer is compelled to produce it himself.

In the double-pot procedure, two earthen containers are buried in the ground, one above the other. Over a small pot, which later serves to catch the pitch, is a somewhat larger pot, perforated at the bottom, which is heated by fire all around. The birch bark or similar resin-rich wood is placed. To avoid cracking, the lid is normally fitted with a protective layer of lime (*Lutum sapientiae*). As the temperature rises, the bark begins to give off gas, since the tar steam cannot escape through the lid, it goes through the holes in the bottom into the lower pot, which is considerably cooler from the soil around it, and finally condenses on its walls.

The quantity depends essentially on the temperature; if it is too low, nothing or very little condenses. If it is too hot, the back burns to ashes in the pot, and the valuable pitch in it is destroyed.

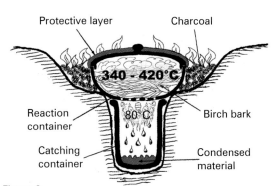

Figure 8
Double-pot procedure

In a simpler method, the lower pot is eliminated. The lid has a small hole, so that no excess pressure can build up, and instead of burying it in the ground, you use your garden grill. Charcoal is ignited (no flames), and so the steam cannot condense so well here, the process must be interrupted after a short time (10-15 minutes).

The pitch obtained is scraped from the bottom and sides with a wooden spatula; then you repeat the process until the bark is all used up. For this process, it is best to use Mother's best metal cooking pot (ca. 20-25 mm thickness), with a lid that closes very well (weight it if necessary), or that comes far down on the pot (inverted lid). Here too, constant watching is recommended; check the temperature with an exhaust-gas thermometer (available at home improvement stores) and check how near the owner of the pot is.

In technical terms, birch pitch is a molten adhesive (physical binding system > solvent-free adhesive. Ferr L-Tite, Beman, Pattex hot glue sticks, etc.).

The work amounts to the following:
• Bring the adhesive to a melting temperature with a candle,
• Also warm the obsidian or bone point briefly,
• Apply the adhesive,
• Stick the objects together,
• Let it cool and it is finished.

As with all hot adhesives, water is the best means of separation. So be especially careful that the objects are dry. On the other hand, the adhesive can be shaped very well with wet fingers without sticking to you.

Natural Adhesives

Gluten or fish glues are made by first softening the scales or plates in lukewarm water. The time thus depends on the size of the particles and takes 2 to 4 hours. For this reason, plates should be made much smaller in advance, so as not to require too much time.

Only when the raw glue has fully emerged is it carefully heated. Remember that the glue must not be heated over 60 degrees C, so as not to destroy the egg-white chains. Normally an enameled steel or stainless steel pot is used for heating. If uncoated iron or copper is used, major color changes can occur.

The viscosity is affected by adding water or cooking slowly, and is a matter of experience (ca. 25-30% solid content). The flowing ability of normal artificial resin paint is a reference point. If our glue runs from the brush at about the same rate, the viscosity is about right.

The unbinding time depends strongly on the water content of the glue (viscosity) and the composition of the basis. Rule of thumb: if the glue in the pot has attained the toughness of leather, the glue layer should have been dissolved, too. This can extend over weeks and months, so don't be impatient.

Two recipes for reducing the water-solubility after unbinding:

GLUTEN GLUE

Skin or bone glue (plates or flakes)	100 parts
Water	200 parts
Urea	8 parts
Glycerine	8 parts

FISH GLUE

Fish glue (plates or flakes)	100 parts
Water	10 parts
Benzoic acid	0.22 parts
Methyl alcohol	0.75 parts
Boiling water	8 parts

Photo: Cooker with pot in pot; gluten glue is best tempered in a water bath.

I hope you find this little introduction to adhesive technology interesting and helpful in evaluating the adhesives as to their uses and properties.

In general, the first rule of adhesives was introduced in the New Stone Age and has never been changed. It is:

Glue sticks best
To your hands
To your vest,
To your pants!

With adhesive greetings, Boris Pantel

GLOSSARY OF ADHESIVES

Accelerator: Substance that, in slight concentration, increases the speed of a chemical reaction. The use time and hardening time are thus shortened.

Activator: Chemical substance that can induce chemical reactions which would not occur without it. Unlike catalysts, activators take part in the chemical reaction.

Adhesion: Sticking power between the surfaces of two objects. In a gluing, the adhesion describes the sticking power between the object and the adhesive.

Adhesion Breaking: Failure of adhesion on the surface between the glued object and the adhesive. In such a process, the adhesive has loosened from the object's surface. This indicates insufficient surface preparation.

Airing: Pre-drying of an applied solvent or dispersion adhesive by partially dampening the substance.

Binding: Setting the adhesive surface of physically binding adhesives. It involves processes like cooling (stiffening) or steaming of the substance. No chemical processes occur.

Cleaving Space: Space between the pieces to be glued, filled as completely as possible with glue. The spaces depend on the glue and generally measure 0.02 and 0.3 mm.

Cohesion: The binding force in the glue itself. The cohesion describes the bonding of molecules and is composed of intermolecular attracting forces and purely mechanical cohesion of the polymer chains.

Cohesion Breaking: Failure of adhesion in the glue itself. In such a breaking process, the adhesion of the glue to the glued surface remains successful. In most gluing, cohesive breaking behavior is sought.

Contact Cement: Adhesive that acts as Newtonian fluid and attains a comparatively unspecific adhesion (like a kind of suction) on non-porous surfaces in this relatively highly viscous state. The adhesion results from reversible physical adhesive forces. Typical adhesives of this kind are used for sticking bands.

Contact Medium: Usually highly thinned solution of basic materials of adhesives used afterward to improve adhesion and/or long-term stability. Every adhesive needs its own special medium. *See also Primer.*

Exotherm: Physical or chemical processes that occur under release of energy (usually release of heat).

Filler: Inorganic or weakly flowing organic additive to adhesives, filling materials, such as ground quartz, chalk, soot, metal powder, glass fibers, etc. The purpose is the increase in viscosity, hardness, firmness, stiffness, decrease of shrinkage, improvement of stability, electric or heat conducting ability.

Final Stability: Maximum attainable firmness that an adhesive can attain under normal conditions. The values, sometimes given in data sheets, are based on precise comparison of all parameters.

Gas Discharge: A form of exhaust behavior which occurs in the hardening of Cyanacrylates. Slightly liquid adhesive components give off gas and precipitate as a whitish matter beside the point of adhesion.

Glass Transition Time: Temperature range that characterizes the transition in high-polymer artificial substances (like adhesives) from a less elastic, stiff, firm state to an elastic, less stiff and firm state. *See also Softening Temperature.*

Hand-firmness: Firmness that allows further work on a glued piece without additional fixing. The adhesive is not yet quantitatively hardened at this point.

Hardener: Adhesive component that effects chemical hardening by polycondensation, polymerization or polyaddition. In German two-component adhesives, this means accelerating the B components, the A component being the means of binding. In British or American adhesives, it is just the opposite. The accelerator is the A component, the binder the B component.

194

Hardening: Adhesion of the glue layer of chemically hardening adhesives such as epoxies, phenol, polyurethane, or silicon resins, whereby the cohesive powers occur. It depends on irreversible chemical processes.

Hardening Time: Length of time in which the adhesion with chemically hardening adhesives has attained a specific necessary firmness after contact, and chemical reactions no longer occur.

Loosening: Failure of adhesion outside the gluing surface. In such a break, the firmness of the adhesion is greater than the inherent firmness of the material of the object.

Mixing Ratio: Relation by weight or volume, in which components A and B of an adhesive must be mixed to attain optimal results.

Monomer: Small molecules, existing alone, that represent the building blocks of the resulting macromolecules (polymers). According to their structure, the formation of the polymer occurs through polycondensation, polymerization, or polyaddition.

Networking: Properties of an adhesive to fit into molecular dimensions of the contours of a surface. The tendency increases with decreasing surface energy (surface tension) of the adhesive. The goal is to attain the greatest difference between the surface energy of the adhesive (small) and that of the glued object (great).

Post-bonding: Reactions usually improved by warmth, which complete the actual hardening, which is cut off at room temperature and cannot continue, via remaining not-yet-reacted molecule parts.

Primer: Strongly thinned (5-20%) solution of the adhesive, which is applied to fresh surfaces of objects. It completely networks the surface and thus causes additional protection from uncleanness. It also improves the adhesive properties and slows aging processes.

Resin: Technological collective term for solid or tough fluid organic non-crystalline products. In the adhesive industry, epoxies, polyurethane, and Polyester resins are known.

Shrinkage: In the formation of polymers there is, because of the chemical hardening reaction, a volume decrease of the adhesive.

Skin Formation: Strengthened reaction of an adhesive from outside influences, which can be moisture in PUR adhesives or oxygen in methacylanth-containing adhesives. Through the formation of skin, the networking of surfaces is prevented by the adhesive. The pieces must thus be in contact before the skin building occurs.

Softening Temperature: The softening behavior of thermoplastic materials. At this point their mechanical properties, such as firmness, change dramatically. The softening range, as it might better be called, is about 40 to 60 degrees C.

Structural Adhesion: Adhesion that provides the essential contribution to the securing of the function of a component in a technical adhesion.

Surface Energy or Tension: Properties of solid bodies and liquids of making their surfaces as small as possible (in solids this is not possible, though they obey the same laws). Liquids try to make their surface into a spherical form. The best-known example is mercury, which forms spherical drops because of its very high surface energy.

Surface Picture: Appearance of the broken surfaces in an adhesion. It lets one see whether errors were made in gluing or the glue is very aged.

Tempering: Warming to make the adhesive network subsequently and remove inner tensions.

Use Time: Extent of time in which an adhesive can be used after mixing. It depends on the speed of the polymer formation and the external conditions, and should be followed strictly.

Viscosity: Criterion for describing the flowing ability (fluidity) of a substance (Pascal Seconds). In the literature, mPas (milli-Pascal seconds) is used. A small value describes a thin liquid, low-viscosity substance such as water (1mPas), a high value indicates a thick fluid. Highly viscous substances such as an epoxy resin are 170,000 mPas.

THE AUTHOR

ACHIM STEGMEYER

Born in 1960, Achim is a trained motor vehicle locksmith. He got into traditional archery in 1987 and began in the same year to make his first self-taught bow-building experiments.

Since 1989 he has sold his bows; since 1995 he has earned his living as a bow builder. The highest handcrafting quality, aesthetics, and best performance qualities are his inspiration and goal. Thus he puts great value on the praise and recommendations of his customers.

THE LAMINATED BOW

Producing a bow of laminated construction is a relatively modern way of building a bow. Today it involves the gluing of several thin layers of wood between two layers of fiberglass, whereby a preformed piece of heartwood, which formed the handle area, is also glued in.

All the components (wood strips, fiberglass strips, handle) are glued together in one work process in a special bow form. The essential advantages of this kind of bow building are the relatively "simple" construction, the endurance, permanent pulling power, and very good performance of the bow, and the many possible variations of bow wood and bow design.

Since the job of producing a glued, layered bow is the same for all models (longbow, flat bow, recurve), I shall describe just the building of one bow below. First, though, let me describe the different materials that are used for it.

LIMB WOODS

The most important properties for optimal limb wood are high elasticity, high bending firmness, high shearing firmness, low weight, and good gluing properties. There are great numbers of wood that are suitable for laminated bows, of which I'll state just the most important here: bamboo, yew, Osage orange, elm, locust, mountain maple, ash, walnut, hickory, and cherry.

Yew, bamboo, Osage orange, locust and elm, according to my experience, rank among the best limb woods, and I prefer yew and bamboo. They are somewhat lighter in weight, thus they cause less hand shock and allow greater arrow speed.

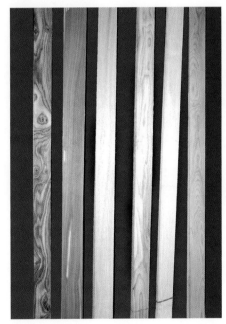

On the other hand, bows made of Osage orange, locust, and elm have very good shooting performance for heavy arrows, are very robust and enduring, and very insensitive to temperature changes.

In recurve bows, very high shear pressures occur in the limbs, for which reason one chooses a wood here that is equal to them.

These include the mountain maple, which thus ranks among the most often-used wood for recurve bows. But in my opinion, it also has commercial reasons why it is preferred for use in recurve bows. These are: good drying properties, good machine workability, little spoilage, good gluing characteristics, and good lacquering ability because of its fine pores. And it is inexpensive and easy to obtain.

I personally use it very seldom and prefer Osage, locust, or elm, since they are just as shear-resistant but have an attractive appearance under clear fiberglass and allow faster shooting. The other listed woods are medium-weight woods, from which one can also make good bows.

I recommend that the beginner in bow building try maple or ash first. These woods are easy to obtain, somewhat less expensive, and produce very satisfactory bows, normally not so fast and comfortable, but very enduring and robust.

Figure 1. Tapered wood strip

To make a bow limb as efficient as possible, it is advantageous to taper the individual wooden strips, which means making them steadily slimmer. This considerably decreases the mass of wood.

One can surely leave these strips parallel, and thus with the same thickness from one end to the other, but such a bow would produce more hand shock, a less even drawing performance, and would also shoot less quickly.

How much the wood should be tapered always depends on the bow design. It is best to carry out a few tests. In my own bows, the difference between the thickest and thinnest points of the limbs of a recurve is about 2 to 3 millimeters, and ca. 3-5 mm for a longbow. This always depends on the strength of the reflex and the length and width of the limb.

It is true of all woods that they should be air-dried, and the longer they are stored, the better (some 6-7% wood moisture). The wood should naturally be as faultless as possible, straight-grained, branch-free, and without cracks.

HANDLE WOOD

In the choice of handle wood, it is important that it be very hard, heavy, and thick. There is a wide variety of good-looking, variously colored hardwoods available from well-supplied wood dealers, for example, ebony, rosewood, Brazilian rosewood (bocote), kingwood, purple heart, snakewood, cocobolo, olive, to name only a few of the nicest and heaviest, but also most expensive, types.

Bubinga, red paduk, wengé, or zebrano are also very hard, but a little lighter in weight and lower in price.

Here you have all kinds of wood combinations, and even a handle piece of glued layers is possible.

Caution is always urged with very oil-rich woods, since this can cause problems with the glue adhesion (wood must be well degreased on the gluing surfaces; see also the previous chapter about adhesives).

FIBERGLASS LAMINATES

Fiberglass is a modern composition material that has been used in bow building since the 1940s. Countless one-direction glass fibers (about 70% in the longitudinal direction) bedded in epoxy resin produce an extremely flexible material, though only in the direction of the fibers.

Fiberglass is made transparent and in colors (black, white, brown, green, gray, red), and in various lengths, widths, and thicknesses. I recommend exclusively transparent fiberglass, through which the wood can be seen, and through which I can see whether my gluing work has turned out well.

This glass, made especially for bow building (Gordon Bo Tuff), can be obtained from the USA through several wholesalers (Bingham Projects and Old Master Crafters). Many types can also be obtained from various ski manufacturers. I personally use Bo Tuff from the USA, in 0.8, 1, 1.2, and 1.5 mm thicknesses, and in various lengths and widths.

ADHESIVES

Two-component epoxy resin is surely the best material to stand the high stress of a bow. These adhesives are available from various dealers, with various mixing conditions and properties.

Most of them can be used well and have a very long "open time" of about one hour before they begin to harden. When you use them, pay strict attention to the directions.

These adhesives can generally be obtained where fiberglass is available.

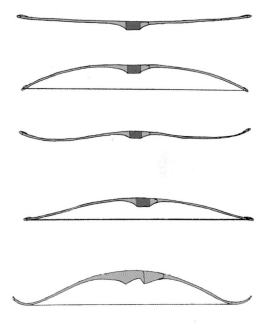

THE BOW DESIGN

Longbows, flat bows, and recurves can be made in a variety of lengths and designs. Finding the right bow for yourself is a matter of personal needs and preferences, and depends on your own shooting style. As a rule, a shooter with a short draw, who likes to go hunting or to "hunting-like" tournaments, will gladly use a short bow, but if he has a long draw, he would rather have a longer bow or a recurve.

Example: When a shooter has a draw of 26-27 inches, he could choose a flat bow with a length of 58-62 inches, a longbow of 64-66 inches, or a recurve of 56-60 inches. These standard values naturally vary for different versions.

The shorter bow offers more freedom of movement in the field, is very fast, but requires good shooting.

The longer bow shoots more quietly and forgives shooting mistakes, but is sometimes a hindrance in the field. Before you decide in favor of one type of bow, you should get good experience with all types of bows, since the practical impression can be perceived very differently.

Note: A straight bow is simplest to build. A bow with reflex-deflex or a recurve bow, on the other hand, is much more trouble to build.

THE BOW FORM (GLUING FORM)

The bow form is the basic need for a laminated bow. Since all components are glued to each other on this form at the same time, the later bow will exactly represent this form.

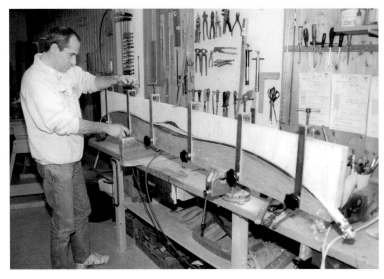

Adjusting the bow form

This form should be made of plywood (multiplex or beech plywood) or of metal, and wood is generally less expensive to obtain and simpler to work. With forms made of a single grown piece of wood, there is a danger that it may warp during the high temperatures involved in the gluing process.

To prepare the gluing form, you first cut the bow contour onto millimeter graph paper and transfer the whole thing to a piece of multiplex board. (Dimensions for longbows: 4 cm thick, 15 cm high, and some 10 cm longer than the overall bow)

After cutting out the contour with a band saw, grind down the raw surface completely to measure on an angle-grinding machine. If you have no such machine, you can ask a carpenter. Make sure that the whole form is completely angled correctly and has no uneven spots.

It will go even better and quicker with a stencil of 5 mm thick plywood. Using this contour, trace the whole thing on a piece. Finally, sand the form slightly and finish it with PU lacquer.

There are various ways of pressing the laminate layers into the form. One is the use of screw clamps (Figure 2).

Screw clamp

Pressure wood
Pressure plate
1-1.5 mm

Pressure rubber
8 mm thick

Bow laminate

Rubber hose

Multiplex
bow form
(one piece)

Figure 2 Bow form with screw clamps

Another is a compressed air clamp (Figure 3 and photo at left). I personally prefer the compressed air method, because the pressure is divided completely evenly. The whole apparatus is also not too heavy, since you need several clamps for the clamp method.

The upper half of the two-piece form can be made out of full wood or be glued together out of two or three carpenters' plates.

The surfaces of the form, on which the components lie, can still have thin rubber (such as old cut-up bicycle tubes) glued onto it, which evens the pressure out better.

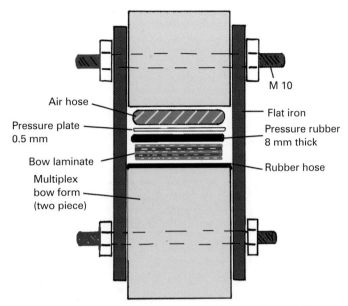

M 10

Air hose

Pressure plate
0.5 mm

Bow laminate

Multiplex
bow form
(two piece)

Flat iron

Pressure rubber
8 mm thick

Rubber hose

Figure 3. Two-piece
compressed air clamp.

THE WARMING BOX

Most epoxy resin glues attain their greatest firmness when they are brought up to a certain temperature. This varies from one manufacturer to another.

So you build yourself a big box, in which you can place the whole bow form comfortably and warm it at the same time.

To warm it, use four or five light bulbs of 150 watts each, which can be controlled by a preset thermostat. The whole thing is placed in the lower part of the box, and the inside of the box will also be coated with reflective material, so the warmth will spread evenly.

For the professional bow builder, electrically operated flexible heating plates will also be useful; they can be used directly in the bow form. Thus you also save the space for the big warming box.

Figure 4. Warming box with bow form

THE ACTUAL BOW-BUILDING PROCESS

The measurements for the following description apply mainly for a longbow 66 inches long, with some 50 to 55 pounds of draw, with two-inch reflex and 3/4-inch deflex. In principle, though, the description applies to all laminated bows.

Handle

We are seeking a piece of handle wood and trimming it to the dimensions of 1.5" x 1.5" x 18" (4 cm x 4 cm x 46 cm), and marking the handle section by the standing annual rings.

Figure 5. Handle

Standing annual rings

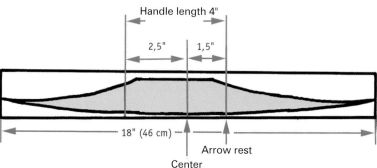

After that, saw the handle out crudely and polish it so that it fits perfectly into the bow form.

Make sure that the fadeout (thinning) tapers very smoothly, becomes paper-thin, and is all at the right angle.

Limbs

For the limbs, three pairs of precisely measured wooden strips measuring 92 cm by 0.5 cm (36" x 1.5") are used; they must now be tapered from 3.4 mm at the thick end to 1.8 mm at the thin end.

Figure 6. Wooden strips are glued together

After that, two pieces, each 182 cm long, are made of two strips, each 92 cm long, by simple splicing (at the thick end).

202

The fiberglass strips have strips of adhesive paper glued onto the outside, which protects the glass, and you see the later marking lines better on it. One of the glass strips gets cut into two halves, since they, along with the two shorter wooden strips, will be glued onto the inside of the bow (the belly of it), where they are interrupted by the handle.

Now you clean all the glued joints with thinner or acetone. For any dirty spots of grease or dust on the gluing surfaces interfere with the best possible gluing, which can lead to delamination or breaking of the bow.

The individual components before gluing

The Gluing

Now you mix the appropriate amount of epoxy resin glue and carefully spread it on all (!) gluing surfaces.

After that, the components are placed in the bow form, which is lined with plastic wrap and fixed with adhesive strips so it cannot slip. You must make sure that the centers of the form and handle piece match up exactly with each other.

When the pressure components, like the air hose, rubber, sheet metal, and the upper half of the form, are fixed and screwed in place, you slowly apply pressure to the hose until you have reached some 6-7 bar, and then put the whole form into the warming box.

At about 70 degrees C, the glue has harden after 3 to 4 hours, and you can take the raw bow out of the form after it cools.

Now the excess glue can be removed (careful—sharp edges).

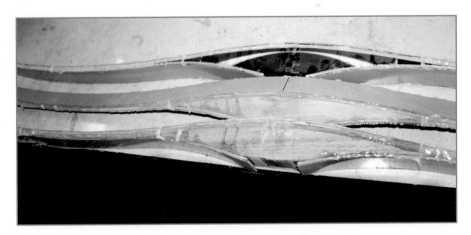

Finished glued bow blanks with remnants of glue.

Bow Dimensions

The center lines are marked on the back of the raw bow for length and width (Figure 7.1).

Working out from the middle of the bow, now mark the bow length and handle length with the handle area. Since the bow will measure 66 inches from string nock to string nock, one inch has to be added on each end for the tips (Figure 7.2).

Then mark the desired bow width at the tips and the ends of the handle, and connect the points with each other.

All material beyond the length and width markings can now be removed (Figure 7.3).

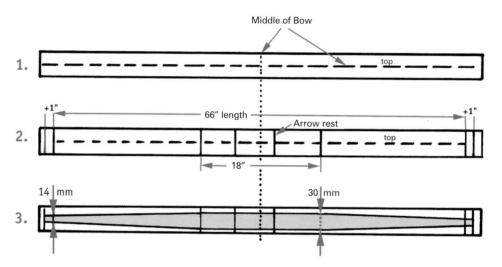

Figure 7 Bow back with dimensions

Tip Overlays

After taking off the remaining material, glue the so-called tip overlays onto the ends of the limbs. These are not absolutely necessary for the use of Dacron bowstrings, but if you use Fast Flight strings, it is necessary to use overlays of fiberglass, micarta, bone, horn, or a combination thereof.

When you file the string nocks (string beds), be sure that the side depths (ca. 3-4 mm) are the same on both sides, and that no sharp edges remain on which the string could wear through over time.

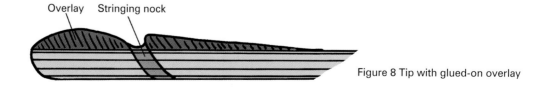

Figure 8 Tip with glued-on overlay

Tillering

Before you draw the bow the first time, all the fiberglass edges on the limbs are to be rounded, as the glass could break otherwise.

On the drawn bow, check now to see if the movement of both limbs is the same in terms of length. If this is not the case, take some more material away. Since the limb always leans to its weaker side, take some material off the opposite, stronger limb.

Then check the so-called tiller of the limbs, which means make sure that they bend equally strongly.

That is done best on a tiller wall, on which parallel lines are drawn, so that you can thus see clearly how the limbs are bending.

The arrow pass lies above the center of the bow, nearer the upper limb, which puts somewhat more pressure on it. But since the upper limb does not give off more energy than the lower one when shooting, the upper limb has to be made a little weaker.

This difference can be measured. With the bow drawn (brace height: 6 to 7 inches), measure the distance from the string to the end of the handle. This should be 3 to 7 mm greater on the upper limb.

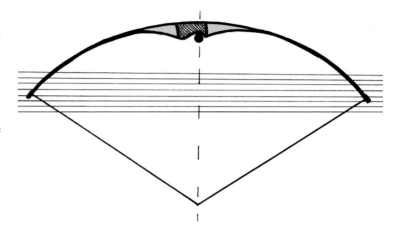

Figure 9. Bending behavior at tillering stick.

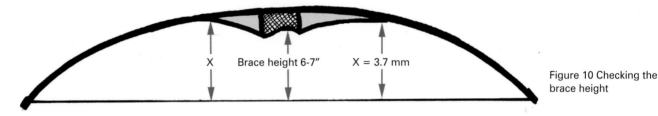

X   Brace height 6-7"   X = 3.7 mm

Figure 10 Checking the brace height

Draw Weight

Now test the draw weight with a pull scale when it is drawn to 28 inches, measured from the front edge (the back) of the bow.

If the weight is still too high, you can reduce it by scraping down the edges on the belly side of the limbs or by cautiously scraping the fiberglass layer on the belly side. But always make sure that flight and tiller still agree.

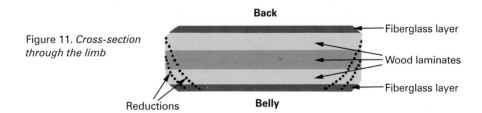

Back

Figure 11. *Cross-section through the limb*

Fiberglass layer

Wood laminates

Fiberglass layer

Reductions   **Belly**

If the draw weight turns out to be too low, there is only one possible way to reach the desired weight. One must shorten the bow a little, glue on new tip overlays, and repeat the procedure of tillering.

Thus it is an advantage when the draw weight at this stage is still 2 to 3 pounds more that desired, since something can still be removed through working out the handle and arrow shelf and finely polishing the bow, which will reduce the weight.

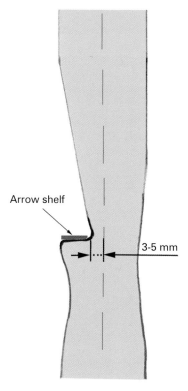

Arrow shelf

3-5 mm

The Arrow Shelf

The next step is making the arrow shelf. This lateral cut must not go too far into the handle; its deepest point should still be 3 to 5 mm short of the middle of the bow.

Then work the handle, in which it must be absolutely sure that the fiberglass layer on the back of the bow is intact and undamaged.

Finishing

After the last fine polishing, the bow is lacquered. Polyurethane lacquer, two-component acrylic lacquer, or various parquet lacquers will do a good job.

It is important that the lacquer remains elastic, adheres well, and does not rub off.

So the bow will not slip in your hand, you can cover the handle with soft leather by using contact cement.

And so the arrow does not leave traces on the arrow shelf when shot, you can also put a piece of leather, pelt, or felt here.

As a string for this bow, either a Dacron string with 12 to 14 strands, or a Fast Flight string with 14 to 16 strands, is recommended.

Notes

To be able to turn this description into fact, I consider handcrafting ability and a feeling for material and technique to be necessary. All the descriptions are based on my personal experience in bow building.

In principle, though, everyone must gain his own experience.

I hope I have helped you make your dream of making your own self-made longbow come true. In this spirit, I wish you lots of success and happiness.

Longbow forever!

Achim Stegmeyer

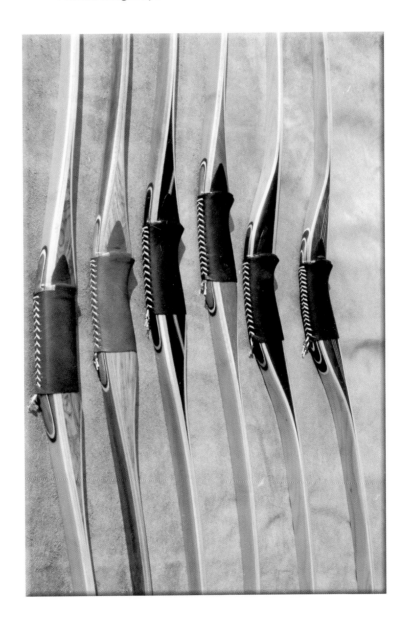

THE TERMS USED IN BOW BUILDING AND SPORT

Agincourt: The site of a famous battle in 1415, where English bowmen won a resounding victory over the French.

Aiming Point: Chosen point at which the head of an arrow is aimed, above or below the actual target.

Anchor Point: The point, usually in the archer's face, to which the bow is pulled; it serves to regularize the draw length.

Annual Rings: Yearly growth rings in wood, of great importance in bow building.

Archer: A person who shoots a bow.

Archer's Paradox: The phenomenon when an arrow bends when shot, curves around the bow, and then straightens its course in free flight. This explains the meaning of the spine value.

Armguard: It protects the archer's forearm (bracer).

Arrow Plate: A small piece of material placed on a bow to protect it from being worn by arrows sliding past.

Arrow Rest: Device used to hold the arrow until it is released.

Back: The surface of the bow facing away from the archer.

Back Set: The slight, natural curve of an unstrung bow. *See Reflex and String Follow.*

Backing: Wood or other suitable material added to the back of a bow to stabilize and strengthen it and avoid breakage.

Bamboo: A very good material for bows and arrows.

Barebow: A bow without sights or other assisting features; it is aimed "instinctively" or by a system.

Barreled Shaft: An arrow shaft that is widest in the middle and tapers to the front and rear.

Belly: The inside of the bow that faces the archer.

Birch Pitch: Stone Age adhesive derived from boiling birch bark without the presence of air.

Blunt: An unsharpened arrowhead for roving and small game.

Bodkin: A thin needle-like three- or four-sided point capable of penetrating armor.

Bolt: A short arrow shot from a crossbow.

Bowyer's Knot: A simple, easily released loop used to fasten the string to the bow.

Bow Hand: The hand that holds the bow, as opposed to the Drawing Hand.

Bow Length: Usually the length of an unstrung bow from tip to tip; can also mean the length of the string from nock to nock, which is more practical.

Bowstringer: A device used to string a bow.

Bowyer: A person who makes or repairs bows.

Brace: The stringing of a bow.

Brace Height: The distance from the belly of the bow to the strung bowstring.

Broadhead: A sharply cut arrowhead made for hunting.

Bull's-eye: Innermost circle of a circular target.

Button: Adjustable contact to adjust the place of arrows.

Checker: An aid for checking and adjusting the brace height and nocking point of a bow.

Clout Shooting: A competition involving shooting at a distant target.

Cock Feather: Differently colored feather that indicates a right angle to the nock.

Composite Bow: Any bow made of a combination of materials; often refers to a classic type of Asian recurve bow composed of horn, wood, and sinew.

Compound Bow: A modern bow type that allows easier drawing and faster shooting.

Compression Crack: Crack in the wood of a bow's belly resulting from too much bending; can decrease performance but is usually not dangerous.

Crécy: Site of a famous battle in 1346 won by English bowmen.

Creeping: Relaxing pressure on a fully drawn bow, decreasing the draw length.

Cresting: Colored rings on an arrow shaft for decoration and identification.

Crowndip: Coloring applied by dipping the rear end of an arrow in paint.

Dacron: A modern synthetic fiber with little elasticity, popular for making bowstrings.

Damper: A bundle of fur, wool or rubber plaited into the bowstring to dampen sound.

Dechsel: German name of a tool with a transverse blade, used to build bows in the Stone Age.

Deflex: Bending of part of the limb toward the archer.

Deflex-Reflex: Curving bow shape of modern longbows, to increase performance and comfort.

Dip: The transition from the grip area to the limb of a bow, also called Fade-out.

Dogwood: A tree, *Cornus*, providing good arrow material, heavy, hard and tough.

Dominant Eye: The archer's stronger eye, used for aiming.

Draw: Pulling the bowstring towards the anchor point.

Draw Blade: Hand tool with a straight, angled surface, used to remove small amounts of wood from a bow.

Draw Knife: Two-handled tool with sharp blade, used to remove wood from a bow.

Draw Length: Distance from the outside of the bow to the string when the latter is fully tensed before shooting, depending on the length of the arrow and the archer's arm.

Draw Weight: Power of a fully drawn bow, measured in English pounds.

Drawing Hand: The hand used to draw a bow; as opposed to the Bow Hand.

Dry Shot: Shooting a bow without an arrow; can be destructive to the bow.

Drying Crack: Longitudinal crack in a wooden stave, result of too-fast, uneven drying.

Endless String: A bowstring made of a single cord, with loops at the ends.

Epoxy: Two-component epoxide resin, the adhesive used most often in bow building, very firm and easy to use.

Face Walking: An aiming technique in which the anchor point is raised or lowered on the archer's face depending on the distance of the shot.

Facing: Strengthening material on the inside of a bow; counterpart to Backing.

Fade-out: The transition from handle to limbs in a bow, also called Dip.

Fast-Flight: Popular modern bowstring material, made of synthetic fibers with minimal elasticity for fast arrow flight.

Feather: The wing feather of a goose or turkey, or the portion of it attached to an arrow.

Fiberglass: A modern material made of glass fibers, used as the backing and facing of laminated bows; extremely flexible and used for new bow forms such as deflex-reflex.

Field Point: Traditional arrowhead for field target archery.

Field Shooting: Shooting at various targets and ranges in a natural environment.

Finish: Coating of oil, wax, or lacquer applied to a finished bow to protect it from moisture and other weather effects.

Fistmele: Distance from the belly of the bow to the string when the bow is braced; also Brace Height.

FITA: International archery organization for Olympic archery.

Flat Bow: Bow with flat, wide limbs, making shorter bows than classic longbows.

Flemish Splice: Medieval technique of making loops at the ends of bowstrings.

Fletching: The pieces of feathers attached to an arrow to stabilize its flight.

Flight Shooting: Competition for shooting arrows to maximum distances.

Flu-Flu: An arrow with especially large fletching, for quick braking of the arrow's flight.

Flying Anchor: Style of drawing and releasing a bow without pausing.

Footing: A spliced-in foreshaft made of hardwood.

Foreshaft: Front part of an arrow shaft, either made of more stable material than the rest of the shaft, or made so as to release from it when hunting.

Fps, ft/s: Feet per second, initial velocity of an arrow on being released from a bow.

Full Draw: An archer's position when the bow is fully drawn.

Game Trail: Simulated hunting competition in which the archer must find the targets and best shooting positions.

Grain: Unit of weight (100 grains = 6.47 grams); also the ring pattern of wood.

Grip: The enlarged central part of a bow held in the archer's hand, also Handle or Riser.

Hand Shock: The kick, recoil, or vibration of a bow when shot, disturbing to an archer.

Heartwood: The strong, stable wood from the inner part of a tree trunk.

Hemp: Historic fibrous material used to make bowstrings.

Holmegaard Bow: Oldest known type of bow found in Europe, made of elm and having characteristic shoulders in the limbs.

Horn Tips: Pieces of horn, including string nocks, attached to ends of bow limbs.

Horsetail (*Equisetum*): Plant useful for smoothing wood surfaces.

Hunter Round: Competition in which only one shot is allowed at each target representing animals.

Hunting Bow: Strong bow for shooting heavy arrows, usually shorter than a longbow for greater mobility in the field.

IFAA: International Field Archery Association.

Inch: 1 inch = 25.4 mm.

Instinctive Shooting: Shooting from instinct, without deliberate aiming.

Judo Point: Blunt arrowhead with extended claws, used to prevent disappearance of an arrow in grass, etc.

Kill Zone: The innermost area of a target that represents an animal; striking it symbolizes a kill.

Kyudo: Japanese traditional archery.

Laminated Bow: Bow made of several layers of material glued together.

Lb.: English abbreviation for pound; *see Pound.*

LH.: Abbreviation for left-handed.

Limb: Either limb of a bow, running from the grip to the end.

Linen: Flax fiber, historical material for bowstrings, offering much strength and little flexibility.

Longbow: Traditional straight bow without recurves.

Mary Rose: English warship sunk in 1546, from which 137 longbows were salvaged; also the name of the type of bow found in the ship, with unusually heavy draw weight.

Mediterranean Grip: Style of holding the string with two fingers below and one finger above the arrow shaft.

Nock: Notch near either limb end of a bow, for attaching the bowstring, or at the rear end of arrow, to fit over the bowstring.

Nock Wrapping: Wrapping of cord around the rear end of an arrow to prevent it from splitting at the nock.

Nocking Point: Marked spot on the string where the arrow is set.

Pistol Grip: Especially shaped grip of a bow, giving a firm hold.

Plane: Tool with a sharp horizontal blade, used for removing wood from a raw bow.

Point-On: Distance at which an archer sights the tip of his/her arrow upon the point of aim and hits the targets.

Popinjay: Competitive, almost vertical shooting at bird targets.

Pound: English weight measure, approximately 453 grams, symbolized by #.

Pre-aiming: Pointing the arrow at the target before drawing the bow.

Propeller Wood: Warped wood; a bow stave made of it would look like a propeller.

Push-and-pull Method: Method of stringing or unstringing a bow by bracing the lower tip against the left foot, pulling the upper limb with the right hand, which also slides the bowstring to the upper nock, also a shooting technique.

Pushing Wood: Especially stable wood on a bow that causes uneven balance of the limbs.

Quiver: A container for carrying arrows.

Raw Bow: A crude bow carved from wood, before tillering.

Recurve Bow: Bow with curved or bent limb sections.

Recurves: The parts of bow limbs bent forward on a recurve bow.

Reflex: Parts of the limbs bent in the direction of the target.

Release: Letting go of the bowstring to shoot.

RH: Abbreviation for right-handed.

Roving: Wandering shooting at natural targets such as tree stumps, leaves, etc.

Sapwood: The outer wood of a tree trunk, between the bark and the heartwood

Scraping Plane: Small plane with side grips used to remove wood in bow building; intermediate between a drawknife and a draw blade.

Self-bow: Bow made of a single piece of wood.

Self-nock: Nock carved into an arrow shaft, rather than being set on it.

Serving: Wrapping of cord on the middle of a bowstring to protect it from wear.

Shaft: Arrow material, to which the head, fletching, and nock are added.

Shelf: Lower angle of the window, on which the arrow rests.

Shooting Glove: Three-fingered glove used in sport shooting.

Silex: Quartz stone used for arrowheads in early times; includes flint, obsidian, etc.

Siyah: Stiff, angled part of the limb of a classic Asian bow. Works as a lever.

Spine: Resistance of an arrow shaft to bending.

Spine Value: Measured resistance of an arrow shaft to bending, stated in pounds.

Spine-tester: Device for measuring an arrow shaft's resistance to bending.

Splicing: Technique of combining two pieces of wood by gluing to form a complete bow component or arrow.

Spring Scale: Device used for weighing the pulling power of a bow.

Stacking: Excessive increase in draw weight at the end of drawing.

Stave: Piece of wood or laminate out of which a bow is made.

Stellmoor Bow: Presumed fragment of a bow from the Stellmoor site, Northern Germany, ca. 9500 B.C.

Step-through Method: Method of stringing or unstringing a bow in which one leg passes between the bow and string, to avoid the danger of straining the bow unevenly or twisting the limbs.

String: Cord with which a bow is strung; also Bowstring.

String Board: Device used in making bowstrings.

String Follow: Permanent slight curving of a bow after frequent shooting; it decreases the bow's performance.

String Helper / String Keeper: a loop of cord that prevents the unstrung string from dropping far down the bow.

String Walking: Aiming technique in which the drawing hand's position on the string varies according to the shot distance.

String Wax: Wax with which a bowstring is impregnated to preserve and protect it.

Stringer: Cord loop used to string or unstring a bow.

Stump Shooting: Type of Roving in which tree stumps are used as targets.

Swing-draw Method: Shooting style in which the bow is raised as it is drawn.

System Shooting: Deliberate style of aiming at a target, opposed to Instinctive Shooting.

Tab: Simple leather or fur, finger protection for the drawing hand.

Take-down: Bow that can be dismantled, coming apart in the grip.

Tapered: Bow limb or arrow shaft that becomes regularly slimmer in one direction.

Target: Object at which an arrow is shot and into which it sticks.

Target Bow: Bow made to shoot light, fast arrows at targets.

Thumb Ring: Form of protection for the thumb, used in Asian shooting.

Tiller: Bow's state of being trimmed so that both limbs bend equally.

Tillering: Fine removal of wood to equalize bending of bow limbs.

Tillering Board: Device to hold a bow for tillering.

Tillering String: Overlong bowstring used in early stages of tillering, shortened or replaced by a standard bowstring later in tillering.

Tips: Strengthened pieces added to the limb ends of a bow.

Traditional Bow: A bow made in traditional style, performing and shooting like bows from olden times.

Tuning: Adapting bow, arrow, and string to one's shooting style for smooth, straight shooting.

Undergrip: Holding the arrow on the string with three fingers under the arrow; *see String Walking.*

Unfeathered Arrow Test: Test made to determine correct spine value by shooting unfeathered arrows; useful only with good shooting style.

Viburnum: Shrub popular in the Stone Age as a source of hard, tough arrow wood.

Warming Box: Large heatable box used to dry bow wood or laminated bows.

Window: Cutout area in the grip of a bow, to assist aiming.

Wooden Bow: A bow made completely of wood (= self bow), without fiberglass, etc.

Yard: English measure of three feet; = 0.91 meter.

Yew: Tree whose wood was preferred for bow building from the Neolithic Era through the Late Middle Ages.

TIMELINE

Prehistoric and historic types of full bows and important discoveries from the Stone Age to the Renaissance in Europe.

Name/Site	Earliest Date	Location of Specimen
Holmegaard Bow	ca. 8000 B.C.	Danish National Museum, Copenhagen
Tybrind Vig Bow	ca. 5300–4000 B.C.	Moesgaard Museum, Aarhus, Denmark
Bodman Bow	ca. 4000 B.C.	Rosgarten Museum, Konstanz
Egolzwil Bow	ca. 3800 B.C.	Swiss Landesmuseum, Zürich
Hauslabjoch Bow	ca. 3300 B.C.	South Tyrol Archaeological Museum, Bozen, Italy (Ötzi's bow)
Aamosen Bow	ca. 3000 B.C.	Danish National Museum, Copenhagen
Meare-Heath Bow	ca. 2700 B.C.	Museum of Archeology and Anthropology, Cambridge, England
Lötschen Pass Bow	ca. 2000 B.C.	Lötschental Museum, Kippel, Switzerland
Nydam Bow	ca. 200–400 A.D.	Archaeological Landesmuseum, Schleswig
Oberflacht Bow	ca. 550 A.D.	Württemberg Landesmuseum, Stuttgart
Altdorf Bow	ca. 650 A.D.	Uri Historical Museum, Kippel, Switzerland
Haithabu Bow	ca. 900 A.D.	Haithabu Viking Museum, Schleswig
Burg-Elmendorf Bow	ca. 1050 A.D.	Archaeological Landesmuseum, Schleswig
Schloss Hohenaschau Bow	ca. 1480 A.D.	Germanic Nationalmuseum, Nürnberg
Mary Rose Bow	1545 A.D.	Mary Rose Museum, Portsmouth, and Tower of London, England

ADDRESSES

AUTHORS

Flemming Alrune
"Langsbjerggaard," Vindebaekvej 3, DK-4792 Askeby, Denmark
E-mail: paterson-alrune@c.dk

Wulf Hein
ARCHAEO-TECHNIK, Buchenstrasse 7, D-61203 Dorn-Assenheim, Germany
www.archaeo-technik.de
E-mail: info@archaeo-technik.de

Jürgen Junkmanns
Authentic bows and arrows, bow building classes
Frankenstr. 45, D-50374, Erfstadt, Germany
www.pfeil-bogen.de

Boris Pantel
E-mail: boris.pantel@archery.de

Holger Riesch
Bergstrase 32, D-55595 Roxheim, Germany
E-mail: holger@riesch.info

Achim Stegmeyer
Traditional bows
Mühlstrasse 43/1, D-71576 Burgstetten, Germany
www.stegmeyer-bogenbau.de

Ulrich Stehli
Englische Langbogen & Handgeschmiedete Pfeilspitzen
Thingslinder Strasse 62, D-58566 Kierspe, Germany
Telephone +49 (0)2359-49 58

Konrad Vögele
Bow of wood, bow building classes
Hohbaumleweg 18
D-88416 Bellamont, Germany
www.holzbogenbau.com
E-mail: Konrad-Voegele@gmx.de

Jorge Zschieschang
Bows and bowls, bowbuilding classes
Ernst-Schulze-Strasse 2a, D-37081 Göttingen, Germany